Writing by candlelight

Writing by candlelight

E.P. THOMPSON

Cartoons by Gabriel

MERLIN · LONDON

© The Merlin Press 1980
This edition first published by
The Merlin Press Ltd
3 Manchester Road
London E14

ISBN cloth   0 85036 257 1
       paperback 0 85036 260 1

Cover designed by Louis Mackay

2nd impression June 1980
3rd impression September 1980
4th impression June 1981

Printed in Great Britain by
Whitstable Litho Ltd
Millstrood Road
Whitstable, Kent.

CONTENTS

Introduction

The essays and articles in this book were, with two exceptions, all written in the 1970s. They generally arose unbidden and without premeditation, because 'events' seemed to insist that something should be said. This something was generally intended to controvert, and if possible to discomfort, the purveyors of received wisdom, and to contest the official descriptions of reality presented in the media.

The events will be remembered and the pieces should explain themselves. They concern such matters as the power workers' strike of 1970 and the first miners' strike of 1972; Harold Wilson's apologetics and the referendum about 'going into Europe'; the ABC Official Secrets trial of 1978 and the current attack on the jury system.

Taken together, they have (somewhat to my own surprise) an undeniable thematic unity. All are concerned, to greater or lesser degree, with the means employed today to manufacture what is then offered as a consensus of 'public opinion'. I commence with 'The Segregation of Dissent', although this was written twenty years ago, because it describes this process, and may now seem prescient.

In watching these manufacturers at their work I have on occasion made use of very ephemeral matter, such as the correspondence columns of the press, passing levinities in *The Times*, or chat shows on TV. This may be related to my own conditions of work, as a writer living in the provinces. But many millions receive the official description of reality in this way. I argue in the final piece, 'The Doomsday Consensus', that this manufacture (and suppression) of opinion has now acquired an unprecedented reach, which threatens the democratic process, not at its margins but at its very centre — and which, in the case of nuclear missiles, directly threatens our lives. I will add that the need has been so manifest, for more than a decade, for direct contestation with the media — including the need for *at least* one alternative daily newspaper — that I cannot understand why this is not at the top of every democratic agenda.

The second uniting preoccupation, forced onto the pages by the events themselves, gives rise to equal dismay. This is the steady increment in the powers and presence of the state, the closure of 'consensual' political life, the incorporation of democratic process or the diversion of this into harmless ritual forms: in short, the advance of authoritarianism not only as ideology but as fact.

It was only after some hesitation that I decided to include a section on Warwick University. Some aspects of this ten-year-old affair are now dated, and readers may prefer to pass the section by. But I have included the section because the affair of 'the files' appears in retrospect to reveal in microcosm processes enacted during the subsequent decade within the general life of the nation. One notes the attempt to impose a new style of business management (which has now been carried through, at great expense and with much alienation and inefficiency, in local government); the specious appeal to the ideology of 'modernization', and the hostility to practices of democratic self-government, as instanced by the Tyzack Report (which has subsequently found expression in the 'modernization' of the judicial system and in attempts to manage or eliminate the jury); the rendering ineffective of dissent by building it into the body-walls of a managed system, and the scrutiny of students and staff by the collection of files and even by espionage — all these seem now to illustrate, not the local case of one new university, but the general case of the nation.

It is true that the case of Warwick University offers also more heartening evidence on the other side. The response of the students, and then — in more prolonged and complex episodes — of many academic staff, as well as administrators, was sharp and effective, and this met with some support outside the University's walls. While Warwick University today is very far from the democratic utopia dreamed up by some of us in 1970, it is, I believe, a place governed by rules in which democratic process has some part, and it is a place where serious and scholarly educational work goes on. The moment of encroaching authoritarianism provoked a moment of euphoric libertarian revolt, and when 'order' was at length reasserted (in part through the agency of Lord Radcliffe) authority was clipped of some powers and placed under more watchful controls.

One would be less anxious if one thought that this could be a paradigm for the state of the British nation in 1980. We are very certainly now within the authoritarian moment. For two decades the state, whether under Conservative or Labour administrations, has been taking liberties, and these liberties were once ours. In the section on 'The State and Civil Liberties' I comment on this process, and in 'The State of the Nation' I argue that we are now approaching a point of crisis in which not fascism but a peculiarly British form of authoritarianism, working behind the back of the democratic process, is now bringing national life within its general closure. This closure is named 'consensus', and the media manufacture that. Britain, as we enter the 1980s, has the most reactionary government in Western Europe, which is simultaneously attacking the livelihood and democratic rights of its own people, and accepting, with bellicose subservience, a client role for the state as a station of NATO. In compensation for the abject collapse of traditional British influence and power, Mrs Thatcher is repeating history as farce, and attempting to mimic (before bored auditoriums) Churchill's post-war role as the leading ideologist of Cold War in the Western world.

I wrote 'The State of the Nation' in October 1979, and I wrote it out of a pessimistic mood. It was a bad moment. On every side it seemed that the rules of the traditional democratic game were being struck out. The extraordinary and repressive Official Information Bill (which had clearly been drafted by security) had already been introduced in the House of Lords. Mr Justice King-Hamilton had referred the *Guardian* to the Director of Public Prosecutions for divulging the remarkable rag-bag of irrelevant information dredged up from police files in a new case of jury vetting. Wherever one looked in the media, Mr James Anderton or some other over-mighty chief constable was holding forth.

It seemed to me then that Britain might be in the final year or two of its own 'Weimar' — let us say, at such a moment as 1930, when Karl Jaspers wrote his *Die Geistige Situation der Zeit* with, not the Nazis, but a crowd of officious extras — police and security chiefs, 'modernizing' civil servants and political cynics, NATO and military personnel — waiting in the wings. No conspiratorial coup would be necessary. Massive unemployment, heavy industrial conflict with massive police response, racial provocations — and perhaps counter-provocations by increasingly desperate groups on the extreme Left and in threatened immigrant communities — heavy security measures and McCarthyite terrorization of dissent: all this would lead, by a series of swift degenerative stages, from the liberal managed society (where we now are) to a very foul, policed and managed, authoritarian state.

Now, as I write in January 1980, this pessimism may seem excessive. There has been a twitch or two in the inert body of democracy — resuscitation might still be possible. In an extra-ordinary comedy of official errors, the Blunt affair (which was very probably deliberately leaked by elements in security in the expectation of provoking a spectacular witch-hunt) back-fired on its own promoters: it directed attention to the security services themselves, and to their arbitrary, elitist, secretive and bungling procedures. The Official Information Bill was withdrawn, although it may very soon return in some new form. And there have been other encouraging signs. A general fight is at last being put up to defend the jury, inclu-ding — a most heartening sign that we still have a political culture — by jurors themselves. There is to be a jury in the inquest upon Blair Peach after all, although we do not yet know how this will be selected. A more general concern is being expressed, on many sides, as to the rising presence of

the police. And a stubborn fight is being enacted in the
Labour Party, which -- if the conference and the constituencies should be successful against the managers of the parliamentary party — could move a great national party outside
certain critical 'consensual' sanctities (the sacred consensual
silence as to NATO, Cruise missiles, the security services,
'law and order'), and thus directly challenge the legitimacy of
the means through which, for two decades, we have been
managed.

I wished, when writing 'The State of the Nation', to indi-
cate the gravity of the situation and to summon up resistance. I do not intend to suggest that the issue is settled.
Countervailing forces do exist. I do not wish to nourish pessimism. At the present moment of writing, our political life
seems to be in a state of radical instability. We receive contra-
dictory signals every week. Matters are in a most delicate
equilibrium, and any sudden deterioration in the general
political context -- such as renewed international crisis
(which is now arising in the aftermath of NATO's aggressive
nuclear strategy and the Soviet occupation of Afghanistan),
or industrial break-down (if it is not attended by a revitaliza-
tion of our older democratic culture) -- could lead us, very
swiftly, into political disaster.

This is a concern of all democrats, and not only of 'the
Left' (not every part of which has unambiguous democratic
credentials). There is, however, one factor in the situation of
a part of the Left, and also of the feminist movement, which
could possibly weaken the necessary response to this situation. For at least a decade (since 1968 or thereabouts) a part
of the Left has turned in disgust away from national political
life and opted for building an alternative culture. A part of
the feminist movement, for evident reasons, has taken a
similar option.

This turn has sometimes been activist, on single-issue cam-
paigns, and it has sometimes been more detached, intellectual
and even introversial in character (the self-examination and
self-elaboration of theory). In either case, achievements have
been made in building an alternative culture during the last
decade. Minorities may have gained in confidence, some

intellectual inquiries have had vitality, new styles of living have been developed, and the women's movement has exerted a new kind of presence. I am certainly not offering any polemical rejection of what has been done.

But, ineluctably, the official culture of power goes on its way: and perhaps it has its way even more easily when some part of the opposition confronts it with only a disgusted back. Opting for an alternative can, in certain circumstances, also be opting out, by leaving a vacuum into which power can move. We are not allowed an indefinite period in which to construct an alternative culture, which will then re-emerge into national life, after three or four decades, in the form of a 'revolution'. For during that time the official culture of power is not politely waiting for the Left to return, so that the game can start fair again. It is busy all the while. It is arming the police, preparing contingency plans with the army, vetting the juries, perfecting its files and its surveillance, plotting provocations, undermining the trade unions, repealing abortion acts, selling off national resources, destroying the urban environment, and establishing centres of genocide, under the sole control of United States generals, at Upper Heyford and Lakenheath.

The 'alternative culture' *must* find ways of influencing again, in active ways, the national political life. I am not asking any group or movement to surrender its values or its autonomy. I don't think that there is only one 'correct' or useful way to act, such as joining the Labour Party (where I happen to be myself). I am not, for example, asking sisters in the feminist movement to stop acting together as sisters, but to think more urgently of their other roles as citizens, jurors, trade unionists or electors as well.

The notion has got about that one's gender or colour or preferences must always, in every situation, be the primary existential facts, and that these differences must be nearly-insurmountable barriers inhibiting common political action in a hundred other kinds of situation. This may start from valid premises. But when the notion is pressed too far, and when those who are under common threat of nuclear war, of loss of rights and of work, or under the common exploitation of money, can no longer work effectively together because they must always nurse primary differences in the form of grudges, then this is dangerously divisive. It marks the end of important affirmative traditions of radical, socialist and labour politics. Granted that very significant primary demands, especially of women, got hushed or annexed in mass movements of the past, then the answer is to convert such movements (and their organizations) to a new kind of attention to these demands, which I am confident that these sisters are tough enough to do. It is certainly not to throw away the possibility of a general movement, and leave us as a lot of fragmented and quarrelling pieces in the face of power.

This is realized well enough by many in the women's movement today, as the authors of *Beyond the Fragments* show, just as it is realized by many of the Asians of Southall. If the police state arrives, then, whatever our gender or our colour, we will go into much the same crowded prisons, and if the nuclear missiles are fired we will all go together when we go. It would be better not to go, and if the 'alternative culture' can find ways, without loss of principle, to reconnect with an active national political culture, this will bring reinforcements at a time of need.

It might even help us to do more. For the continuous downward pressures of the last decades — the pressures of modernizing bureaucracies, of Official Secrecy, of the manipulative media, of the police — have at length called forth a spirit of resistance, with a new interest in democratic forms and a new accent on libertarian values. If we can find ways of co-ordinating this resistance, and of articulating this rising consciousness in new political forms (both as theory and as policies), then it is possible that my pessimistic scenario is overdrawn. One can even glimpse the possibility of a quite new phase of democratic and socialist insurgency somewhere ahead — a resurgent movement with new priorities, which would turn its back on the old statist norms and bureaucratic forms to be found in the orthodox traditions of both communism and social democracy, and which would address the critical problem of the restructuring of our institutions (national, industrial, judicial, local, and in communications and education) with a quite new democratic inventiveness. That may be more than we can hope for, but it would be worth working for, together.

My thanks are due to the editors and staffs of the following journals and publishers for permission to republish pieces which at first found hospitality in their pages: *New University*, the *Sunday Times*, *The Observer*, *Vole*, the *Guardian*, the *New Statesman*, *State Research* and Julian Friedmann Publishers. My particular thanks are due to Paul Barker and to *New Society*. More of these pieces appeared in *New Society* than in all the other places put together, and on occasion I was given the support of a determined editorial decision in the face of difficulties. Thus 'The Business University' was published in the face of an injunction, and several of the later pieces in the face of a judge's frown of contempt.

New Society's hospitality to a dissenting view, and Paul Barker's editorial advice, have been heartening evidence that the closure of our democratic traditions is not yet complete. My particular thanks are also due to Bruce Page of the *New Statesman* for his editorial advice with 'A State of Blackmail' (another piece which ran along the edge of the law); to Sarah Harrison, Tony Bunyan and the team around *State Research*; to Dorothy Thompson for suggestions and criticisms throughout; to many Indian friends who are suggested in 'The Nehru Tradition'; to the defendants (and the defence committee) in the ABC Official Secrets trial; to John Griffith, John Saville, Patricia Hollis, Phil Jeffries, Rodney Hilton and Julian Harber for advice on particular points; and to Martin Eve, David Musson and Antonia Owen of The Merlin Press.

A final note. When I published *The Poverty of Theory* (Merlin, 1978), I suggested that I would publish a second volume of *Reasoning* shortly. This is not that volume, although I have included here some pieces which might have gone into it. I still hope to present a volume with more theoretical writings from the 1950s and 1960s, and with some retrospective analysis of the first New Left. But this has been delayed. Just now there seem to be more important things to do.

20 January 1980   E.P.T.

The Segregation of Dissent

In this talk I want to discuss the familiar problem of mass communications. But I want to deal with it from an unfamiliar angle: from the standpoint of those who inhabit the underworld of British political life. For nearly twenty years I have taken my share of door-knocking, committee work, and of organizing thinly attended meetings on behalf of minority causes; and of producing more or less ephemeral minority journals. I don't want to labour here the physical and financial difficulties encountered by minority political groups, nor the hundreds of voluntary and apparently unrewarding man-hours entailed. There are thousands of people in this country who know this from their own experience.

But it seems to me that the position of this kind of dissent in our society is becoming increasingly precarious. Where the minority group once had a significant function within the wider democratic process, it has now become so effectively isolated by changes in the means of communication that its activities are well on the way to becoming a harmless form of intellectual self-expression. This process has already gone so far that commonly-held notions of the 'free society' are so much at variance with British actualities as to serve as an impediment to the practice of democracy. But, first, let me take some examples from the predicament of a dis-

---

This talk, rejected by the BBC, was published in *New University*, May 1961.

senting political group with which I am associated — the New Left.

The New Left has been learning the hard way how difficult it is to penetrate the bland, fair-minded defences of the Establishment. Of course, any rising unorthodoxy — in any society — must expect to encounter the inertia of received opinions and entrenched institutions. What is new is the problem of 'take-off' for a minority group. Does a movement of dissent, which challenges not this or that policy of the parties but *the kind of politics* in which all parties are implicated, stand any chance of breaking into the world of actual political decisions?

One hundred years ago — from the standpoint of formal democracy — we were an under-developed country. But within this limited democracy political heresy abounded and was often surprisingly effective. The minority had direct access to its own means of communication. The cost of launching a newspaper was not prohibitive. From the press, the public meeting, or the chapel, a determined minority could conduct a sustained propaganda, on the issues which it selected and according to its own strategy.

Today orthodox political thought assumes the viability of our formal democratic procedures. But these procedures are becoming more and more empty of real content, public life more enervated, and controversy more muffled. We all know some of the reasons for this drift — the centralized control over the major media of communication; the power of the party machine, together with the gross conforming idiocy of two-party parliamentary routines; the manipulation of opinion by the techniques of the salesman — the brand-image, persuasion by association, the play upon status anxieties . . . 'Get on, get ahead, get up! ' say the advertisers. 'The Opportunity State', says the Conservative Party. 'Equality of Opportunity', says the official Labour echo. In this orchestration of competitive values, how is incipient heresy to be heard at all? To say that our aim should be, not equality of opportunity within an acquisitive society, but, a society of equals; that we need, not more ladders, but, more generous patterns of community life; to say these things is simply to proclaim one's political irrelevance.

One consequence of the elimination of heretical opinion is the ghostly nature of such controversies as do from time to time arise. A year or two ago it became clear that the Campaign for Nuclear Disarmament was winning wide public support, and that its success carried implications derogatory to NATO. Now, allegiance to NATO is part of that religious area behind the Establishment which one may not question. It seemed self-evident to editors, commentators, and most politicians that if it was only pointed out that a unilateral initiative might endanger NATO, then the heresy would be extinguished overnight. And for a year prior to Labour's Scarborough Conference this *was* pointed out — patiently but firmly in the 'quality' press, abusively in the popular press, truculently by television interviewers.

But where *was* the heresy? Apart from the odd splutter in a correspondence column, it was invisible. It was a spook. The fact that the spook was not exorcized may be due in part to the activity of the New Left in proposing constructive policies for British neutrality — policies widely canvassed in the netherworld of Campaign meetings and trade union branches to which the Establishment rarely descends. But so far as the main media are concerned — the daily and weekly press, radio and television — these policies had no existence. There *were* no serious neutralists in Britain.

I think it is a very serious matter when an issue can have come to the point of commanding millions of votes at a party conference while it still lies under the prohibition of our major media. And I want to note a parallel here between the predicament of 'neutralists' in this country and of 'revisionists' in the Soviet Union. The arguments of 'revisionists' are never actually allowed expression in the Soviet media. They, also, are views held by spooks — 'certain persons', 'immature elements who . . . ' At the most, they are suggested obliquely in specialist journals, virtually encapsulated from the general public. What is achieved in one case by direct political controls is achieved in the other case by public and financial monopolies. But the result is much the same.

The similarity points to differences. There is no need in this country to suppose any active apparatus to suppress dissent, any Zhdanov with an office in Portland Square. It is more simple than that. These heretical opinions (let us say, neutralism, or Welsh nationalism, or the advocacy of rent strikes, or — indeed — orthodox Communism) have no effective 'party political' existence. Indeed, if certain of them were permitted to emerge from the netherworld it would be highly embarrassing to all parties. And the convention has been established that opinions which have no party-political existence have no real political existence. The press is generally subject to the influence of one or other of the parties. Radio and television are subject to party-political agreements. The measuring out of opportunities to dissenting groups (which are likely to be uncouth and labouring under a sense of grievance) is administratively a nuisance — and, anyway, watchful party officials and a party-political Parliament stand in the background, ready to defend their monopoly of the rights of political citizenship.

As the arteries of parliamentary life have hardened, the arteries of communication have hardened in sympathy. One process has reinforced the other. A bewildering variety of opinions must somehow be compressed into one or other pack, under an authorized party brand-image. Constitutional procedures become confused with the expedients of voluntary institutions. The breach of party or trade union discipline becomes confused with a breach of law — and may indeed entail effective loss of political rights. Outraged morality and outraged orthodoxy adopt the same tone of reproof to the 'proscribed' organization, the 'unofficial' striker, 'extra-marital' relations, and actual illegality.

In such a climate, the possibility of propagating an alternative ('unauthorized') diagnosis of our social problems becomes more remote. And it is made doubly remote by the conformity of those media which — in classic liberal theory — should have been the first to resist the insolent encroachments of party and Parliament upon the political rights of the citizen. It is true that a world of discrete political discourse continues, in which all questions are open and the ailments of mass society are itemized. But it is a world of small circulation journals, student societies, enterprising publishers, 'intellectuals'. BBC and ITV, quality and popular press — these inhabit the world of 'responsible', practical politics. Of course — for it is a world which they have created.

It is not only the *number* of 'responsible' views which are determined by the media. They also determine, to great degree, the questions which it is possible to have views *about*, and the *form* in which these questions arise. An issue which arises outside the media — let us say the Clause Four controversy in the Labour Party — is taken up, shaped, and altered out of recognition when it is admitted to their vast distorting hall. Some voices are magnified, others silenced; some issues seized upon, others dismissed; the view of Mr Gaitskell or Mr Crosland may be reported *in extenso*; other views may be personalized, caricatured, or dramatized not as arguments but simply as a Row.

Thus even those who initiate controversy lose control over its course at the moment when the media take it up. We are all familiar with the methods employed by the press to trivialize, personalize, or sensationalize an issue. But the methods of radio and of television have been the subject of less criticism. It is not a question of the absolute exclusion of dissent. So long as unorthodox opinion stops short at the point of adding 'colour' or 'human interest' to a programme it can even be a commercial asset. A tinge of 'angriness', an image of rugged independence — these are marketable qualities in favour with viewers. What is noxious to authority today is not the profession of unorthodox principles but their earnest and effective advocacy. And dissent of any kind cannot appear on these media except through the intermediary of the producer. And the producer selects the participants, arranges them in interesting patterns (Mr X of the Bow Group against Miss Y of the Young Fabians), and determines questions of emphasis and tone. Dissent can never present its views in its own way and in its own tone — it is assumed that the British public would be bored by ten minutes of consecutive argument. But, for dissent, tone is as important as content. It must say, not only that these ideas are *true*, but that they *matter*. How can one think of Paine or Cobbett or Hazlitt apart from their tone? And which programme could accommodate any one of them today?

The examples may seem marginal. But they are part of a process which serves at every point to consolidate the formal status quo and to accelerate the actual decay of democratic life. One hundred years ago Mill warned of the danger of dissent being stifled by 'our merely social intolerance', which:

> kills no one, roots out no opinions, but induces men to disguise them, or to abstain from any active effort for their diffusion. With us, heretical opinions do not perceptibly gain, or even lose, ground in each decade or generation; they never blaze out far and wide, but continue to smoulder in the narrow circles of thinking and studious persons among whom they originate, without ever lighting up the general affairs of mankind with either a true or a deceptive light.

Today the effects are worse: there is less intolerance, because dissent is scarcely communicated at all. It can never gain access to the media for long enough to present a sustained and coherent image. Between the potential and the actual, between the heresy of the minority and the great agencies which shape the opinions of the majority, between the islands of dissent and the mainland of mass communication, there is a gulf across which the bridges are falling into disrepair.

But without this traffic any claim to democracy is spurious. The quality of democratic life is revealed not in the existence of certain institutions but in the way these institutions are used. Formally, the institutions may appear admirable; controversy of a kind may take place within them; the odd licensed radical may even give an air of openness to a system which is in fact three-quarters shut. It can even be important for the occasional 'spot' to be reserved on the media for more fundamental dissent, since its very appearance serves to legitimize the system. But, all the time, essential conditions of free controversy are absent. If dissent is to stand any chance of self-propagation, then it must appear

— not as sensational 'copy' nor as a gimmick in some 'free speech' corner, but — again and again. It must present its arguments systematically and continuously, in its own tone, according to its own strategy, selecting its own points of engagement, over a long period of time. If equality of access by all minorities to the media is inconceivable, there must at least be *sufficient* opportunity of access for the minority to be able to make up for the poverty of its resources by the energy of its advocacy and the force of its arguments.

These are exactly the conditions which were satisfied — however imperfectly — by the cheap printing-press, the hustings, the soap-box and the public hall. The crucial growing-point of the democratic process is the point at which a minority may propagate an opinion intolerable to the majority. Milton was confident that equality of access to the press provided adequate means within a limited democracy, if certain forms of censorship were removed. Mill — although deeply aware of the resources of orthodoxy — hoped that the opinion of minorities, if effectively organized and pressed with vigour, might in the end prevail. But neither could envisage the rise to power of the private or public corporation, like mammoth turnpike trusts controlling the main arteries of communication — trusts with the power to grant or withhold licences to all road users, a power exercised in practice very much in the manner of Milton's state licenser whose 'very office and his commission enjoins him to let pass nothing but what is vulgarly received already'.

I am far from belittling the importance of our formal liberties. It is in the archipelago of dissenting islands — the journal, the trade union branch, the experimental theatre, the library, the voluntary society — that the only forces are mustered which may at some time liberate the mainland. But the right is specious if the means are denied; and it is the mainland which is my concern. While commentators engage in elaborate psephological inquiries, the agencies which condition public opinion and which inhibit contrary opinions from arising go unchallenged. And in effect, if not in intention, these agencies are becoming increasingly authoritarian. Politics may soon settle down into a game of power at the top, with the media conditioning public attitudes to which the politicians adjust their 'images' in the hope of floating the marginal voter their way. From image to echo and back to image, it is a system of political tautology into which principle need not enter. It might, indeed, be called 'tautocracy'.

I have spent time on this argument because the task of creating an *alternative* means of communication has, from the start, been a major preoccupation of the New Left. Before the outlawed vehicles with their socialist contraband may travel, we have had to build our own road network and our own bridges to a wider public. But these considerations are also crucial if we are to understand the failure of nerve within the liberal tradition. Why is it that liberal-minded intellectuals have submitted so tamely to these processes?

The truth is that our liberal intellectual often does not notice the real forces which determine our political life, because he does not feel *himself* to be unfree. In his island of mild dissent he is able to speak, to argue, and to communicate with others like himself to his heart's content. Where he has a grievance, there is generally a remedy to hand which does not entail any major appeal to public opinion. He may say what he wants because he wants to say so little; and the more intemperate radical can often be 'nobbled' before he becomes an irritant within the system. If the intellectual thinks of the forces of conditioning, he thinks of them as something done *to* other people — the masses — *by* other people — the advertisers or the press — not as something which is also being done to him, and in the doing of which he has active complicity.

Moreover, what he wants to say serves only too often as an intellectual gloss upon the status quo. How else are we to describe this curious dichotomy in our intellectual life, whereby a profound spiritual pessimism is found at one pole, and a complacent belief in the efficacy of piecemeal reform at the other? Both attitudes coexist within the same minds. It is because man's nature is evil (so the argument runs) that we must shelter behind institutions from our own propensities. The experience of this tormented half-century has taught us that stability is the supreme social value. Since any major structural change would entail a social imbalance in which forces of irrationalism might assert themselves, we are condemned to accept the established fact. We are like impotent passengers within a delicate social mechanism where any sudden lurch might trigger off unforseen forces — we must move on tip-toe with hushed voices, dusting and polishing here and there, but never daring to redesign the machine. To look for major structural change is dangerous and 'apocalyptic'. Since we are limited to piecemeal reform, we must apply ourselves to the existing institutions and agencies of change. The two-party system may be imperfect, but at least it appears to be safe; and the end of politics is no longer the good life but stability — a system of checks and balances upon original sin. No matter how cynical our liberal intellectual may be about the actual conduct of our political life, he finds himself assenting to a system which silences effective dissent. He has sailed a salty ocean of philosophy only to paddle in a brackish puddle of psephology.

The energies of liberal dissent have declined to little more than a facile piecemeal progressivism and a naive faith in democratic institutions — the admiration of a model of the democratic process which has long since ceased to bear relation to the fact. The angry courage of Mill has gone but the periods of his prose remain. Our democratic safeguards and institutions have ceased to play any significant part in the dynamic processes of a changing society — but they still serve a purpose. They have become the solace of the intellectual's conscience and, only too often, his excuse for inactivity. As such they may be actively harmful — not, of course, in themselves — but insofar as they provide a formal act of legitimacy which disguises the actual unfreedom of the central process of opinion-formation.

From the hurricanes of violence which have swept the last decades, the liberal conscience has fled to the shelter of institutions. But authoritarianism has not only arisen in the aftermath of revolutionary upheaval — it has as often been the outcome of political stasis. Trapped in the reactive pattern provoked by Stalinism, too many of our liberal intellectuals fail to see the encroaching authoritarianism of the Business Society, with its growing retinue of intellectual retainers. In the sixties the threat to the living organism of democracy comes — not from the illusions of the thirties, but — from these new concentrations of financial and of governmental power.

We may now have reached a point where the concentration of power is such that we must either subject it to new democratic controls — which will involve changes of a revolutionary order — or change will go on, willy nilly, in directions both authoritarian and irresponsible. So long as the liberal tradition suffers from this depressive reaction, which derives from the traumatic disenchantments of the Stalin era, so long is it likely that our society will suffer from a paralysis of will. Perhaps it is this which the generation who first approached politics on the Aldermaston road have been finding out.

1961

WARWICK
UNIVERSITY

The Business University

When student unrest erupts at a British university, two standard reactions can be expected. The first assumes that the students are alone responsible, and leads on to speculations as to their motives. The second assumes that responsibility may be charged to old-fashioned elements in the university administration and among senior academic staff, who have responded too slowly or too clumsily to legitimate student demands.

There is, however, a third explanatory hypothesis, which most observers would overlook as being too improbable.

This is the explanation that dominant elements in the administration of a university had become so intimately enmeshed with the upper reaches of consumer capitalist society that they are actively twisting the purposes and procedures of the university away from those normally accepted in British universities, and thus threatening its integrity as a self-governing academic institution; and that the students, feeling neglected and manipulated in this context, and feeling also — although at first less clearly — that intellectual values are at stake, should be impelled to action.

Such a hypothesis seems unlikely, but it might be worth sketching — in an abstract way — how it might come about. An old provincial university is often immersed deeply in

This article first appeared in *New Society*, 19 February 1970.

local business and civic life, and is subject to many utilitarian (and sometimes improper) pressures. But it also employs large numbers of teachers and administrators who have, over the years, established traditions intended to safeguard certain academic priorities; and its affairs are governed by a high formality of bureaucratic procedure. The vice-chancellor, while wooing private and public money, is also expected to defend his academics from external non-academic pressures, and to represent the independence of his university institution as a place of learning.

A new university might be established, however, to which a new kind of vice-chancellor was appointed, who saw it as his particular mission to establish a new type of intimate (and subordinate) association with 'industry'. He might see himself not so much as an academic organizer and arbitrator as the managing director of a business enterprise.

Such a man would hold quite exceptional power, and would have commanding influence over an input of some millions of money — mostly public, some private. Having a decisive say in the appointment of his first professors, he could also virtually nominate at his pleasure approved laymen to the university's governing Council: or he could do this if he had a close working understanding with the Council's chairman. A raw university Senate (comprised of members who, for the most part, depended upon him for favours without which their academic plans would be frustrated) and a complaisant Council (in part comprised of his own nominees) would offer no serious check to his power.

If the university also raised several millions of pounds in private-appeal moneys, and if the allocation of these moneys lay effectively within his control, his ability to secure his own power by dispensing influence would be enlarged. It would be possible for him to decide — without close regard to student demand, national need, or the logic of academic development and achievement — which areas should expand and which should be held back, which new subjects should be introduced, what public image the university should project.

Difficulties might arise if his senior administrative staff

should — out of professional integrity — resist this manipulation and insist upon open academic decisions and due procedure; or if an element in his academic staff should resent his decisions enough to question them repeatedly and forcibly on committees. But these difficulties could be surmounted — the first, perhaps, by changing the terms of employment of administrative staff so as to make them employees virtually subject to dismissal by the managing director: the second, perhaps, by intimidating some staff, by releasing financial favours to others for some cherished project, or, possibly, by confusing academic and policy issues by routing and re-routing them through an opaque complexity of committees, by rewriting minutes and by disguising where, when and how the critical decisions of policy are taken.

It might even be possible to adopt some of the seedier methods of certain business firms, by replacing face-to-face human relations and formal committee decisions by telephonic exchanges and a security-conscious administration, who were told to mark certain staff and students as 'disloyal' to the organization.

Such a corruption of the purposes of a university could take place — it should be noted — without any violent fracture of legal proprieties and even without irregularities which call for the attention of the auditors. The academic body would exhibit, at the higher levels, either accommodation to the system or a resentful paralysis of will; little would be heard in the corridors of pseudo-power other than the dull thud of academic knives in other academic backs; while at the lower levels there would be confusion and unfocused resentments.

In such a situation, only the students could defend the university's intellectual integrity, and they could only do this by the now classic forms of student 'revolt'. Such a revolt, in such a context, would — it could only be expected — display a mixture of motives, offer a confusion of objectives, and have unhappy as well as idealistic and heroic features.

If such a revolt were to occur, then the position of the university teacher would seem to be clear. He could not confine his role to that of making clucking protective noises on behalf of the rights or good intentions of his students. As an intellectual worker, in whatever field of study, he must be unconditionally opposed to the mystification of the truth. He could no longer, by his silence, assist in the mystification of the very institution in which he and his students work. He should come to the side of the students by telling them what he knows of the truth.

Such an institution could not exist on this side of the Atlantic. We may heave a sigh of liberal relief.

There does, however, exist, in the mid-Atlantic of the Motor Industry, the new University of Warwick. Pitched in cold fields three miles from any urban facilities, its staff and many of its students are week-day visitors. The students stand waiting in the wind for the inadequate public service transport, or rely on hitches from friendly citizens from their digs in Coventry, Kenilworth or Leamington Spa. The white-tiled buildings straggle across more than a mile, the University's administrative block standing at the opposite pole of the site to the main teaching buildings, laboratories and library.

The students' own living, eating and recreational facilities are segregated again, like the cafeteria and service stations on a detour from a motorway; and the students' social building has the lack of privacy, noise and dehumanized utilitarianism of that kind of public convenience. The Administration calls it Rootes Hall: the students call its main area 'the airport lounge'. There is no central campus, no quadrangle or social facilities where the staff and students can easily intermingle on their normal occasions. Whatever other instruments the architects may have used on their drawing-boards, they certainly made lavish use of a divider and a ruler.

The Vice-Chancellor, Mr J.B. Butterworth, MA, JP, is a lawyer whose previous post was as a bursar of an Oxford college. The keynote of his planning, from the first initiation of the University, has been clear: this was to be a forward-looking institution, with exceptionally close relations with industry, employing advanced methods of internal business management, with an ambitious rate of growth towards a target of 20,000 or even 25,000 students: this was to be a

Massachusetts Institute of Technology for the Midlands.

There is nothing exceptionable in this, and much that many people might approve of. In one or two respects the Vice-Chancellor achieved spectacular successes: the citizens of Coventry through their then Labour-controlled City Council presented the University with a handsome quarter-million-pound site on the periphery of the city's limits, and the Warwickshire County Council donated land comparable in extent and value, adjoining the city's lands. An initial University appeal fund raised some £2.5 million, mainly in covenants from local industrialists.

The success of the Vice-Chancellor's policies is indicated by the roll call of chairs endowed by outside funds. These include the Barclays Bank Professor of Management Information Systems, the Clarkson Professor of Marketing, the Esmée Fairbairn Professor of the Economics of Finance and Investment, another Clarkson chair in economics and the Volkswagen Professor of German.

Well and good. Well and good also to the Institute of Directors Professor of Business Studies and to the Pressed Steel Fisher Professor of Industrial Relations who have recently received massive injections of public and private money for their research programmes, the latter programme being supported to the extent of some hundreds of thousands of pounds by the Ford Foundation, the Social Science Research Council and the Leverhulme Trust.

This is itself the state of the current academic game, and reveals only somewhat more than the normal pattern of the distortion of academic growth in the directions which private or earmarked endowments dictate. It is only to be expected, also, that the disposition of these endowments, as well as the uses to which the University's foundation appeal have been put, have occasioned some jealousies among professorial staff — unconvincingly concealed from the knowledge of their juniors and their students. (The University's foundation fund is administered separately by trustees, and does not form part of the annual published statement of accounts.)

The effects of this channelling of money are, of course, felt most acutely in the arts and several of the social science subjects. In the fifth year of the University's development, these subjects are still housed in crowded and unsatisfactory accommodation at the top of the library building, while the sciences have substantial, well-equipped new buildings. But, in terms of the 'end product' of the whole process, 264 first degrees were awarded in arts and social science subjects in 1969, as against 127 in the sciences.

The University's published accounts show that by 31 July 1969 there had been, in capital expenditure on equipment, £437,498 for engineering science, £319,249 for physics (furniture, books and equipment), £321,553 for the molecular sciences and a further £101,150 for the workshops. The total that was allowed for the library in furniture, books and equipment, over exactly the same initial period, was £171,858. (This does not, of course, take account of *current* expenditure.) The researches going forward in the scientific laboratories are, no doubt, valuable and of general scientific and technical importance; but with work going on in such problems as metal fatigue (Massey Ferguson), vehicle instrumentation (Rootes and Ford Motor Company), fatigue in tyres (Dunlop), and high-speed machine-tool cutting tips (Alfred Herbert), local industrialists may be forgiven if their interest in the University is largely as a laboratory for their own research and development.

What is, perhaps, not wholly traditional in old-fashioned university terms is the constitution of the University's governing body, the Council. At first sight this is constituted on the usual lines. There is a majority of laymen; a minority of duly appointed academic representatives (this even includes two students). The laymen include three representatives each from the Warwickshire County Council and the Coventry City Council; and there are nine co-opted lay members. It is generally understood that nominations for co-option emerge through the Vice-Chancellor or else emerge through the Chairman of Council (the Pro-Chancellor).

With one exception (the Bishop of Coventry), all nine co-opted members are representative of very substantial business interests. Sir Stanley Harley is Chairman and Managing Director of Coventry Gauge Limited and director of fifteen companies, mostly concerned with machine tools: he is also President of Coventry Conservative Association. Gilbert A. Hunt is Managing Director and Chief Executive Officer of Rootes Motors Limited (now American-owned, by Chrysler International), and also a director of the Reed Paper Group. Lord Iliffe is Vice-Chairman of the *Birmingham Post and Mail* and Chairman of Coventry Newspapers Limited. Sir William Lyons is Chairman and Chief Executive Officer of Jaguar Cars Limited, Chairman of Coventry Climax Engines, Guy Motors (Europe), Daimler Company and Henry Meadows, and a director of British Leyland. J.R. Mead, an accountant, appears to be a director of some forty smaller companies. Lord Rootes explains himself. A.F. Tuke is Vice-Chairman of Barclays Bank, and R.D. Young is Chairman of Alfred Herbert Limited and a director of Rugby Portland Cement.

No impropriety here, of course: a lack of tact, perhaps, to co-opt only one part of the spirit to eight parts of mammon. A lay body has a role to play in the running of a university, and sympathetic industrialists have a place on it and can lend experience. But . . . perhaps the people of Coventry or of Warwickshire might not feel themselves to be wholly represented. (Since Labour lost control of Coventry City Council, no individual from Coventry's strong labour movement has in fact held a place on the University Council.)

Two other powerful figures complete the Council: R.J. Kerr-Muir, a director of Courtaulds, who is the University's Treasurer; and Sir Arnold Hall, Chairman and Managing Director of the Hawker-Siddeley Group, who is the University's Pro-Chancellor and the Chairman of its Council.

These are all very busy men, and some of them, no doubt, can do little more than grace the Council with their names and offer to it their goodwill. But several have lent to the University their very active services — notably Sir Arnold Hall, R.J. Kerr-Muir and Gilbert Hunt. The latter is Chairman of the University's Building Committee, while Mead, Tuke and Kerr-Muir serve on the crucial Finance and General Purposes Committee.

The Council is generally held to have — both in plenary sessions and (even more so) through its committees and executive officers — more direct and continuous influence within the decision-making levels of the University's government than precedent normally sanctions in other universities. This cannot be found out by reading the University's statutes. It is more a question of a certain style of management techniques.

The Vice-Chancellor has said, more than once, and at meetings of Assembly (the congregation of the full academic staff): 'We must remember that Council is our employer.' On more than one occasion decisions which (in conventional practice) might be assumed to be the concern of the University's academic governing body — the Senate — have been overturned by Council.

Trivial academic politics, no doubt. But there has been growing, among staff and students, an increasing sense of the opacity of the University's decision-making procedures, as critical decisions — affecting finance, social policy, building, university development, student representation — are moved from committee to committee, and decided in places where the Vice-Chancellor and one or more of his powerful co-opted Council members themselves have overriding influence.

Attempts by staff to influence future academic development, after protracted and sometimes enthusiastic discussion in the academic schools and boards, have, more than once, disappeared into the upper air with little explanation.

More than two years ago Professor Zeeman, the distinguished mathematician carried an overwhelming majority of Assembly in support of a resolution favouring an independent student-controlled union building (a commonplace in most universities). The proposal was upheld, by smaller majorities, in Senate. The Vice-Chancellor and his close Council associates were inflexibly opposed to this, in part because they wish to employ student social facilities during vacations as a conference centre, rather more (one suspects) because they have an understandable dislike of the word 'union'.

The proposal was shunted through delaying procedures and eventually was to come up for decision on Council. Some days before the Council meeting the Vice-Chancellor informed Professor Zeeman that if he, Zeeman, could see his way to remaining silent when the matter was debated on Council, the Vice-Chancellor, for his part, could see no reason why certain mysteriously-delayed building conversions — essential for housing an international seminar of mathematical scholars — should not, at the next building committee, be rapidly advanced. Outraged, Professor Zeeman circulated an account to members of Council in advance of their meeting, suggesting that he had been subjected to improper pressure. When Council met, its Chairman severely rebuked the Professor for his violation of procedure: the proposals for a union building were defeated.

Sad stuff — and in violation of procedure to mention it. In any case, it is often suggested to staff that they should be grateful that they are able to call upon such expert industrial experience, in managing their affairs and finances by the most advanced managerial techniques. Warwick has spent a high proportion of its public (UGC) resources upon administrative costs, but the benefits accruing to them have not been immediately apparent. Since scarcely any Council members are known to have attended academic or open social events in the University, it is hard for staff to know what their managerial skills consist in.

Page after page of the evidence taken during the parliamentary inquiries in the case of Bristol-Siddeley Engines, when investigating that company's overcharging of the British public by some £3.5 million in excess profits on defence contracts (in the repair of aero-engines), give rise to an uneasy sense that managerial techniques may be only too much like techniques which academics have experienced nearer home:

'You see, this again is one of these rather curious examples of perhaps my language being imprecise. I say "when this matter was brought to the board room" and I do not say that it was discussed by the board. In fact, it was discussed by Mr Davidson, first with me and then with Sir Arnold Hall and, for reasons which I have explained about the constitution of the company, in a matter of the greatest importance our decision was really final . . . and I think you will find that Sir Arnold probably consulted his financial director and I probably consulted mine, and we told Mr Davidson to get on with it . . .' (evidence of Sir Reginald Verdon-Smith, 21 March 1968, *Third Special Report from the Committee of Public Accounts*, p. 55).

Sir Arnold Hall, the Chairman of the University Council, was of course Managing Director of Bristol-Siddeley during the three years when it seemingly did not come to the notice of senior management that defence contracts were running at the satisfactory rates of 120 per cent profit (Sapphire 6), 124.9 per cent profit (Sapphire 7), 135.2 per cent profit (Viper) and 142.6 per cent profit (Proteus). Such matters (his fellow directors explained to the committee) might never have been important enough to have come before their notice.

Early in 1968 the University Council engaged a firm of industrial consultants, John Tyzack and Partners, to carry out an investigation into the administrative structure of Warwick. Their report — which is clearly being implemented by stages — was presented in a style, and revealed a manner of thinking, somewhat strange to academics. 'Taken as a whole, the University is certainly inefficient by normal commercial or industrial standards.' (Alas, no lecturer's profitability could compare with that of Sapphire 7.) Assuming for no stated reason that the University's policy demanded a rapid rate of expansion it cautiously recommended 'economies' to further this by means of an increase in the ratio of students to staff. (To a university teacher this means more work or poorer teaching to larger groups; the student's 'economy' is to find staff less available.) The Vice-Chancellor (the report said) was heavily engaged in 'maintaining the momentum' of the University, 'nurturing its reputation for high academic achievement', and in:

> fostering its interests in the highest circles, attracting financial support, and enhancing its status by playing a part in the public life of the University world at large both inside and outside the United Kingdom. His image is its image.

He was so busy in these many ways that he required the services of an assistant or deputy Vice-Chancellor. This post (it was recommended) should not carry security of tenure: 'the reasoning here is that this is primarily an administrative appointment, and we see no reason why it should not be treated by Council in the same way as a board of directors would treat the appointment of a general manager'. The University was to be structured according to the principle of absolute loyalty and responsibility to its chief executive, the Vice-Chancellor. The Vice-Chancellor should have the power to veto committee decisions and refer them back to Council or Senate. Indeed, Messrs Tyzack perceived very little to recommend itself in the University's structure of academic policy-making:

> We have been told that democracy has a special place in university life, and that there is constant political pressure from the rank-and-file of the academic staff claiming the right not only to be consulted more but to 'have a hand in decision-making'. The result in practice is already an amorphous and time-wasting system which has led to needlessly protracted argument, dilatoriness in the taking of decisions, uncertainty regarding the effective centres of power and action, and at times to conflicts of policy . . .

No firm could increase its output in this slovenly way. 'Sooner or later the University of Warwick will have to come to terms with the age-old conflict between democratic principles and effective government.' Indeed, academic committees would not stand up before time-and-motion study. 'Committees absorb not only the energies of salaried members of the academic staff whose primary function is supposed to be teaching and research, but also the time of registry staff who have to service the committees.' 'We cannot emphasize too strongly . . . that whatever a committee's area of authority it has no power to seek implementation otherwise than through the Vice-Chancellor.'

If committees could not actually be abolished, the smaller the better: 'the bigger the committee the less desirable it is that there should be frequent meetings, for the man-hours consumed will be proportionately higher'.

A section of the report was devoted to the products of this new, forward-looking operation: the students. 'The University must somehow put across the message that the

My dear Vice-Chancellor...

TUTORIAL

student is considered important as an adult member of the community, and that the authorities care about him and value him.' Representation of students on any important policy-making committees was not commended: but a student liaison committee might be set up, 'whose main function would be to provide a working link between the students and the administration rather than the University at large'.

At the end of Warwick's last academic session, the Registrar — an officer who, in most universities, is to be measured in power beside the Vice-Chancellor, and one who is, above all, concerned to ensure that all formal procedures are properly observed — tendered his resignation and accepted a post at another university. Several of his senior administrative staff left with him. Neither the Senate nor the Council instituted any inquiry into the reasons for their departure, and their own professional code commands their silence. They were universally respected by the staff, as honest, accessible and hard-working men.

On Tuesday 10 February *The Times* carried a three-page supplement (for which the university paid some £1,500 — as much as three student grants or an assistant lecturer's annual salary) on 'Science at Warwick University'. 'Tailored to industry's needs', wrote the Technology Correspondent. 'Projects ... directly related to modern industrial needs', was the theme of a short message from J.B. Butterworth. On Wednesday 11 February the students invaded the Registry, infuriated by the prevarication about student control in their three-year pursuit of humanized surroundings — not meaning only union buildings.

Opening a file in an unlocked office next to the Vice-Chancellor's they came, almost at once, upon the astonishing report of the Director of Legal Affairs of the Rootes Organization on the visiting American professor, David Montgomery. Knowing that he was my colleague, a student rang me. I went in, inspected the letters, and decided immediately that they must be made public to the academic staff. As I left the registry, some 150 students were holding an intense but responsible discussion. The issue: should they —

despite any promises which some felt that they had made to an administrator — force the Vice-Chancellor's door and inspect all files that he and his assistants had not hurriedly taken away earlier in the day. They were very angry.

This is, of course, the corporate society, with all its ways of adapting and tailoring men to industry's needs, the corporate managerial society, with its direct access to legal process to prevent the truth from being published, making the very air of Warwick this week crackle with tension, as we have been waiting for that alignment of forces to move in on us.

It might be thought that we have here already, very nearly, the 'private university,' in symbiotic relationship with the aims and ethos of industrial capitalism, but built within a shell of public money and public legitimation. (The University's published accounts for the year ending July 1969 show that it has already expended from HM Treasury £8,620,519 in non-recurrent grants alone, as against £1,307,856 in private gifts.)

There are issues enough to be pondered here. The integrity of a university as a self-governing institution, which now seems like a fading episode of liberalism. Personal rights of privacy and academic liberties. The question of due representation on the lay bodies of institutions primarily dependent upon public money, as well as the powers of such bodies — and of administrative officers — in relation to the academic staff. And other issues. The attitude of the labour movement towards this kind of spying.

There will be time to think and talk about these things. But, as I write, the first need is for public opinion to give support to our students. Despite all its unhappy history of manipulation, the University of Warwick has kept the services of many very good and — it is now becoming plain — more than a few courageous staff. There are human and material resources here in abundance, capable of making the University a first-rate and modern centre of learning, if its independence and internal self-government can, in this crisis, be asserted. Such a university might properly develop far wider and more differentiated relationships with the people of industrial Warwickshire. Until recently the system was so opaque that few can be accused of seeing it in more than an episodic way. The staff could only see its consequences — these rows, these frustrations, this or that administrative hang-up. Collectively, all of us — all we liberal academics — were struck with a paralysis of will as the system not only grew round us, but built us into its own body-walls. Once inside there it looked as if we were running our bit of the show: but the show itself was being directed towards other ends.

We have been luckier than any of us had the right to deserve in the quality of our students. They took the initiative. They asked the right questions. They began to understand the answers.

They stood firm against rhetoric, against threats, against the special pleading of those with large interests to lose. They have — by now in scores — put their academic careers at risk. It is they who have reasserted the idea of a university. They may well need help.

A Report on Lord Radcliffe

When one is involved in controversy — as I have been at Warwick — one inevitably attempts to construct some mental picture, some cultural 'identikit' of one's opponent. One wishes to understand, not only his opinions and actions, but also the nexus of belief or policy out of which these flow.

No doubt all such mental constructs, attempted in a situation of conflict, are unfair; and no doubt I have as little likelihood of understanding the mind of Lord Radcliffe as he has of understanding that of a militant student leader. But in any event the attempt is being made, and I have spent some part of the last three or four days in his company.

I don't mean in his physical company. I have met Lord Radcliffe only once, a few weeks ago, and I found him to be an eminently courteous gentleman, easy in his manners, and wearing his great distinction lightly. As Chancellor of the University he had been called out of his well-deserved retirement to perform what he could (increasingly) see to be a complex and even distasteful inquiry — small change, perhaps, after the series of great national inquiries of which he has been chairman, but time-taking and delicate all the same — and it was clear that he intended to do what he considered to be his duty.

I have tried, by turning to his writings and his public life, to form some estimate of how such duty would be considered.

This article first appeared in *New Society*, 30 April 1970.

If one turns to *Who's Who*, one is confronted with a distinction that is formidable: the Viscount Radcliffe, GBE, PC (1949), life peer (1962); educated at Haileybury and New College, a QC at the age of thirty-six (1935); Lord of Appeal in Ordinary, 1949-64; an address off the Duchess of Bedford Walk, a country place called Hampton Lucy House (some literary reminiscence here — wasn't Shakespeare supposed to have done his deer-poaching on a Lucy estate?); club, Brooks's.

Lord Radcliffe has said firmly (in the Rede lecture at Cambridge University in 1961): 'Let a fairy grant me my three wishes, I would gladly use them all in one prayer only, that never again should anyone using pen or typewriter be permitted to employ that inane cliche "Establishment".' But even Cambridge University could not come up with a fairy with this power, and the word forces itself onto the page. It is scarcely possible to think of any living man who has been accorded such trust, by successive governments and by diverse public bodies, as has been accorded to Lord Radcliffe.

He was Director-General of the Ministry of Information between 1941 and 1945, handling massive exercises in public relations and screening the most secret information. He was Chairman of the Royal Commission on Taxation of Profits and Income (1952), of the Committee of Inquiry into the Monetary and Credit System (1957-9), and he was again accorded access to the inmost confidences of the state as Chairman of the Vassall Case Tribunal and, above all, the inquiry into security procedures in the public services (1961-2).

This is only a part of his work in the direct line of public service. Less directly, he has served as Chairman of a number of quasi-public educational or cultural bodies: of the BBC Advisory Council (1952-5); of the Board of Trustees of the British Museum (1963-8) — a post which he left with a display of public indignation at government policy which earned him the respect of all scholars; Chairman of the Board of Governors of the School of Oriental and African Studies (from 1960); Chancellor of the University of Warwick (from 1965).

I have a literary habit of imagination, and already there comes to my mind those passages of a Buchan novel, where politician, lawyer and serving officer enjoy a camaraderie of action: or, perhaps, the opening of *Heart of Darkness*:

'The Director of Companies was our captain and our host ... The Lawyer — the best of old fellows — had, because of his many years and many virtues, the only cushion on deck, and was lying on the only rug. The Accountant had brought out already a box of dominoes ... Marlow sat cross-legged right aft.'

And Lord Radcliffe himself gives one a certain licence to improvise such fantasies, in his own brief reminiscences of his time as a Fellow of All Souls (1922-37), whose non-resident fellows were 'strategically placed at the important centres of our public life':

'A minister or secretary of state ... an archbishop and here or there a bishop, the permanent head of this depart-ment of state or that (preferably Treasury or Foreign Office), one or two headmasters from really important schools, the editor of *The Times* and someone from the inner circle of the City: and, of course, several of the leading lawyers of the day.'

Lord Radcliffe's literary productions are slender. As he notes himself, the greater part of his output has been 'sub-merged' in the reports of committees or in legal judgements. He has delivered (in 1951) the Reith lectures, on *The Problem of Power*: three lectures on *The Law and its Compass* at Northwestern University, Illinois (1960): and a series of addresses, for the most part on occasions of distinction, collected in *Not in Feather Beds*.

All confirm the impression of a man who is both cultured and judicious: of a lawyer who observes the law in its his-torical evolution and who is aware of its limitations. The assumptions (which are conservative) are rarely stated directly and never stated stridently. One is aware, in his style, of a need for privacy which goes beyond reticence, even of a certain loneliness (to sit in judgement may be a lonely occupation) which is, in a personal sense, endearing. One responds to a certain fortitude with which he repudiates the modish cries of liberal individualism and reaffirms, with quiet emphasis, unfashionable opinions.

He is entitled to these opinions. But many, at Warwick and beyond, are also entitled to inquire into these opinions, since he is inquiring into theirs. And here I can't do other than return to a passage of his Cambridge lecture of 1961 where he defines a certain kind of 'Establishment people':

'There are those who consider that they are by some natural decree of tradition or inheritance appointed to occupy and retain the seats of power. Such persons are generally found to be somewhat indifferent to the purposes or principles for which they exercise their power, the great thing being that the natural order should not be violated to the extent of their losing control.'

Indifference to principle we may leave aside: this must always be a matter of degree, and Lord Radcliffe's writings leave one in no doubt that there are certain principles which he would defend to the end. For the rest, one may put it beside a certain tone in Lord Radcliffe's writings. Addressing the Law Society on 'Law and Order' in 1964 he declared:

'Out of the few institutions of this country that ought to be accorded national status, one blindly perpetuates a radical myth that finds its natural enemy in all authority, and the other clings to an outmoded formula that denies the acceptance of any law beyond that of its own will . . . Indeed, it is a serious question whether England is not rapidly becoming, in the strict sense, an ungovernable country.'

In the context of the address it is difficult not to conclude that the two national institutions so delicately alluded to are the Labour Party and the TUC: they are not, at least, the Church or the Bank of England. 'We need more leadership than we get,' he declared in an Oration at the LSE in 1965, 'in the sense that at all levels of society we need more persons of experience and authority to speak and act boldly and sincerely, without deference to the subtleties of public relations or the imputed susceptibilities of youth or of egalitarian opinion.'

'As a matter of principle', he notes in his report on the Warwick 'files' (paragraph 59), 'I retain some doubts in my own mind whether there may not be teachers so far committed to particular socio-political systems as to disqualify them from the objective analysis of their subject that the university tradition itself assumes.' It is a chilling doubt when one recalls that it does not arise in the mind of *any* retired judge, but in the mind of the judge who was Chairman of the Committee on Security Procedures in the public service, who knows as few men in this land do what exactly is entailed in the 'positive vetting' procedures to which civil servants are subject.

The brief of this committee was to inquire into the measures of safeguarding information in the civil service against the Intelligence services of foreign powers, and against 'subversive organizations in this country, of which in current conditions the most formidable is the Communist Party of Great Britain, with its fringe of associated bodies and sympathizers'. One wonders what kind of brief, in the 'current conditions' of 1970, a similar committee might take: would it have to add Trotskyists, solidarists, anarchists, situationists, Maoists, yippies, and all their associated fringes? Or would it use some admirable formula like that used by this Radcliffe committee: 'For the sake of brevity we have followed the common practice of using the phrase "communist" throughout to include fascists.'

I have moved a good way from the Communist Party since I left it in 1956, but not far enough — not far enough by a very long chalk — not to remain angry at that established judgement. When I was a Communist I was fortunate in working for a university which did not (it seems) share Lord Radcliffe's doubts (my active membership was perfectly open). At the height of the Cold War there were unpleasant incidents at several other places, and I have no doubt that some vetting went on of new appointments; but most universities adhered, if lukewarmly, to the view of the Association of University Teachers that such vetting was improper, and that the proof of the pudding was in the eating — a university teacher was qualified to teach if he showed himself, in his work, to be so qualified. This position saved British universities from the savage political and cultural consequences of the McCarthyism which swept their fellow institutions in the United States.

The findings of that Radcliffe committee were (as with all his committees) judicious. A 'more active policy in departments' was recommended 'with regard to suspected cases of communist association and sympathy', with 'more frequent resort to the purge procedure in marginal cases.' 'It is not satisfactory just to sit back and feel unhappy.' (For some reason I sense an echo of this phrase in Paragraph 65 of the Warwick report, where Lord Radcliffe defends the Vice-Chancellor's right to collect in his files any matter which might bear upon the good order and discipline of the University: 'There is no rule either in equity or of common sense that one ought to wait to be blown up by an explosion before trying to detect the likelihood of its occurrence.')

At the same time the recommendations of the security committee were, by American standards, humane. Suspected subversives were not to be sacked but to be given innocuous jobs. Since people might change their propensity to subvert as they grew older, their positive vetting should be subject to reappraisals every five years or so. (Several of my senior colleagues may heave a sigh of relief at this.)

In any event, Lord Radcliffe knows deeply what security procedures entail and the complex issues involved. As he said in the House of Lords (6 July 1967):

> Telephone tapping ... the opening of letters; the scrutinizing of cables ... all are forms — as most Intelligence work is — of prying. It is an opprobrious phrase, prying, if you do not agree with the activity at all or with the purpose of the activity. It is a harmless phrase, if you agree with the exercise of that right, which was plainly conferred on the government by the act of 1920, and if you think that the exercise of that right is justified and is being done for a right national purpose ... The activity itself is a form of scrutiny.

And so, no doubt, was the attention with which Mr Gilbert Hunt and Mr Catchpole of Rootes Motors pursued Dr David Montgomery. Lord Radcliffe gives no hint in his report as to whether he would regard that scrutiny in an opprobrious or in a harmless light. As a judge he might not be called upon to do so, although as Chancellor of a university he might have been expected to record an opinion. He was, however, relieved from this difficulty by Mr Gilbert Hunt who assured him that 'throughout he regarded himself as making his protest on behalf of Rootes and not in his capacity as a member of University Council or as Chairman of its Building Committee'. It is a charitable distinction, and the report gives many other evidences of such charity.

Charity is present, however, only when dealing with the problems of men of authority and of established position, when confronted by the threat of subversion. It is always assumed that these are the people who must 'scrutinize' those beneath them. It is not a question of any gross unfairness, but simply the *tone* of the Establishment. Discussing the Vice-Chancellor's response ('I would like to be kept informed') to informations sent in to him from influential outsiders, Lord Radcliffe finds: 'To have asked to be kept in touch or be informed of any further incident, though it may mistakenly have encouraged the recipient, was neither here nor there in a personal exchange.'

It is, surely, once again, a matter of tone? If the Secretary of a Coventry trade union had written to the Vice-Chancellor, reporting upon a professor who had made a speech advocating legislation to curb the unions (complaining, perhaps, about the Chancellor himself, who appears to be supporting such a review of the law in his address to the Law Society in 1964), then perhaps the matter would never have risen to the chummy level of a 'personal exchange'. In any case, one is fairly confident that its outcome would have been either 'here' or 'there'. The phrase implies a certain ambience where 'personal exchanges' occur between men of established authority who share a common outlook, a common disposition, a common need to handle their own subversives, and in which whatever is said is 'neither here nor there' because here and there are, despite differences in roles and in the rules within which each operate, within very much the same ideological circle of here-thereness. If there had been any serious ideological abrasion, if the Vice-Chancellor had felt it to be his proper role to defend his staff or students against rather unusual kinds of scrutiny, then a tension would at once have been set up strong enough to have pulled here and there apart.

I have neglected to note one of Lord Radcliffe's many distinguished services. In 1947 he acted as Chairman of the Punjab and Bengal Boundary Commissions, and, in this capacity, he drew the critical dividing line between India and Pakistan: India was to be here, and Pakistan there. The incident has been recorded in Auden's poem, 'Partition':

> . . . in seven weeks it was done, the frontiers decided,
> A continent for better or worse divided.
> The next day he sailed for England, where he quickly forgot
> The case, as a good lawyer must. Return he would not,
> Afraid, as he told his Club, that he might get shot.

Auden may be unfair. Very likely he is. In my mental picture of Lord Radcliffe I cannot see him as forgetting easily this case, since, in his writings, there is one place where the reticence of his style is shed altogether, and that is where he recalls the historic record of the Anglo-Indian governing class. His collected papers include warmly coloured lectures in memory of Henry Lawrence and of Elphinstone; 'Thoughts on India as the Page is Turned.' and a tribute to Kipling. One of his Reith lectures was given over to the same theme — 'the wind has blown, the hot wind of the Indian plains, and the dust is already drifted over the memory of their achievement'.

And this reminds me, sharply, that I am here, and that Lord Radcliffe is there. For he belongs securely to — and has been a distinguished member of — a governing class. He is not ashamed of that, he shares its *esprit de corps*, and he has an unusual sense of its difficulties and duties. And I belong — much as I may try to disguise the fact even from myself — to a kind of shabby sub-Establishment, part literary, part academic, part Dissent, part (perhaps?) poaching, which has been watching *that* Establishment for some hundreds of years, resisting its pretensions, throwing back its encroachments, but never, finally, challenging its power.

Lord Radcliffe must have gained some of his allegiance to

his class at Haileybury, with its close links with the Indian Civil Service. And I must have learned some of my allegiances from my father, himself part academic, part man of letters, who spent so much of himself in the twenties and thirties writing books, pamphlets, letters to the press, and stumping half-empty halls, in the cause of Indian independence. He never received, nor would he have dreamed of receiving, any honours for such service; he gained — what he valued far more — the friendship of Tagore and of Nehru.

Brought up in such a tradition, in a household some of whose most distinguished visitors had served terms of imprisonment under British rule, it would be surprising if I shared Lord Radcliffe's assumptions as to the good intentions of governors, when 'scrutinizing' their inferiors. I see them as much the same as then, somewhat curbed in the open expression of their power, the older generation giving way to men with a new managerial style, for whose brashness, amorality, and open celebration of money and success I suspect that Lord Radcliffe himself may feel some distaste.

To describe him as a member of the ruling class, and as a very highly trusted member, is not to offer a personal or moral judgement. One may respect Lord Radcliffe precisely because he has been, on occasion, more blunt than is fashionable, less devious than is common in a society of opportunistic and managed public relations, ready, at times, to recall his own class to its duties. But to say this is also to resist the specious notion that any judicial impartiality, any here-thereness is possible, in matters which involve dispute, not over fact, but of principle. Lord Radcliffe has said himself ('Law and Order', 1964) that a judge 'must strip himself of all prejudices ... except, I ought to add, those prejudices which on consideration he is prepared to stand by as his sincere convictions'. His convictions as to what is necessary for the government of an academic institution are, without doubt, sincere. And so are the convictions of those who find scrutiny opprobrious and who are attempting to develop new modes of self-government. The report does not even serve as a hyphen between them. We (the governed) are here and he (the governor) is there.

Sir, Writing by Candlelight . . .

Let the power workers dim the street lamps, or even plunge whole districts into utter darkness, the lights of righteousness and duty burn all the brighter from 10,000 darkened drawing-rooms in Chelsea or the Surrey hills.

> Sir,
> May I, writing by candlelight, express my total support for the government in their attempt to halt the unbelievably inflated wage claims now being made?

inquires one correspondent to *The Times* (12 December). Undoubtedly he may and will.

Historians have often paid tribute to this peculiar character of the British. It is in grave adversity, in states of emergency, that they have noted this flaring-up of the British spirit. Only then do those proper guardians of the conscience of the community — the retiring middle classes — shed their usual reticence and openly articulate their values and commitments.

One infallible signal of such a time of bourgeois renaissance is the epistolary *levée en masse* of the readers of *The Times*. Such *levées* are infrequent; when they occur, one senses the presence of History. One such took place in February 1886 after the 'Trafalgar Square Riots', when unorganized unemployed demonstrators — after listening

From *New Society*, 24 December 1970.

to some exciting rhetoric from John E. Williams, John Burns and H. M. Hyndman of the Social Democratic Federation — broke into a brief rampage through the West End, smashing shop windows, looting and even throwing bricks at select London clubs. Worse riots occurred, in most years, in some parts of the country: but not on such sanctified ground as Pall Mall.

'Sir', wrote one unfortunate gentleman, whose carriage windows were smashed in the rioting: 'I am a subscriber to various charities and hospitals, which I shall discontinue. I have always advocated the cause of the people. I shall do so no more.'

But wounded and long-suffering righteousness, on these occasions, takes second place to the firm disciplinary mode. 'Sir', demanded one correspondent in 1886,

> What is the use of having a highly-paid Commissioner of Police, with proportionately highly-paid deputies, if they are afraid of the responsibility attaching to their posts? . . . When there is a kennel riot in any kennel of hounds, the huntsman and whips do not wait to get the special orders of the master, but proceed to restore order at once.

Another correspondent (11 February 1886) produced an example of the genre so rich that it has to be quoted at length:

> Sir,
> On returning from the Prince's Levée I was walking through Pall Mall, in uniform. It was gradually filling with very suspicious-looking 'unemployed' at that time, two of whom, turning towards me, one said, rather significantly, 'Why, who the —— is this chap?"
> As I passed the War Office entrance, formerly the Duke of Buckingham's, a blind fiddler, led by a little girl, came by . . . playing some odd tune or other, when a young guardsman on sentry stepped out and said, in a commanding tone, 'You stop that noise' . . . I thought, 'Now there is a man of common sense and of action.' It was a little thing to stop at the time, but when the snowball which a child or a blind fiddler could set rolling on the top of the hill reaches the bottom it has become in this country an immovable monster, in other countries a destroying avalanche.
> On the 10 April 1848, I was sworn in a special constable between

Buckingham Palace and the House of Commons. At the former we had a battery of Horse Artillery hidden in the stable yard. I asked the officer commanding what he was going to do? His answer was, 'We have our scouts, and if we hear of any gatherings we could run out and sweep the Mall or the Birdcage Walk in two minutes, or command St James Street and Pall Mall in three.' He would not wait till mischief was done. Are those days quite gone?
   Your obedient servant,

           Wilbraham Taylor

Such high heroics can rarely be repeated, just as the true, physical *levées* of the bourgeoisie against the plebs (the Volunteers against the Jacobins in 1800, the Yeomanry against the poor of Peterloo, the Specials against the Chartist 10 April, the debs and Oxbridge undergraduates against the General Strike) are too few to satiate the desire dramatically to beat the bounds of class. So the epistolary cry goes out for someone — the government — to discipline *them*, and put them back in kennels.

John E. Williams had been reported, in 1886, as having deplored that the unemployed were not well enough organized — not to riot and destroy property, but — to occupy the banks, Stock Exchange, and government offices. 'Sir', wrote one *Timesian*, 'if correctly reported, Williams must be an atrocious miscreant, compared with whom Gashford in *Barnaby Rudge* is a virtuous person.'

December 1970 has produced little in this genre of comparable quality, perhaps because electrical workers' leaders are scarcely typecast as communist or Trotskyist fiends. (Perhaps the nearest was the letter — 14 December — from Nicolas Bentley, suggesting that Robert Morley, who had dared to declare his solidarity with trade unionism, must be a 'callous reprobate'.) But the old theme of 'there ought to be a law against . . .' has been fully orchestrated. This was very evident in another vintage epistolary year, 1926.

One mine-owner addressed himself (5 June 1926) to the subject of the mineworkers' officials: 'Their one object is to squeeze as much money out of the industry as it will stand, to the detriment of the proprietors who have taken all the risk incidental to coalmining.' (A rigorous statistical examination of the number of coal-owners killed in mining disasters might not bear this out.) The Bishop of Durham came baying up behind (22 June): 'Trade unions now include in their ranks a great number of young men whose boyhood was spent during the war, when every kind of discipline was weakened . . . These lawless youths are well-fitted to become the janissaries of Communist Revolution.'

Trade unions were 'the mocking caricature of anything . . . democratic', and their rank-and-file were 'the hopeless tools of the ruling clique'. They could only be held down by stronger law. The compulsory secret ballot, then as now, was one grand recipe for the extirpation of strikes, from correspondents pathetically anxious to believe that if only the workers expressed their minds *in secret* they would turn out to be chaps just like themselves — or, rather, chaps *convenient to* themselves, compounded of all bourgeois virtues of prudence, self-help, and deference to property, but emasculated of the bourgeois reproductive system — the drive for *money*.

Such themes, announced in 1926, have, if anything, become more pronounced with the epistolary *posse comitatus* of 1970. Should strikes be forbidden by law? asks Sir H. T. Smith, from Wallingford (11 December). On the same day the 'long-suffering public' found a spokesman in H. P. Rae: deeply perturbed about invalids dependent upon 'continuously functioning kidney-machines' (which they aren't), he demanded: 'why the hesitation in putting in troops *now*?' 'The vast majority of the public', he assured *Times* readers from his Chelsea address, 'are sick to death of the squalid attempts by the unions to tyrannize', etcetera. Mr Tennet of Shottermill Ponds, Haslemere, also found (12 December) that the workers were 'misusing their monopoly position', and Richard Hughes, from the United University Club, suggested 'a national one-day token lock-out [by employers] in support of the . . . Industrial Relations Bill'.

Mr Flamank of Solihull (also 12 December) wanted to see the formation of 'an emergency service corps', which could, at the Home Secretary's whistle, 'move in and run the services'. Those encouraging industrial unrest, 'be they communists, shop stewards or militant students, are just as much our enemies as were the Nazis'. (Perhaps one can hear an echo of

Wilbraham Taylor and the Horse Artillery over Birdcage Walk?)

Such situations tend to make the bourgeois feel, with a sudden flash of insight, their own value in the world: they bear its weight and (*vide* the coal-owner) its risks upon their shoulders. 'Think what the feeling would be', exclaimed Lord Midleton (28 June 1926), 'if any pit were closed for the day and all wages lost to the men because the managing and controlling staff required a day off!' A similar thought occurred to Mr Reade (14 December 1970): 'Sir, If manual workers can work to rule, why not wages clerks too?' Aha! The argument is final: what if we, who *have* the money, stopped letting you rotters have it ! ! !

It is not to be thought that, in such national emergencies, the bourgeoisie is solely concerned with such paltry matters as money or comfort or class power. Not at all: the full moral idealism blazes out. Thomas Hughes, the Christian Socialist author of *Tom Brown's Schooldays*, came unhesitatingly to his post in the correspondence column in 1886: these modern socialists he found to be 'notorious ruffians', and 'If Mr Chamberlain will consider why he cannot be getting Messrs Hyndman & Co a year or two's oakum picking instead of "receiving their views in writing" he would be doing all honest folk more service, in my judgment.'

At such moments *Timesian* correspondents always know unhesitatingly what are the thoughts and needs of 'all honest folk' or of (see *The Times*, 14 December 1970) 'the welfare of the entire community' (Rose Cottage, Westhumble, Surrey). But it was left to the honest folksman, Sir Alan Lascelles (The Old Stables, Kensington Palace), to come forward as shop steward of 'an immensely larger union — namely, the union of British citizens' (17 December).

In 1926, however, the immediate requirements of the 'entire community' were pointed out to the striking miners in more dulcet tones, since they had made the tragic error of being manoeuvred into a bitter, wasting strike during the summer months, and the readers of *The Times* were suffering, not from empty grates, but from an over-full sense of moral outrage. At such a time, the clergy select themselves as the

proper admonishers. The Dean of Worcester advised
the miners (8 June 1926) that if they capitulated to the coal-
owners' terms they 'will have won a great victory — a victory
of their nobler over the lower self'. The Archdeacon of
Chester addressed the same homily with greater fervour:
capitulation by the miners 'would be good Christianity . . .
an act of personal self-denial . . . of personal self-renunciation
for the sake of others, following the supreme example of the
Greatest Figure in history'.

One has yet to notice, in 1970, correspondents congratula-
ting the power workers, who called off their work to rule, on
their good Christianity, or likening Frank Chapple to the
'Greatest Figure' in history. (Nor did *The Times* publish such
congratulations from rural deans in 1926, when the miners
returned to their pits defeated; after all, such letters, if read
at the pithead, might have induced moral complacency, and,
as events were to show, the nation was to expect a good deal
more Christianity from the miners in the coming years.)

But — let us be fair — there has been one change in the
genre in recent years: the clergy, generally, do not push
themselves forward so obtrusively, nor do they presume so
readily to express the conscience of the nation on socially
divisive issues. Their role, as national conscience and admonishers of delinquents, has been passed over, in good part, to
David Frost and Malcolm Muggeridge. Some small part, perhaps, has been taken over by that new conscience-bearer, the
middle-class housewife, who being out of the hurly-burly and
puerility of industrial warfare, can watch all things with a
wholly objective eye and instantly detect from her kitchen
the national interest. Thus, on 11 December, a correspondent
from Prescot, Lancs:

> . . . the radio is dead. The television is dead. The electric heaters are
> dead. The kettle is dead. The fridge is dead. My washing machine is
> dead. My iron is dead. All the street lights are dead . . . Goodness
> knows how many *tragic* deaths may result . . .

It is (she concludes) 'an exhibition of power surely grotesque
in its selfishness'.

All dark and comfortless: we stalk the drear world of the

psalmist or space-fiction writer: all that inanimate world of consumer goods, animated each quarter by the insertion of money, lies inert, disobedient. All flesh is grass, we know; but what (O ultimate of horrors!) if all gadgets turned out to be grass also? It is the Rebellion of the Robots, recorded by the author of Ecclesiastes.

Grotesque and selfish the power workers' action may have been. How can one know? Facts have been scarcer than homilies. Reading the press one learns that one has been living through little less than cosmic disaster. One had thought that one's neighbours had suffered little more than power cuts for several hours on three or four days, but the mistake is evident. Outside there, in the darkness, the nation had been utterly paralysed for week upon week; invalids dependent upon 'continuously operating' kidney-machines lived two or three to every street; armed robbers prowled the darkness with impunity; not a hospital in the country that was not lit solely by candles, with surgeons operating upon month-old babies by the light of a failing torch.

A comparatively few individuals, wrote a correspondent from Richmond (12 December), were inflicting upon the public 'catastrophic injury'. Why not 'issue an order *withdrawing all legal protection* from the persons and property of the workers concerned', and the officials of their unions? 'Let the community get its own back.' This 'whole community' (another correspondent, 16 December) 'has long been renowned for its patience and forbearance. But surely the time has come', etcetera. 'We are sick and tired . . .', 'the time has come', 'irresponsible' . . . irresponsible *to us*!

What is, of course, 'grotesque in its selfishness' is the time-worn hypocrisy of the bourgeois response to discomfort. Anyone familiar with the Victorian and Edwardian press cannot fail to detect, in these tones of moral outrage, that old bourgeois theme for moralisms: the 'servant problem'. But the servants now are out of reach; an electric light switch is impervious to the scolding of the mistress; a dust-cart cannot be given a week's wages in lieu of notice.

And anyone who has read his E. M. Forster or his Angus Wilson knows the old British bourgeois propensity to moralize his own convenience and to minister to his own comforts under a cloud of altruism. For 95 per cent of the bluster and outrage was the miasma arising from tens of thousands of petty material inconveniences. The electric alarm failed to go off, mummy fell over the dog in the dark, the grill faded with the fillet steak done on one side only, daddy got stuck for half an hour in the lift on the way to a directors' meeting, the children missed *Top of the Pops*, the fridge de-froze all over the soufflé, the bath was lukewarm, there was nothing to do but go early to a loveless bourgeois bed. But, wait, there was one alternative: 'Sir, Writing by candlelight . . .'

But to mention the *real* occasions might seem petty. It was necessary to generalize these inconveniences into a 'national interest'. The raw fillet steak became an inert kidney-machine, the dripping fridge an unlit operating theatre, the loveless bed became a threat to the 'whole community'. No matter: now the emergency is over, these moral fantasies will shrink back to their proper size. The shivering old-age pensioners (many of whom will continue to shiver all winter through on their inadequate pensions), the imperilled invalids (many of whom will continue in peril from inadequate medical provision) will cease to obtrude themselves in the correspondence columns of *The Times*.

It has been a notable state of national humbug. It was concluded, as in an obligatory ritual, by David Frost, at peak viewing hours on a Saturday night, bullying a few power workers, with a studio audience, handpicked for their utter insensitive self-righteousness, baying at his back.

Occasions were found, not only to express moral disapprobation, but also approval; the audience applauded to the echo nurses who, underpaid as they are, would never strike because of the needs of their patients.* David Frost who, from what one has heard, does not face the same financial dilemmas — and the withdrawal of whose labour would scarcely induce even this government to declare a state of 'national emergency' — was evidently delighted. The bourgeoisie has always been ready to acknowledge virtue in the servant class when it finds it: pliant, loyal, living patiently in

*Ha ha! [1979.]

the attic, carrying on dutifully a service to the 'whole community'. Aubrey Leatham, physician at St George's Hospital, Hyde Park Corner, saluted the same virtue among the cardiac technicians at his hospital (*The Times*, 16 December) who, earning 'as little as £415 a year, would like to strike, but they do not, because they are humanitarian'.

And how noble they are, indeed, to pace the hearts of emergency patients in the acute care area for only £8 a week! But, surely, if this is so, this also is an outrage, which we should have heard of before, and insistently, and not only as a stick to beat the power workers with? Has Mr Leatham taken up his pen before, to press the astonishing case of his cardiac technicians? Or will he, and the other militant correspondents to *The Times* and so many other papers, relapse into silence now that the inconvenience and discomfort is over?

The grand lesson of the 'emergency' was this: the intricate reciprocity of human needs and services — a reciprocity of which we are, every day, the beneficiaries. In our reified mental world, we think we are dependent upon *things*. What other people do for us is mediated by inanimate objects: the switch, the water tap, the lavatory chain, the telephone receiver, the cheque through the post. That cheque is where the duties of the good bourgeois end. But let the switch or the tap, the chain or the receiver fail, and then the bourgeois discovers — at once — enormous 'oughts' within the reciprocal flow.

But these 'oughts' are always the moral obligations of other people: the sewage workers ought not to kill fish, the dustmen ought not to encourage rats, the power workers ought not to imperil invalids, and — this week it will be — the postmen ought not to deny bronchitic old-age pensioners their Christmas parcels from grandchildren in Australia. Why, all these people owe a duty to the 'community'!

What the duty of the community is to these people is less firmly stated. Certainly, those whose lolly is the theme of the business supplements — those whose salary increases (like those of admirals and university teachers) are awarded quietly and without fuss, and which (it seems) create no national emergency and no dangerous inflationary pressures — have little need to compose letters to *The Times* as to their own moral obligations and duties.

It is the business of the servant class to serve. And it is the logic of this reified bourgeois world that their services are only noticed when they cease. It is only when the dustbins linger in the street, the unsorted post piles up — it is only when the power workers throw across the switches and look out into a darkness of their own making — that the servants know suddenly the great unspoken fact about our society: their own daily power.

Yesterday's Manikin

This first sentence of Harold Wilson's book runs: 'This book is the record of a Government all but a year of whose life was dominated by an inherited balance of payments problem . . .'

Not all of the book's contents confirm this allegation. Stricken sterling, it is true, presided over many Cabinet meetings; suffered dramatic haemorrhages on the steps of the House of Commons; was subjected to unnumbered 'frenetic' attacks, was stabbed in the back by a disloyal Opposition, was refused blood-transfusions by General De Gaulle; but still gamely dragged its gory limbs back again and again through the corridors of power, dictating this rise in the Bank Rate, that delay in extending the school-leaving age, these cuts in the social services and those imposts on their consumers.

But sterling did not dominate the Government single handed. For some 200 pages of its 800-page life, it appears to have been dominated by Mr Ian Smith. And for another 200 pages (perhaps the more important ones) it was dominated by the Presidents Joxon.

Thanks to the book, however, we are able finally to dismiss a ridiculous rumour assiduously fostered by Tory lobby correspondents: that the Government was dominated by *Mr Wilson*. No one could struggle through even one hundred

---

* Taken from *New Society*, 29 July 1971, reviewing Harold Wilson, *The Labour Government, 1964-70* (1971). Some passages of my original typescript — cut for reasons of space — have been replaced.

pages of its life, and still maintain that illusion.

The book starts badly, but it gets a great deal worse as it goes on. In his acknowledgements Wilson thanks all those who helped in its 'compilation'. It is an apt term, if the emphasis is placed on the *pile*. It certainly cannot be said to have been *written*, in the sense that (like it or not) Churchill's or Macmillan's were. It has been piled up, one damn thing after another: 'while the Vietnamese crisis was at its height, work was going rapidly ahead on the Budget'. Here we have the style —

> After a short Easter break I was back at Downing Street ... I found the usual accumulation of red boxes, and took the opportunity of seeing a number of ambassadors, high commissioners and foreign visitors, and also of interviewing those I was proposing to recommend for life peerages ...

Agonizing international crises, petty party intrigues, Crawfie-like revelations, jostle one against the other. Contingencies follow pell-mell upon one another's heels: the Ford's strike; Angouilla; John Silkin replaced as Chief Whip; Biafra; the borough elections.

At times the pace quickens, as when Lord George George-Brown stomps around, and even challenges Presidents Sterling and Joxon for his moment of preposterous dominance:

> Messages were coming to me from the Leader of the House and the whips saying that the tea-room at the House was seething, and letters, telephone calls, round robbins and memorials were going to George beseeching him to stay in the Government.

Since he was being such a thundering nuisance, he clearly had to be promoted. A real issue of principle suddenly surfaces: George enters a party meeting in the House and finds someone else sitting in his seat:

> George sat below the platform. Later that evening he telephoned my office, holding me responsible. He now knew where he stood, he said, but he was not going to resign; he would wait for me to sack him. Little did he know that I was about to offer him the one job within a Prime Minister's gift which, above all others, he wanted.

A lollipop for George: the Foreign Secretaryship of Great Britain. An expensive condiment, perhaps, for the loss of a seat on the platform. But, then, Wilson had not been 'responsible'. It was a Contingency who had sat down on George-Brown's seat, hence letting him know where he stood (or would have stood, had he not found a seat below the platform).

Indeed, this is the great unifying theme of these 800 pages. Wilson was responsible for *nothing*. Everything happened *to* him; for six years he himself happened nothing, except the re-arrangement of his ministers (fortunately he was surrounded by men of enormous virtuosity, like Michael Stewart, 'a wise and authoritative figure capable of filling any position in the Government'), and the ultimate happening of deciding on the election date ('before finally deciding, I needed to refresh my memory about the incidence of wakes weeks and other local holiday periods').

Apart from this, the book is a record of one accident and eventuality after another trooping into the Cabinet room, ever thicker upon each other's heels — the Prime Minister of Great Britain, a sandwich in one hand, a hot line to Washington in the other, dictating to a Garden girl a speech to a fractious TUC, as one after another they come: oh gosh, Ian Smith has diddled me again! oh lumme, the Torrey Canyon! great grief, sterling has had a coronary! oh golly, the Scots Nats have got Hamilton! yes, Mr Joxon! no, Mr Joxon! George, try a lollipop!

In such a throng, even President Sterling is in the end forced to sit below the platform. This book is the record of a Government all of whose life was dominated by President Contingency.

This is not to say that the book may not find an audience. Messrs Weidenfeld might survey the market addressed by Roget's *Thesaurus*, Partridge's *Dictionary of Slang*, etc., with a view to promoting this as Wilson's *Longer Dictionary of Cliché*. For here we have an evident master: Wilson never uses one cliché when two or three will suffice. He is never discreet; he 'draws a veil'. Ministers are moved 'from square leg to cover point'. International gatherings gnaw 'bones of contention'. The Chancellor of the Exchequer gives 'a touch on the tiller'.

What is more alarming is the growing conviction that the author apprehends the universe as cliché. The eye is mesmerized by the circumstances, or the febrile rituals, of power: the White House, Number 10, the seething tea-room. The power itself, and its occasions — the war in Vietnam, the conflict on the shop floor at Fords, the Biafran tragedy — are for ever obstructed from view by the machinery, and devalued of all intrinsic significance. It is not only that Wilson sees them wrongly: it is that he never sees them steadily and in themselves at all. They are points which may appear on the Order paper at Question Time, to which the Prime Minister must bend his mind only in search of an inscrutable evasion, calculated to silence the critics in his party.

When visiting De Gaulle, Wilson asked him how he spent his time at Colombey. The General replied that he walked in the woods and thought deeply. 'I said that I liked to walk, but not to think about public affairs — hence my preoccupation with golf.'

Wilson was, of course, preoccupied with other things as well as golf. He was preoccupied throughout — and to a ridiculous and pitiful degree — with his public image and his press, especially that part of the press which added afflatus to his self-image of 'responsible government' and which shared his own impeccable sense of cliché. During his futile dogsbodying attempts to 'mediate' over Vietnam, between an American government which concealed its intentions from him and disowned his initiatives and a Russian government which clearly found his exercises in agile political weightlessness to be meretricious, he found enormous comfort in a 'very obvious briefing to a trusted British correspondent' by President Johnson: 'How Wilson gained President Johnson's trust'. And how? 'Johnson has every confidence that Wilson is practical enough not to propose anything he could not accept.' Of an earlier, self-advertising and ill-prepared attempt to offer himself as 'mediator', Wilson comments: 'the Peking *People's Daily* modestly contented itself with calling me a "nitwit"'. One has the sense of having stumbled for a moment, out of endless dimly-lit circular corridors, into the light of the real world.

Returning doggedly to the corridors once more, one should note that here or there scraps of serious political information have been left for the reader to pick up. Those who have long studied the enormous power of the Civil Service and financial establishments will find abundant exemplification of their theses here. Mr Wilson entered into 'power' and found the Queen's Speech already drafted and awaiting on his desk (p. 20). The Foreign Office appears more than once as interpreting too literally and precipitately Wilson's intentions, as on 31 January 1966 when the Americans resumed bombing in North Vietnam: 'The Foreign Office, falling over itself to get into line, issued a press statement supporting the President's action. By an error, this was not submitted to me for approval' (p. 204). But the error (it transpires) was not one of political or moral principle; it lay in issuing a statement insufficiently opaque, at a time when Wilson was already embarrassed by his parliamentary 'Left' on the eve of an election.

Mr Wilson was also, as is proper in a responsible first minister of the Queen, preoccupied with problems of 'security'; not — as is manifest — security against the agents of that foreign power which was notoriously sapping British independence and self-respect at that time (one recalls that at this moment an agent funded by the CIA was even in control of *Encounter*), but security against revolutionaries in the labour movement. 'The moderate members of the seamen's executive were virtually terrorized by a small professional group of Communists or near-Communists' (an odd situation when even Wilson must admit that there were then — during the strike of June 1966 — no Communists on the seamen's executive). The British seamen, after decades of near-company unionism, had accomplished that most difficult of all industrial actions (in an industry whose members may be scattered at any point across the seven seas), a national strike, with high morale and solidarity.

A seamen's strike, more than any other industrial dispute, must be settled decisively. Once the men have put out to sea once more, the possibility of solidarity on a national scale may not recur for years or decades. Hence it is in the interests of the employers to parley, to procrastinate, to offer Courts of Inquiry, interim and partial resolutions; and it is in the logic of their situation that the men will be intransigent, demanding a maximum settlement. This — and not any Communist 'terrorization' — underlay the situation of June 1966. In any case, the spine-chilling tactics of 'this tightly knit group of politically motivated men' consisted in the demand for no settlement without either a ballot of the union membership or a recall delegate conference.

It was against the threat of this democratic process that Wilson proclaimed a State of Emergency, and used the full resources of the national media to smash the strike. Throughout the affair he was fully briefed by the 'senior people responsible for these matters' as to the information of spies (and perhaps of at least one *agent provocateur*?) within the seamen's and dockers' movement. From the sweepings of these *voyeurs* he constructed a sensational whodunit for presentation to the House (and thence to the more silly tabloids): the Liverpool and South Shields delegates, neither of them Communists, 'when attending the executive council in London . . . have stayed at the same flat as Mr Jack Coward . . . Mr Ramelson has visited the flat when they were there . . .' One wonders what Mr Wilson would have made (had he been Prime Minister in 1889) of the far more sinister comings and goings of Tillett, Mann and Burns during the dock strike of that year?

Even Mr Heath was unconvinced by this taradiddle, or thought it politic to pretend to seem so. This distressed Wilson far more than the manifest and caustic scepticism of the entire non-Communist labour movement (long habituated to not only Mr Ramelson but also to the emissaries of Mr George Woodcock and of Catholic Action running round visiting flats). So what did Wilson do? He arranged a special meeting for Mr Heath, 'on Privy Counsellor terms', where not only the 'senior people' (i.e. chairborne industrial espionage) but also 'one of the operators "in the field" ' were brought in to convince the Leader of the Opposition. (Mr Heath, as it happens, remained unconvinced — or thought it politic to seem so — which has a certain interest: a certain kind of sick social democracy has often proved itself to be more hysteric in its anti-Communism, more ideologically motivated and less capable of realism, than the authentic capitalist executive.)

The whole sad episode is set out on pages 233-41. What is astonishing is that so many in the labour movement appear to have forgotten it. They should not.

But I must correct myself; we do not, of course, have the *whole* episode, but only so much of that episode as Wilson feels disposed to offer, in the effort to afflate his 'responsible' image. Which raises the question of such memoirs in general. Historians find that the memoirs of politicians are among the least valuable source-materials of history, except insofar as they include materials (original correspondence, documents) not available elsewhere. For such purposes this example is almost useless. Politicians belong to that special class of liar who seem to be genuinely unable to discriminate between special pleading, the suppression of material evidence, and outright falsification of the record. The interval between action and the presentation of that action to a public in the most favourable possible light is so miniscule that the first becomes inextricably confused with the second.

Historians may begin to set about the work of threshing out the grain of the man from the bulky husk of his image in some thirty years time. One of the few reforms for which Wilson may be given personal credit was the shortening of the statutory limitation upon the inspection of Government papers; and he claims this credit in complacent terms. But, alas, unless some revolutionary change intervenes, neither I nor my readers will live long enough to test Wilson's account of the seamen's episode against the documentary record. For (Wilson neglects to tell his readers this) the thirty-year rule does not extend to matters which affect the 'security' of the state; and espionage into the trade union and socialist movement is precisely one such matter. Before my fellow tradesmen may sit down in the Public Record Office and open the files of the 'operators in the field' they must still wait for seventy-five or hundred years; and in the interim a good deal of ash will have gone up from the incinerators of the 'senior people responsible for these matters'.

One other preoccupation might be noted: I have been around the labour movement almost as long as Mr Wilson (although not in the same rarified regions), and after some thirty years of witnessing treasons one grows a skin of cynicism as thick as that of a Fabian tortoise. But even I was astonished at the unashamed admission (pp. 131-2) that the decision to introduce legislation against trade union wages-pressure was taken at the instance of Joe Fowler, the American Secretary of the Treasury:

> He was extremely helpful to us, but was anxious both about sterling and for the dollar, if anything were to go wrong ... While he did not attempt in any way to ... give us orders, he was apprehensive that if further central bank aid were required it would be difficult to mount it if we had no better safeguard against inflation than the voluntary system. It was in these circumstances that we began first to think in terms of statutory powers.

Not only to 'think', as it happens, but also to rush George Brown back from his holiday in the South of France, to hold high-level ministerial conferences and soundings of the TUC. This was in August 1965 ('it was not a welcome prospect with a majority of, at most, three'). Students of rodomontade will be entranced at the manner in which Wilson presents the ensuing tortuous four-year-long débâcle as yet one more famous personal victory in the art of the possible.

It is, after all, an art in which a certain kind of Labour politician should properly excel. Moving among a loosely knit group of men motivated by personal ambition, *primus inter pares*, the political art is reduced to a certain skill in playing off one rival against the other. Habituated by decades of party conferences and parliamentary-party jockeyings to take decisions, not in terms of any fixity of principle, but upon an estimation of block-votes to be garnered, of the balance upon the right and the left of the party, and the proper quantum of ambiguity which may propel a compromise through the centre — it is within such psycho-dramas that Wilson experienced his formative biography.

Propelled on to the national scene, he is apprehensive of polls, of the 'press', of by-elections; but *far* more apprehensive of the balance of forces within the parliamentary party. It is against his estimate of this balance, and not against any analysis of the actual issue before him or the principle intrinsic to it, that his postures (for he is always more ready for a posture than a policy) are struck. Hence he was happier, more secure, even — fleetingly — more decisive, with a majority of three than with a majority of a hundred. And even on the international scene he maintained imperturbably the same mentality of a conference fixer. In a revealing commentary upon Rhodesia (p. 180) he notes:

> Much too often, difficult decisions of government are dismissed in terms of a Prime Minister's reaction to pressure from the Opposition, or minority — sometimes majority — pressure from Government back-benchers, so that the real task of government is almost always reduced to parliamentary manoeuvring ... So far from domestic political considerations swaying our judgement there were, in fact ... four 'constituencies'.

These constituencies were, 1) the dimension of Rhodesian opinion, 2) the dimension of public opinion in Britain, 3) the views of Commonwealth countries, 4) the dimension of world opinion, as expressed in the United Nations. Good grief, *four* dimensions of block-votes, and George Woodcock unable to influence three of them! In such a multi-dimensional universe, the art of the possible ceases to be merely Janus-like and becomes prosenneahedral.* What a field for posturing, for drafting ambivalent statements, for scurrying around the world and making evasive statements at airports! Had the dimension of *principle* been added, the life of a Prime Minister would have become insupportable.

Mr Wilson would like us all to see the universe in his way. Indeed, he would perhaps like to introduce statutory powers to compel us to do so. Recent petulancies have suggested that he is not content with oral and visual media which have increasingly imposed, with their vast resources, the obscene fiction that all politics must be 'party-political' politics; which expropriate the British people of all liberties of address

* Prosenneahedral. I fell upon this happy Wilsonian word by chance in the dictionary: 'having nine faces on two adjacent parts'.

to the media on political matters unless these be approved by the conventions of 'party-political' formulae; and which decree that large and arresting political realities which have not been duly devalued into parliamentary 'party-political' packages do not exist. He would, perhaps, like some statutory watchdogs of the 'public interest', some permanent emissaries from the Whips' offices closeted with the directors of television, measuring out the 'party-political' minutes, sampling the specific gravity of cliché, censoring intruders from the workshop or the university, utterly prohibiting entertainers or satirists who have the insolence to come upon the air without a licence from a Whip.

Some readers will think me unfair. With 800 pages of Mr Wilson in their digestive tract they will think me more so. So compulsive is the philistinism of this book, its celebration of contingency, its resistance to thought, that the reader is conditioned to see all in the same diminished perspectives, and to say, as he lays it down, 'This is what politics is about. Poor manikin, he could do nothing else.'

And yet it is not so; and it is the persuasion that it might be so which makes it so utterly lamentable, the lamentable record of a lamentable administration. De Gaulle may withdraw from NATO and no skies fall. Yugoslavia, with its comparatively sparse economy, may assert its independence for twenty years. But Britain, like a total paralytic, lies inert and without initiative, confined from all movement by the anxieties of the City, the imperatives of the American alliance.

Even an internationalist may feel shame at the devaluation of his own nation's possible initiatives which this book punctuates. The devaluation of the traditions of the labour movement, of the very notion of politics as a dignified human preoccupation, is total.

It is not only the comedy, played through once again, of a 'socialist' administration coming to power, and being instantly stopped dead in its tracks by the discovery that capitalism is in difficulties. This is not what this book even pretends to be about: neither capitalism nor socialism are entered in the index, although sterling receives fifty-nine references. Nor is it only that the book offers no analysis whatsoever as to the character of contemporary capitalism, no perspectives of any kind into the future.

Socialism has been written out of the record even as a peroration. Ramsay MacDonald, in 1924, assured an audience that he had no expectation of fulfilling any socialist pledges, not because he lacked a majority, but because the time was not ripe: 'it would be cutting green corn'; even if he were to be Prime Minister for fifty years, 'the pledges I have given you from my heart would still be unfulfilled — not because I fainted or failed, but because the corn was still green'. Harold Wilson (and for this at least we may be thankful) has dispensed with even this evergreen corny mantle.

What he offers himself as is simply as a Top Executive. He wishes to be seen, in relation to the British people, as Mr Gilbert Hunt stands in relation to Chrysler-Rootes. Nor is this to offer wisdom after the event. In 1967 and 1968 in the midst of that political devaluation, some of us — the prime movers being Raymond Williams and Michael Barratt-Brown — offered an analysis in the *May Day Manifesto*.

It may be worth recalling our description of the process then:

> Consensus politics, integral to the success of the new capitalism, is in its essence manipulative politics, the politics of man-management, and as such deeply undemocratic . . . It is the politics of pragmatism, of the successful manoeuvre within existing limits. Every administrative act is a kind of clever performance, an exercise of political public relations. Whether manoeuvres are made by a Tory or Labour government then hardly matters, since both accept the constraints of the status quo as a framework. Government, as the Prime Minister often reminds us, is simply the determination 'to govern'.

And we went on to note that 'as it is now operating, Parliament is acquiescing, openly, in the disappearance of effective parliamentary government, and in its replacement by managed politics':

> In separating itself from continuing popular pressure, it becomes emptied of the urgent and substantial popular content which would enable it to resist or control the administrative machine. It does not really participate in government; it mainly receives and reacts to

decisions elsewhere . . . The government is then not the people in
power, but a broker, a co-ordinator, a part of the machine. What
can then be achieved — the process is of course not complete —
is the final expropriation of the people's active political presence.
Instead, we shall have a new technocratic politics, fitted into the
modern state.

This remains (with a qualification which I shall make in a
moment) the analysis. The real value of Wilson's book is
when it is seen as a digressive and anecdotal phenomenology
of exactly this process: what it felt like not to run, but to
be run by, the machine.

'I find it hard to resist the view', he writes (p. 45), 'that a
modern head of government must be the managing director
as well as chairman of his team.' But if he fell readily into
this role, one feels that he did so as a somnambulist; he
appears never to have questioned the process of which he was
the captive, or to have asked: if he was managing director,
who his shareholders were, or who made up his Board? Or
perhaps one underrates his perspicuity? Certainly, when Joe
Fowler, of the American Treasury, conveyed his 'apprehension', Wilson was quick to take the message; no doubt Mr
Gilbert Hunt, on receiving the apprehensions of a senior
emissary of Chrysler International, would do no less.

One rises from this book with an enhanced contempt for
parliamentarians, and for the Parliamentary Labour Party in
particular. A qualification of the *May Day* analysis might
perhaps be called for: have we not seen, in a year of Tory
government, a return to authentic politics, a reintroduction
of the pure vitriol of class ideology? Certainly, Mr Heath is
manager of a new team (such changes in management are
not unknown in industry); and certainly the early months
of his 'power' have evidenced not (one suspects) the authentic
mentalities of contemporary managerial capitalism, but the
poujadisme of the Tory little men, the constituency workers,
the *enragés* inflamed by petrol tax and by the burdens of
maintaining their children at Repton and at Cheltenham
Ladies' College -- the Tory middle peasantry of the tobac-
conists' shops and the travelling salesmen's saloon-bars,
whose *cahiers de doléances* were filled with parasites and

wogs on national assistance, long-haired student demonstrators, and Trotskyist shop stewards abusing the national
interest — all these, seconded and underwritten by the more
rapacious elements in the City and in property speculation.

Certainly, there are differences of emphasis, of managerial
technique. The 'art of the possible' would not have allowed
a Labour administration to have handled the Dutschke case
in exactly that way. (But in handling the power workers,
Heath simply followed Wilson's precedent with the seamen:
he did not even have to fabricate a 'Communist' sensation.)
On the other hand, a Labour administration would probably
have been too timid about American susceptibilities to have
engineered a Rolls Royce bankruptcy; after all, some latter-
day Joe Fowler might have expressed 'apprehension'. Even
Heath's Tory government, one feels, might conceivably on
some (probably imperialist) issue assert an independence of
the USA. But one suspects that, after a year, ideology is
running out of steam: the wild men are giving way to the
managers: the machine resumes control.

And so, is this all that politics now is? Is it to remain like
this for our lifetime? One may express, cautiously, a doubt.
For the new style of managerial politics brings with it its
own contradiction, in the growing alienation of the people
as a whole from the machine, and its party-political pre-
tences. And while this alienation inevitably takes many
wholly cynical, negative, and even atavistic forms, it is at
root a thoroughly healthy reaction.

One part of the reaction is of course outside of the formal
political institutions altogether: in the streets, in the press or
theatre, in the workshops: in the activity of particular
pressure-groups or communities determined to make themselves felt as contingencies which the politicians must take
into account.

But I hold to a lingering notion that the practical criticism
of parliamentary institutions may still be attempted. As we
noted in the *Manifesto*, 'the criticism of Parliament is in the
interest of democracy as something other than ritual'.

In December 1965, with American bombing moving nearer
every day to Hanoi and Haiphong, Mr Richard Gott decided

to intervene on the Vietnam issue — and only on the Vietnam issue — in a by-election in North Hull. Wilson's majority was then something less than three. The Labour majority only just topped the 1,000 mark. In terms of the art of the possible, it was a futile intervention. The candidate was unknown in Hull, and had scarcely any contacts and no machine. All the Labour electors' solidarities — against 'letting the Tory in' and even, possibly, endangering the Government — were inevitably called up.

Then something curious took place, upon which Wilson's memoirs throw a shaft of darkness. Wilson 'pressed the President hard . . . to suspend the bombing' (p. 187) and until the eve of Christmas remained 'in direct touch' (p. 192) with Johnson about a proposed truce. The bombing pause commenced in January and remained in effect throughout the by-election.

Since we are dealing with memoirs, let me throw in a crumb of my own. I did not then, and do not now, know much of Mr Gott's politics, but I was convinced that his intervention was right. I spoke at a well-attended meeting on the eve of polling-day, and was impressed by the profound seriousness of the audience — five-sixths of whom were committed Labour men and women *and* committed opponents of American actions in Vietnam — and the seriousness with which they were facing a difficult choice. In the event the great majority applauded Gott's arguments — and voted against him. I have not the least doubt that the decisive argument was the continuing truce. Three days later the American bombing was resumed (the Foreign Office, as we have seen, immediately supporting the action).

No doubt many factors influenced this particular detour of American diplomacy. One wonders, however, whether Mr Gott might not have been one small factor among them? Whether, in these direct contacts, Wilson might not have hinted that, if bombing was to be resumed, it would be an act of courtesy to do it three days after rather than three days *before* a difficult by-election. (On 16 December 1965, Wilson and Johnson had had 'exchanges about domestic politics. The old professional was . . . enthralled by our parliamentary cliff-hanging' [p. 186].) From Johnson's point of view, after all, it may have been of more diplomatic utility to have the subservience of a Labour Prime Minister over Vietnam than the (at that time) even more inevitable subservience of a Tory; and the fall of a British government, simply because a sizable minority of British electors refused to support it on that issue, would have been a large bit of awkwardness.

In any event, I am now more than ever convinced — looking across the six intervening years of monotonous bloodshed, and its continuance — that Gott was right, and that the electors who put their loyalty before their principle were wrong. Who knows? If his intervention extended the pause for only four days, he might have saved a score of Vietnamese lives; and that is a score more than — so far as I can make out — Mr Wilson saved in his whole administration.

Perhaps the only way to make such politicians attend is to take them in their own terms, and hit them where it hurts: in their electoral organs. This is not (as some good friends of mine think) to dismiss the labour movement and its loyalties from one's sympathies. It is to say that this movement will only recover its courage and its directions through a process in which it has to face many bits of awkwardness; not only manifestos but also manifestations on its left flank. The art of the possible can only be restrained from engrossing the whole universe if the impossible can find ways of breaking back into politics, again and again.

A Special Case

In the darkness we can sense people around us, in the Rhonnda, in Lanarkshire, in Durham, whom we had almost forgotten. They don't belong to the jolly world of the business supplements: neither Boots nor Beechams have tried to take them over. Their business is simply to provide power as cheaply as possible, a platform from which the serious business of profit-making can start.

The darkness draws us back also towards our past. For centuries it was the miners who crowded a darkness far beyond reach of the light of any common feeling.

They appear sometimes in the historical records as dastardly materialists, intent only upon their own gain, eager to hold the mine-owner (if not yet the 'nation') to ransom. 'Have no conversation with them,' a Yorkshire coal-owner advised his sons in 1671, 'for colliers hate truth or true dealings as the devil hates a saint or a religious person . . . If the colliers complain, be sure you give them less.'

Three centuries later, and that very religious person Mr Edward Heath has shown similar reluctance to converse with such materially minded men. The historian can sympathize with him. The conversation of miners has often been blunt. In the food-rioting days of the eighteenth century, the miners

---

This article originally appeared in *New Society*, 24 February 1972. Some passages from my original typescript — cut for reasons of space — have been replaced.

would erupt suddenly from their communities upon the local market town, 'a great crowd of men, women and children with oaken bludgeons coming down the street bawling out, "One and all — one and all" '.

They have had for centuries this deplorable communistic tendency, arising from the very conditions of their work and community life, the egalitarianism of necessity. The pit-men of the North-East (it was reported) supported the campaign for the Reform Bill of 1832, but some of them were under the misapprehension that 'universal suffrage' meant 'universal suffering'. More curious still, such a slogan commended itself to them. If times were hard, so that some suffered, then all should suffer alike.

Since it was their proper function in the nineteenth century to fuel the workshop of the world, orthodox economists were always clear that it was in the nation's interests that their wages should be kept as low as possible. Hence the axiom that the prosperity of the nation entailed the unprosperity of the miners. Great pains were taken to explain this theorem to them (in Baldwin's time the explanation took some nine months).

But the miners have always had difficulty in comprehending the simplest of propositions as to the market-regulation of wages, and have clung tenaciously to unscientific notions such as 'justice' and 'fair play'. Hence every major wage conflict has turned into an argument about the 'system' as a whole. If the interests of 'the nation' were always opposed to their own, then they suspected that this 'nation' was only a mask behind which other private interests hid. If the prosperity of the world must be carried upon their own unprosperous shoulders, then it followed that, one day, the world must be turned upside down.

The miners emerged from their darkness into a little light around the 1870s: Mr Gladstone had discovered that they were electors (or, to be truthful, they first discovered this for themselves). In the present century their insurgencies or defeats have, time and again, served as markers for the high or low waters of the labour movement. It was at Mid-Lanark that the new Independent Labour image was first seen. The high tide of articulate syndicalism was expressed, in South Wales in 1913, in *The Miner's Next Step*. The defeat of the miners in 1926 punctuated the worst defeat for democratic forces in this country in a century. *The Road to Wigan Pier* and B.L. Coombes's *These Poor Hands* gives us the resilience of the defeated in the 1930s. The Labour victory of 1945 found its most affirmative moment of symbolism in the Vesting Day of the pits.

The miners didn't always use their new-found influence well. The NUM, controlling as many seats as did Pelham-Holles, the eighteenth-century Duke of Newcastle, in his prime, sent some equally pitiful pensioners to Parliament. Although their MPs represented mining communities, they neglected to send into Parliament their wives. The best intelligence of the miners was reserved for the real business of life, the work of the union, in which Arthur Horner, Will Paynter, the Moffats of Fife, Bert Wynne of Derbyshire served their time. Nor was this influence only economic in any narrow sense: it was often exerted in intellectual and cultural fields. The evidence is still there, in the enlightened educational and health policies of Durham and the West Riding, and in the traditions of university extension and tutorial classes.

At some time in the 1950s the lights were dimmed, and the miners were pressed back again into darkness. Pits were closed, whole communities were dispersed or transplanted, parliamentary fiefs were plucked from their grasp, the industry was in 'decline'. Material rewards declined in ratio, and the stocks of condescension rose. The interests of the miners drifted apart once more from 'the national interest'. Because (it was supposed) the miners bargained from weakness, the market value of coal also weakened. Even the younger Left adopted a tone of patronage. The miners were splendid historical fossils of the 'Old Left'. Get back into history, where we can honour you!

That is where the miners were in January 1972. Their strike was evidently hopeless from the start. Every paid expert knew this. Every official spokesman confirmed it. Since the strike hurt no one the nation could afford to

savour historical sentiment and to be generous. People began,
although not very insistently, to suggest that it could afford
to pay the miners a little more. A formula was found for it;
the miners were a 'special case'.

On Friday 11 February, the *Economist* marshalled its
prodigious expertise to scrutinize the position. 'The strike has
so far done little economic harm,' it concluded, 'a measure of
the extent to which coal has lost its kingdom.'

That evening the 'special case' reached out an arm and
pulled the switches. Never, even in these days of Mr Heath,
had the nation passed from misinformed complacency to a
'State of Emergency' so swiftly. It was a bump. There was a
clashing and grinding of gears as the communications industry
sought to throw public opinion into reverse. The old scripts
and visuals of 1970 were dug up: perishing day-old chicks,
grannies stuck in lifts, kidney-machines and the like. And
two new themes were pushed out into the channels.

The first, about picketing, proceeded by the straight
falsification of suppression. The small proportion of incidents
in which mass picketing with obstruction or actual force
were used were taken to characterize the whole. This made it
easier to present the conflict as something which they, the
miners, were doing to us, the nation. That sizeable proportion of the nation which supported the pickets — the thousands
of engineering workers who joined the picket lines in
Birmingham, the union drivers who refused to cross the lines,
the non-union men turned back by peaceful persuasion, the
power workers, technicians and typists who refused to handle
black materials or jobs — could be eliminated from the
equation.

It is of course possible that there are editorialists and TV
commentators (I know that there are academic sociologists
and experts in 'business studies') who have never been on a
picket line, never seen one, never tried to cross one, and
who don't' know the nature of the conflict, the searching
moral scrutiny, even the crisis of identity (to *which* nation
do I belong?) which they can entail. And so I must withdraw
my accusation: such men aren't paid for falsifying evidence,
but only for marketing their own ignorance in the ways most

serviceable to their employers.

The second theme concerns the miners' leadership. It was first fully sounded by Mr Eric Jacobs, the Labour Correspondent of the *Sunday Times* (13 February). His leading article was headed: 'What it is now "about" is the quality of the miners' leadership'. 'Ever since the negotiations got under way last September', (it seems) Mr Gormley and Mr Daly 'have shown the sort of intransigence that can only be called weakness'. These two leaders, alas, are 'profoundly inexperienced in national negotiations':

> The crisis the country faces is due to a failure of authority within the miner's union . . . Our system of industrial relations depends on a willingness to bargain, to compromise, to play the game of give and take. If union leaders refuse to play . . . then the system breaks down . . .

The last sentiment is especially apt. (Damn, where did I put that candle?)

These themes, diluted with saliva, were tried out in the popular dailies. 'Another Crisis of Leadership', editorialized the *Daily Mirror* (16 February):

> Tough — yes. Gormley and Daly are both that. But skilful negotiators? Resourceful and patient? Regretfully, the answer so far must be NO.

'Where was the tactical skill in *bargaining*?' And so to the punch line: 'Have Joe Gormley and Lawrence Daly the strength of character to rise to the occasion?'

Thus the poor man's Eric Jacobs. In staccato gasps and hiccups of rhetoric he spoke for a consensus of the popular press. Now that it was dark enough for the nation to notice them out there in the further darkness, the miners should do the decent thing, withdraw their pickets and get back to work.

To a plain observer, who is not a Labour Expert, all this is by no means self-evident. One had supposed that the leadership of the miners had been rather good. To commence a strike when there is a massive stockpile of your own products at the pitheads, to enlist 100 per cent solidarity of the membership, to plan and execute a most skilful nation-wide scheme of picketing involving the placing of 60,000 men, to maintain the solidarity of a federal union whose fissiparous tendencies are notorious, to win the support not only of other union members but of a growing sector of public opinion, to put one's case cogently and at the drop of a camera before the media — all these suggest that Mr Jacobs and his hiccuping popular shadow have overlooked some qualities in the leadership of the NUM.

But I mistake their meaning. The qualities which they find requisite are not those of loyalty to their own membership and of firmness in pursuit of their demands, but 'experience' in 'our system of industrial relations'. In 'our' system 'we' have defined the function of the union leader as that of a shabby broker, who only pretends to be acting in his client's interests. His function is to bluster, to temporize, to calculate to a nicety that point at which a settlement can be reached without a serious industrial conflict on the one hand or an explosion among his membership which could rock his own position on the other.

It is convenient for us that we have such an admirable system. It is, indeed, essential to our way of life. It has served us admirably in the past few months. Food prices have soared, it is true, and the standard of their living may have lagged a little. But from this platform of 'stabilized inflation' the Stock Exchange has been bulling, investment trusts have been reproducing with affectionate fecundity, the curios at Sotheby's and Christie's have been doubling in value, unemployment has been rising, the availability of cheap domestic labour has been enlarging, the property speculators have been speculating, the take-overs have been overtaking, the cash registers have been jiving, the equities requiting, money has been making love, and the rich conspicuously consuming. Our standard of living is splendid, thank you. Our system of industrial relations must be defended at all costs.

But we were speaking of the miners' leaders, who have failed to find the necessary courage to sell their own members short, as 'our system' prescribes. I don't know Mr Gormley, but I have no complaint against his recent conduct. He can't be quite what he appears to be on television — a startled wombat caught in the headlights of a motorway, wondering how on earth he got to be there among this unwished-for traffic. He's still close enough to the pits not only to be loyal to his members but to *wish* to be so. He has said his bit well, and to the point. We will be able to judge him by his actions.

As it happens, I do know Mr Daly. I will give you Mr Eric Jacobs's version of him and then something of my own. 'Daly, a former Communist, ... is a tough, burly Scot, who likes his "hauf an' hauf" ... and is ready to say his piece on every left-wing platform.' That is all that is of any consequence from Mr Jacobs, except, of course, that he has 'the sort of intransigence that can only be called weakness'.

I would add that Daly is a Fifer. West Fife was Gallacher's constituency for some ten years. Even sympathetic observers often write about miners as if their solidarity sprang from some sub-intellectual sociological traditionalism, a combination of the muscles and the moral instincts. Tough and burly, with their 'hauf an' haufs'.

But West Fife has had, perhaps, as sophisticated and articulate a political tradition as any in these islands. Even in the late 1950s, before pit after pit closed down and communities dispersed, one could find in a Fife miners' club political discussion raging as furiously as football debate in another district.

Daly gained his education in this highly conscious political culture. I use 'education' advisedly. Whatever may be said about Communist Party policy and organization (and Daly has said some hard things) there was then (and is there now?) no comparable organization in which a young miner could enlarge his horizons both nationally and internationally, advance his political knowledge, effect contacts with intellectuals and with workers in other industries, while exerting a growing influence within his own community.

Daly has never repudiated his own political past. When he broke with the Party, on issues of major principle, in 1956, he did a thing characteristic both of the man and of West Fife. As a pit delegate and a public figure in his own mining village of Ballingry, he thought that his fellow workers and neighbours had a right to know the reasons for his action.

He called a densely attended public meeting, and argued the case through point by point.

He carried a majority of his own community with him, and was elected by them as an independent socialist county councillor. Out of this campaign emerged the small Fife Socialist League. He worked out his theory, not in entire isolation, but with friends in the incipient 'New Left'. He was a very influential member of the editorial boards, first of *The New Reasoner* and then of the early *New Left Review*. As an editor of the first, I remember the manuscripts and proofs which came back from him, expertly annotated and as often as not marked with dust from the pit.

In the General Election of 1959 the League decided to campaign both on issues specific to the Fife mining community and the national issues of nuclear disarmament, and it selected Daly as their candidate. He fought his campaign while working in the pit, and he and his wife used their own council house as committee rooms. The deposit was raised by pit-head and door-to-door collections, along with the business of canvassing. He fought not only the established Labour Party machine but also a very strong Communist Party organization, drafted in to hold on to one of their last electoral strongholds. His own organization was a score of local Leaguers and a few of us who came in, for odd days, from outside. He won, in that election, around 5,000 votes, beating the Communist into third place.

I like to think that this campaign effected something in transmitting an older revolutionary tradition into the future. By conducting a public political campaign against both Labourism and Communist orthodoxy he offered to this most thoughtful, most attentive, and most courteous electorate a possible alternative. He laid the basis of that Scottish-wide standing upon which his subsequent electoral successes within the union (fought, once again, in the teeth of both established machines) were won.

Courage is not, when I come to think of it, a quality in which I had (before Mr Jacobs noticed it) found Lawrence Daly deficient. Nor had I thought that Fife miners were such poor judges of character. But this is beside the point. What I noted, at the pit-head, in the crowded village hall, in the club, was the patient, open, rational manner of political argument. Every case was argued as a rational case which miners and their wives could and should follow and make up their own minds upon. Open-cast mining, unilateralism, Castro's Cuba, Trotskyism, pit closures: each one came up at one meeting or another, and not one of them was ducked. It is the Fifer's way; a way so much at odds with the evasions and half-truths of contemporary official politics that most politicians will deny that such a way is possible in these islands, and will then go on to despise the very electors whom their own currency daily debases.

I would add, then, that Daly is a Fifer. There is, also, that bit from Mr Jacobs as to how Daly 'is ready to say his piece on every left-wing platform'. At that it sounds easy — the tough, burly Scot, with one eye on the popularity-stakes of the Left. But Daly's 'piece' has not always been easy to say; it has sometimes been lonely; it has always been worth listening to.

His piece has had the strength of consistency. If the Fife Socialist League decided to pack up, it was simply because no other comparable Leagues appeared elsewhere. They could not do the thing on their own. Daly's 'piece', since then has included participation with Sartre on the Russell War Crimes Tribunal, the visiting of North Vietnam, the flat and repeated denunciation of Russian action in Czechoslovakia. If he has had Communist support in NUM elections, he has refused to buy it by compromise or convenient silence. He has refused either to be drawn into the vicious factionalism of the Left, or to dissociate himself from any serious section of it. He has been willing to talk to the *Black Dwarf*, the *Morning Star*, or *Seven Days*. Bitterly attacked by the *Socialist Worker* for his failure to support the unofficial miners' strikes of a year ago, he came back and argued the case in its columns. It is the Fifer's way.

To say one's piece on every left-wing platform is easy, if one is prepared to endure the exhaustion of life and the wilful malevolence of the sects. But to say a particular piece, open and thoughtful, defining disagreements while not permitting disagreements to fester into enmities, is more difficult. In his stamina, in his search for the uniting affirmatives, in his sense of solidarity against the real enemy, Daly performs among the trade unionists of the Left something of the same role as Raymond Williams performs among the intellectuals.

Lawrence Daly is no doubt (we now have a formula for it) 'a special case'. If the miners are victorious (and, as I write, it appears that they will be) he would himself be the last to attribute success to his own leadership: he would point to the high morale of his members, the support of other unionists, the balance of forces involved.

But what his case illustrates, and what the entire course of the strike points towards, is the continued existence in this country of two nations, of an alternative to the official culture. Daly himself is no *accidental* leader of the miners, no lump of sociological lava thrown up perforce from a traditional sociological crater. No static quantitative survey, no set of questionnaires however nuanced, would have disclosed in 1956 or 1959 that the leadership of the miners in 1972 would have come from this finely-tempered political culture.

There are still areas of our life available to an open democratic process, in which candidates are not groomed to fit pre-ordained roles (such as 'our system of industrial relations') or selected by appointment committees from on top to reproduce the qualities (or deficiencies) of the committee's members. There is still an area in which, at every stage along the way, there is an open conflict of ideas and values.

It isn't possible to push 280,000 men and their families back into history. In pushing the miners back into darkness their culture was not extinguished. It was simply compressed into a fiercer solidarity. From that compression they have sprung back again (in Daly's words) 'as ambassadors of the mining community in every city and port'. They came, at first, as ambassadors of a past culture, reminding us of whom we once were. They remained to challenge us as to whom we might yet become.

Miners' strikes have had before this way of posing larger

questions: who is 'the nation' anyway? How long can we tolerate, in an economy with such intricate reciprocities, not the right to strike but the vast inequalities in life-style and in material opportunity which are thrust before rich and poor alike on a common TV screen, and which plop in the blatant business supplements, each Sunday through the door of stockbroker and of miner alike? Should we not think again, as William Morris demanded in another miners' strike (1893), of an approach to 'a condition of practical equality of economical condition amongst the whole population'?

The 'special case' turns out, after all, to be the general case of the working nation. It is never safe to assume that any of our history is altogether dead. It is more often lying there, as a form of stored cultural energy. The instant daily energy of the contingent dazzles us with its brightness. What passes on the daily screen is so distracting, the presence of the status quo is so palpable, that it is difficult to believe that any other form of energy exists. But this instant energy must be reproduced every moment as it is consumed; it can never be held in store. Let the power be cut off for a while, then we become aware of other and older reserves of energy glowing all around us, just as, when the street-lights are dowsed, we become aware of the stars.

One tends to think of history as a reserve of the conservative and the 'traditional'. But there is still today an enormous reserve of radicalism stored within our culture. Nor is this hyperbole. It was evident in the past fortnight that there was one possible way for Heath to defeat the NUM, a way which would have warmed young Churchill's heart. The *Daily Telegraph* (15 February) explicitly evoked this course of action: 'the use of troops to break the picket lines around the power stations, and to requisition stocks of coal at the pit-head, will become unavoidable'.

And why was this not done? Not (one may be certain) because the government was squeamish about such intervention. It would surely have considered this if the strikers had been 'unofficial' or less formidable. Not even because Mr Maudling has other uses for the troops in Londonderry and Newry. It was because that energy, glowing in the alternate culture of an alternate 'nation', would have been ignited in a flash. And that ignition would have burned on towards a General Strike more potent of decisive change than that of 1926, a more special and perhaps more implacable case.

The pits of Ballingry and of much of West Fife have now closed down. And we had supposed, poor fools that we are, that all that heroic and intelligent history, all that 200 years of inconceivable stubbornness and courage, was quite dead. But out of that history has come this moment of illumination; we stir uneasily as, once again, there are men in our streets shouting 'One and All'. It is a moment of cultural transmission, as the pent-up energies of the dead flow back into the living. We shall burn that history for many years, as we have burned the black forests which for generations they have raised. For the future historian it will seem that this week of darkness in February 1972 was an incandescence.

A Question of Manners

The National Health Service employs a great many women in responsible and exacting tasks: the matrons who organize the complex societies which consultants from time to time blow through; the nurses; the almoners and other administrators; the therapists; the catering staff.

Since the Service employs so many women it follows that if any issue of principle arises within it, there is bound to be a great deal of subjective argument, confusion, doubling of standards, and emotional *ad personam* reasoning. Indeed, one may safely say that where women impinge in any way on public matters and the public interest, all principle will be submerged in irrationality.

This is because those who define what this 'public interest' is are (mostly) male and conservative. Not only are they unable to take up a rational or objective approach towards anything which affects women, but for several hundreds of years they have practised techniques to foster irrationality whenever women appear in any prominent public role. The techniques are exceedingly simple, and all may be reduced to one: the replacement of every other consideration by the argument of *ad feminam*.

The argument *ad feminam* is radically different from the usually objectionable, although occasionally justifiable, form of argument *ad hominem*. In the latter, we try to fault an

---

This article first appeared in *New Society*, 11 July 1974.

argument of principle by pointing out that the man (or woman) who holds it has some personal circumstances of face, favour or fortune which makes his motives in so arguing suspect. Such rebuttal may be relevant in a way, but it can't be relevant to the question of principle proposed.

But the argument *ad feminam* is usually more dishonourable. It can be both malevolent and prurient. In this, no rational encounter of any kind is even offered. It simply emphasizes that the opponent is *a woman*, and passes directly from that to exploiting whatever conventional prejudices are available in relation to womanhood in general. These usually involve sexual ridicule of one kind or another.

All this was gone through in the 1790s when Mary Wollstonecraft and her friends first raised the issue of women's rights. They endured it with good courage, but there is no doubt that it drew some blood. The clergy were rather good at it. 'A Country Parson' informed his 'flock' in Kent that 'it is notorious that our Reforming Women are ... the most abandoned of their sex'. A Cornish parson, the Reverend Polwhele, excelled the others in a poem on 'The unsex'd females'. He found it difficult — this was to be a continuing dilemma among opponents of the suffragettes — to decide whether to ridicule female reformers because they must be ugly and mannish (and therefore compensating for their unattractiveness to men) or because they were 'ripe for every species of licentiousness' (as he remarked in a footnote on the recently dead Wollstonecraft).

But he managed to cull some sexual excitement out of every possible subject. 'Botany', he remarked in one footnote, 'has lately become a fashionable amusement with the ladies. But how the study of the sexual system of plants can accord with female modesty, I am not able to comprehend.' And thence he swept on, under the proud sail of verse:

> With bliss botanic as their bosoms heave,
> Still pluck forbidden fruit, with mother Eve,
> For puberty in sighing florets pant,
> Or point the prostitution of a plant;
> Dissect its organ of unhallow'd lust,
> And fondly gaze the titillating dust.

The point is not the erectile quality of this clergyman's imagination, who found so many salacious goings-on among his flower beds. It is rather that a woman who had a disposition to study botany had, *first of all*, to clamber over that mountain of irrational subjectivism before she could get to a textbook.

I could go on with examples, over 180 years, but it would strain all patience. One must be fair and admit that when issues arose which turned upon male-female relations — women's rights, the suffragettes, women's lib — not only Reverend Pigs but also male chauvinist angels might be provoked at times to a little *ad feminam* joking. But one could equally well document that when issues have arisen which had *nothing whatsoever to do with women's rights* but in which women were prominent actors, antagonists have repeatedly fallen back on the same devices.

They are used constantly now: a trick of the camera, a caption, an *ad feminam* interview of some public personality (often, alas, on the 'woman's page' by some silly female columnist): not the policies but the hairstyle, not the decisions of the conference but how-did-her-husband-man-age-the-house-and-the-kids-and-the-LAUNDRY-while-she-was-away?

That is the stage-one friendly technique: distract, confuse, belittle, by emphasizing at every point that this is not a writer, trade unionist, politician, but a Woman whatever-she-is. But, with opponents, we move on to the other stages . . . She is sexy. She is ugly. She is easy to make. She is old. She is divorced. She is queer. Whatever else, the reader or viewer must have his attention diverted from her as a human being, acting upon or arguing some issue of public importance; and be made to think of her primarily as a Woman or a sexual object, something bizarre and necessarily estranged from principle, a bitch on her hind legs. Manners change, and nowadays we might be more accurate if we spoke of the argument *ad vaginam*. She has got an argument which we can't answer: let's try to make readers think instead about her cunt.

This train of thought was set off, not by some cheapjack

voyeur in a tabloid, but by a paragraph which caught my eye in *The Times*. And of course *The Times* could not be supposed to condone this sort of journalistic practice.

It was a piece by a journalist unknown to me called Mr B. Levin who, to judge from his style, must be a young man and who perhaps will not mind if I point out to him the misconstructions which might be placed upon his writing.

Mr Bertrand Levin, in the centre page of the paper (5 July), was discussing the serious question of 'Medical evidence of society's sickness.' It seems that he was (perhaps properly) concerned at some recent actions of a certain Mrs Esther Brookstone, which threatened public principles which Mr Levin espouses. I had a little difficulty with his piece, since I had been attending a historical conference in the previous days; and Mr Lewin unaccountably failed to inform his readers as to the exact offence which Mrs Brookstone had given. He simply introduced her, in his first sentence, as 'the Woman with the Saw-Edged Bedpan'. I have now discovered that Mrs Brookstone is the secretary of the branch of the National Union of Public Employees at Charing Cross Hospital, a branch which recommended the withdrawal of labour from certain defined amenities of patients in the private wards. The reports which I read suggested that such withdrawal would not extend to nursing care, and they did not mention that Mrs Brookstone was responsible for bedpans (or for sawing their edges). But Mr Bertrand Lewin may possibly have better sources of information; or indeed, if he has, as I suppose, only recently left public school, he might well think that a mention of bedpans would be amusing to his readers.

Perhaps the fun-reactionaries do enjoy these levities — or may we call them levinities? But there was a subsequent paragraph where I thought Mr Bertrand might have been guilty (no doubt unwittingly) of an error of taste. He was seeking to persuade Mrs Brookstone that direct action by hospital workers, rather than indirect consultative and legislative processes, was mistaken and raised constitutional principles; and he offered to make the point clear to her 'with a homespun analogy': 'Suppose some intrepid Don

Juan should take it into his head inflamed by lust, to ravish her.' And so he goes on, through some more homespinning, to suppose that this erotic violence leads to her rushing to a constable for help, which help is refused: 'Would she not feel that if people are going to take the law, and indeed her person, into their own hands, the fabric of society is in danger?'

The fabric of society has been in danger for a long time: it was (so far as I remember) endangered by Mary Wollstonecraft, Tom Paine, the Chartists, trade unionists (often), birth control, state education, free school milk and Bertrand Russell. I think we may take it that it will once again triumphantly survive the action of the NUPE branch at Charing Cross Hospital, and it will certainly survive Mr Levin's homespun erotic fantasy about Mrs Brookstone being raped without redress.

I am less sure whether other fabrics will survive such passages so easily: and one of them I must call, for want of a better word, the fabric of common manners. I don't ask for *good* manners, since I've never pretended to the standards so evident in *The Times*. But common manners suggest that one does not conduct an argument with someone of the other sex by publicly projecting upon him or her a sexual fantasy. Since I do not know Mr Bertram Levin, I will not speculate as to how it might have seemed, in common manners, if Mrs Brookstone were to reply in kind, projecting upon him an imaginary sexual assault; nor whether such an imaginary assailant would or would not have to be supposed to be 'intrepid' and 'inflamed by lust'. But a casual reader, who did not appreciate Mr Bernard's inexperience (and the editor's unaccountable oversight) might make the error of supposing that this kind of attack, in a prestigious national newspaper, upon someone with little opportunity to reply, was the act of a bully or a coward, in a mode close to pornography. Such a reader would of course be old-fashioned and mistaken. All that has been signalled is a further corruption of the fabric of common manners. The fabric of society is (some social anthropologists tell us) made up of much the same stuff.

No doubt Mr Bertram Levin will forgive my pointing

out this indiscretion to him. But I had wished to argue a little further with him about the point at issue.

He is, as I suppose from his immaturities of style, a good deal too young to have served in the Second World War. He will therefore not remember the Beveridge Plan (in itself an unremarkable document) and the remarkable enthusiasms it developed, and their outcome in the National Health Service.

The Beveridge Plan came to me, in the form of an Army Bureau Current Affairs pamphlet, three or four weeks before the final battle of Cassino. The squadron leader came out of his tent with it in his hand, spotted me, and said : 'Oh, Thompson! HQ insists that we get all the men together and run discussions on this. Do you mind taking it on? I'd do it myself, but it's rather difficult to argue *against* a thing when you don't know anything about it.' I thought his command so funny that I wrote it down at the time. But now I see that Mr Levin is having exactly the same kind of difficulty.

I will not convince anyone now — least of all any young radicals — that those discussions were authentic and deeply significant. But everywhere across Italy, on wall newspapers, in bivvies around our tanks, in supply depots, the argument was going on. This curious half-chauvinist, half-anti-fascist, deeply anti-militarist and yet militarily competent army, debated the principles out of which the National Health Service came. They didn't debate these in terms of Beveridge's Giant This and Giant That, but in the direct terms of their own civilian experience.

No doubt the same discussions were going on in British society generally and in the armies waiting for D Day. In fact, I know they were, I won't convince Mr Lewin and other young radicals by saying so: but historical research will discover it in time.

A few weeks later, the final great battles of the war commenced. Some of those who had discussed were killed. Most were not. A good number were wounded in one way or another. I suppose that hospital workers can confirm that a few of them come in and out with old war wounds still.

I will return to these; but first I would prefer to return to Mr Levin, and ask him if he knows what he is talking about?

He supposes that Mrs Brookstone and her NUPE colleagues
may be motivated by feelings of 'fierce, dark joy at the
thought of a rich woman who has undergone major abdominal surgery trying to struggle out of bed to get to a call-box
telephone because the one in her room has been cut off'.

Well, I take no joy in this thought, but I am not overcome
with pity either. I had a minor abdominal operation a few
years ago. The hospital (an old Poor Law one) had huge
round wards like a panopticon. There were some thirty beds
around the walls, and a few more in the middle. Three men
died in the ward during my fortnight there. One died quietly
in his sleep, but the other two had more difficulty. They
were allowed, for the last hour or two, the benefit of screens
around their beds. I remember, in particular, one who, with
the self-effacing courtesy of some elderly working men, was
clearly mainly embarrassed by the concern he was causing
to his mates in the beds on each side. I think he might, out
of some sense of modesty, have preferred to have died in a
private ward. I think it likely that his next-of-kin (who, until
the last hours, were confined to the usual visiting hours)
would have preferred to have been with him there.

In any case, if I think of priorities of need, I will think
first of such patients as that old man, and it will be a long
time before I get around to worrying about a lady (rich or
poor), struggling to get out of bed to a call box. She will, in
any case, be under medical orders either to stay in bed or
not; and if she is allowed up, why should she not go to the
box? I'm afraid that Mr Levin has developed such a vivid
ideological fantasy life that he finds it very difficult to visual-
ize any human or social situation as it actually is.

What I think that Mrs Brookstone and her colleagues at
Charing Cross Hospital may have been doing is asserting in a
new, affirmative, and (for me) deeply heartening way the
same kind of principles which we once discussed around the
tents in a vineyard before the battle of Cassino. That is, that
we should fashion a Health Service based not upon money
and influence but upon human need, and in which all citizens
could expect humane and considerate treatment equally and
as of right. It is not a question of wishing to deprive anyone

of medical care but of stopping the growth of double standards which are corrupting that principle from within.

All of us are citizens who have paid for these services through public revenue and through contributions seriatim through life. People are entitled — if they should so opt — to die in privacy and not in a flurry of harassed nurses behind screens. And, the dramas of death apart, it is only common manners for those who are suffering least to give priority to those who need attention most. In any case I can assure Mrs Brookstone that most patients will extend to her, as I do, their solidarity — not seeing her as a Woman but as a fellow-citizen acting in a common cause: a cause in which manners, not money, maketh man.

Going into Europe

The first person who enthused to me, some years ago, about 'going into Europe' went on to enthuse about green peppers. This gave a clue as to what the great British middle class thinks 'Europe' is about.

It is about the belly. A market is about consumption. The Common Market is conceived of as a distended stomach: a large organ with various traps, digestive chambers and fiscal acids, assimilating a rich diet of consumer goods. It has no mind, no direction, no other identity: it is imagined as either digesting or as in a replete, post-prandial state easily confused with benevolence or idealism.

The image vegetates in the British middle-class subconscious. This Market has no head, eyes, or moral senses. If you ask where it is going, or why, no one knows; they give an anticipatory post-prandial burp ('it will make us viable') and talk about bureaucratic procedures in Brussels. It has no historical itinerary. It lies in a chair, hands on its tummy, digesting a *pasta* of Fiats, a washing-up machine *meunière* and (burp!) that excellent *concorde thermidor* which may not have been as fresh as it should have been.

This Eurostomach is the logical extension of the existing eating-out habits of Oxford and North London. Particular arrangements convenient to West European capitalism blur into a haze of remembered vacations, beaches, *bougainvillaea*, business jaunts, and vintage wines. At the referendum the sky will darken with charter flights from the Dordogne, each

From the *Sunday Times*, 27 April 1975.

passenger's mouth puckered into a *oui*.

At a poor second, the middle class thinks the Market is about Culture. Bob of the *Likely Lads* has long been taking Thelma earnestly to Fellini and Godard. The academic and television Bobs and Thelmas, after their long and abject mid-Atlantic enchantment, have entered a no less abject enchantment with 'Europe'. But it is the same image. Culture is what we *consume*; it is bestowed, without participation, engagement, dialogue — a common cultural stomach.

For 'going into Europe' is also a Magic. It is the Necessary Miracle. Utterly without self-confidence, hemmed in at every side by the defensive organizations of a humane working class (the 'English disease'), the British bourgeoisie prepares, as its last hope of survival, to surrender its identity to the larger rapacity of the European bourgeoisie. It may not survive itself: but at least it will make sure that Money does.

What is sick about this is that, in national as in personal matters, only an individual with a firm identity can make effective relationships. This 'going into Europe' will not turn out to be the thrilling mutual exchange supposed. It is more like nine middle-aged couples with failing marriages meeting in a darkened bedroom in a Brussels hotel for a Group Grope. The *gruppensex* will rejuvenate no one. But in the recriminations of the bitchy afterglower we can expect a resurgence of bourgeois nationalist rancour of sensational intensity.

The offence of the 'going into Europe' humbug is fourfold. First, we are there already. Second, Europe is not that set of nations but includes also Warsaw, Belgrade, Prague. Third, the Market defines the diversity of European cultures at its crassest level as a group of fat, rich nations feeding each other goodies. Fourth, it defines this introversial white bourgeois nationalism as 'internationalism'.

It will not, of course, work. But the spoof about internationalism remains offensive. And dangerous. For when an altruistic glint gets into the bourgeois eye one can be sure that someone is about to catch it. Once replete, the euro-stomach will want to euronate. The present idea is to do it on the British working class. 'Going into Europe' will mean 'rationalization', 'winds of competition', getting rid of 'restrictive practices' (i.e. humane safeguards and self-protection), 'facing up to things'. We can be sure that the things faced up to will be very different through the open shutters of the Dordogne and a bedroom window in Bolton.

These arrangements of capitalist convenience have nothing whatsoever to do with internationalism, political or cultural. What they will do is distance decision-making from its subjects and mystify what remains of democratic process. They provide no opportunities for common fraternal action or intellectual exchange which could not be conducted better without them. And have been, for some hundreds of years. Surely Hugh Thomas knows that his 'White Anglo-Saxon Protestants' have been happily absorbing 'a few doses of latinity' periodically for centuries, without any licence from a Treaty of Rome?

Some sillies in the labour movement suppose the Market will facilitate socialist and trade-union unity. It will do the opposite. It will put the bourgeoisie twenty years ahead at one throw. Luigi and Kurt and George and Gaston, with their secretaries, their linguistic skills, their massed telephones, their expense-account weekends, their inter-locking euro-directorships, their manipulation of the rules and of the Brussels spouters, will always be smiling at the table, with the agenda cooked, the day before the workers get there. And British labour will cast away its one incomparable historical asset (a united movement) in anxious negotiations with its fragmented and ideologically embittered counterparts.

Meanwhile the Dutch elm disease (Europe's most viable export to England in the past decade) is nothing to the beetles being bred by the bureaucrats in Brussels to blight what remains of our active democratic traditions. True, there are plenty of people high in the British state who would like to do the same. But that's the point. The enemies, as well as the friends, of democratic process are everywhere and anywhere: internationalism falls along the line of that horizontal fracture, not within a set of vertical alliances.

There is a more momentous point. As British capitalism dies above and about us, one can glimpse, as an outside chance, the possibility that we could effect here a peaceful transition — for the first time in the world — to a democratic socialist society.

It would be an odd, illogical socialism, quite unacceptable to any grand theorist. That is perhaps why most British Marxists have long ceased to attend to British actualities and, at a time of unparalleled socialist opportunity, play to each other their amateur revolutionary theatricals.

But the opportunity is there, within the logic of our past itinerary. The lines of British culture still run vigorously towards that point of change where our traditions and organizations cease to be defensive and become affirmative forces: the country becomes our own. To make that leap, from a market to a society, requires that our people maintain, for a little longer, their own sense of identity, and an understanding of the democratic procedures available to them. It requires also the holding open of every international option: for trade with the developing world, for dialogue with the Communist world, for informal intellectual exchange.

It is fear of *this* transition — of Money toppled from power — which makes our good bourgeois contort his face into an unlikely expression of internationalism. And, equally, the effecting of this transition is the most substantial contribution to internationalism which our people could make.

That is what we could offer to the European dialogue. And to a Europe which includes Oslo and Belgrade. Long, very long after that, a true idea of 'Europe' might return: as a cautious federation of socialist states. It will develop slowly, tetchily, with jealous regard for individual identities. And so it should.

THE STATE AND
CIVIL LIBERTIES

An Elizabethan Diary

Mr. E. P. Thompson, the historian, has recently discovered behind a panel in his library the diary of a remote ancestor, a minor landowner in Worcestershire, and a JP. The diary is undated, but — despite certain discrepancies — it would seem that the extracts published below date from late September or early October 1593.

Such a Year for Fruits is not in Memory, no, not the oldest Grandame about Episcopi can report the Like. My Lord of Ledbury hath this Yeer a Bushel of Apricocks against the Manor Wall, engraffed on Stock brot from Jerusalem in the late Crusade. There be Coddlins & Pippins on every Side, so that the very Bows do Break. As for the Plumbs, there be ten Bushel at Winchester Measure on any well-set Tree.

*

But here's the Rubb. Fruit cannot go to Markett, not for Money nor even yett as Charitye for the Poor. Some say it be through a Sort of Monopolisers in the Dealing Trade, wch wd keep all Price at its Customary Heighth as it is set in any Leen Yeer. And that these Dealers wd rather that the Poor Starve, the Fruits fall Rotted and Wormey, and the Husbandmen & their Familys Toile & Swinke for no Reward — all so that their Proffits be not Sunke. To wch Effect they have many Foul Tricks in the Regrating & Engrossing Way, wch God &

First published in *Vole*, Vol. 2 No. 5, February 1979.

the Queens Council should prevent.

But Lawyer Grafter of Herefd who hath come but lately from the Innes of Court saith it is Otherwise & that it is (Save the Mark!) the Queens own Council wch is to blame, wch have made a Secret Treaty wth the French & the Low Countries & have thrown the Markett of the Cities wide to em, nay, even given em a Privilege in a Subsidy of the Queens own Revenue, & what is that but the Taxes wch the Industrious pay? So that the Nacion is Taxed to Spoile the Nacions own Tillage. And one Jankyns (he that was once but a meer Schoole Master) passeth privily betweene the Lands & brings the Strangers Wares up all the Rivers of England. And the City Folk run after forrayn Facion & must have the Apples dresst in Papers like Ladyes Sweetmeetes & no Blemish on the Skinnes & all of a Size like Oysters in a Barrel, althow the Fruit be Nothing but Pith & Pulp & a Sort of Natureless Pap without neither Goodnesse nor Taste. So that the Sweete Juices of England, whose Coddlins & Pippins no Land cd ever Equal, are run into the Grownde like an Old Ox pissing in the Mudd.

*

Rode over this two Dayes to the Cotsalls to meet my Cozen, Justice Shallow, for he is indeed now of the Queens Commicion & a Great Man in those Parts. In his Curtesy he made me privy to many great Affaires of State on wch he discoursed wth becoming Wisdom. As that the Plague of Vagabonds, Rogues & Sturdy Beggars is grown to that Heighth that they be now so Insolent as to meet in great Congregacions & upon the open Comons by Day. And that in the North Part of the Kingdom they did meet but last Month & elected a Monarch of Beggars & his Officers. And did demand that the Justices assess all Wages at two d. more in each li. & so in Proporcion to the Prices of Barley Oats & Wheet. Nay, some were there that said that onely White Loavs were good enough for em & Others so Ill-Affected as to say they wd not Work but that they were fed on the best Ale & Beef. And this for onely Twelve Hours Work in the Day wch hath never been known in the Kingdom before. But what Answers the Cotsall

Justices are devizing to bring the Servants into Obedient Condicion, as Whippings Stocks & Brandings & as several Hangings in the Assize Town, Mr Justice Shallow did not disclose to a Full View. But Hangings he said there must certaynly be.

*

Rode into Sessions in Worcester this Day. All the Greatest Persons in the County were there for the Matter before us was Heavy. A cunnyng Artificer in the Imploy of the Queen wch was once a Goldsmith in Perugia hath contrived a Mirrour wch hath two Sides. Wch a Man may sit behind & see through it all that passes before him but wch they that be Observed see not that Man but onely their own Images. So all that it needs is to station a Queens Messenger or other Worthy Person behind the Mirrour & all the Treasons of the Queens Enemys shall be instantly Discovered.

It was agreed that the Principal Persons in the Country, the Lords, Bishopps & Justices do as a great Act of Charitye & Grace freely give & donate Mirrours to the Keepers of Ale-houses, Taverns, Inns, Brothels, Ordinaries & the like, where all great Seditions are Hatcht. For that Tom Nancy & Hobb be so Vain as to sit before the Mirrours preening emselves. And hence all is accomplished at a Double Stroke. For the Rogues & comon Folk be filled with Gratitude to the Great for giving em these Toyes & at the same Time Artists in the Queens Imploy may take down their Likenesses & the Messengers may make Copyes of their Horrid Plots, Blasphemies, yea Heresies wch have never run so High & wch even poor Clerkes of Oxon & piddling Curates do stir up. And other such Matters as privily breaking the Seales on the Mail & stationing Spyes in the Bushes by the comon Highway wch being so long familiar I did not closely attend, in that Squire Western did call me out to inquire the Price of a Yoke of Bullocks at the Fair, and thence with Sir Walter de Coverley to dine at the Swann.

*

Item. As of that Mirrour Sir Walter hath learned that it was
first imployd & to Good Effect against the Treasons of one
Kit Marlowe a poor Scholard of Cambridge Town. Who under
Pretens of Spying against the Papists hath bin in League wth
certain Great Persons in Devon wch were Suspekt as Mortalists
& Republickans to boot. And that this Marlowe was put to
Death for his Treasons, as well it shd be, but that the Queens
Coroner was bidden by Mr Secretary Cecil to give out to the
World that he had mett his Death in a Duell. This Marlowe
was of No Account beeing a Meer Writer of Stage Playes wch
were so ill made as the Players had to make em over again. As
one of Dr Festus his Pact with the Deuill wch onely the first
and last Acts was good enough to Play — & they being poor
enough — but that the Clowne wrote many witty Porcions in
betwixt, as pulling off a Legg that was made of Straws and as
Hornes growing in a Mans Head wch Squire Western who
hath bin in Londn saith made him break his Chair in twain
with Laughing but that the ending of the Deuill coming for
the Dr was Sorry Stuff & put him in Mind of a Funerall &
made Lady Western have the Vapors.

*

Back to the Sessons on Friday. A Messenger hath rode to
Death two noble Horses under him with Newes from the
Council in Londn & all the Talk was what he brot of a Great
Plot Discovered. It does seem a Boatswain who was imployd
a full Eight Yeers Agone on one of the Queens Frigates hath
bin Discovered by Means of the Mirrour a-seated in an Ale-
house wth two Seditious Printers. And he told em about the
Markins on the Buoys up the Channel by wch if known the
Armada wd have sailed up the Thames & anchored off the
Isle of Dogges. And some said that the Spaniards are already
there — the Tower is taken — the Queen & Court fled into
Northumberland to raise an Army — the Inquisition is by
now on English Soile.

The Gentlemen was much astonied at this Newes & there
was a General Call for Warrant of Hue & Cry against all
Cobblers Boatswains & such Disaffected Fellows.

But my Neighbour Admirall Salt took me aside & said this was no more than Landlubbers Talk. For that in Eight Yeers all the Channels have silted & changed & the Buoys bin moved about & that every River Pilot knows more than this Boatswain could know. Nay, that it hath all bin long Published Abroad for Every Eye to read & even the Masters of Petty Forrayn Trading Vessels have it putt down in a little Manual.

But for all that, saith the Admirall, it hath bin a good Stroke to lett the comon Folk suppose that Treasons be abroad in that it may bring em into a better Affecion to the State. Or if Affecion be wanting it will make the Lesser Sort go in More Feer. For if the Boatswain be not Hanged, saith he, what is to prevent Other Men who are privy to Secrets of State disclosing those of more Delicate & Grave Import, as how the Ships Officers make Proffits of the Seamens Victuals & as how Oyls & Spices were run throw the Blockade off the Affrick Coast & our Great Ships of the Line standing idly by? Nay, saith he, Ballads will be stuck up on every Poste agen the Agents of the Crowne & the Disaffected will press Neerer Yett upon the Queens own privy Audience, as asking why Mr Secretary Hal Walsinghame did take Passage of a Sudden helter-skelter back to his Estates in Scilly & what in the Queens own Presence was not said.

'Tis said that a Great Tryal will be had in London to strike Terror into the Hearts of the Queens Loyal Subjects & it is already settled that the Boatswain shall have his Bowells drawn while yett Alive & his Head to be on a Pike outside the Chambers of Mr Secretary in Whitehall. As for the Printers it is not yett agreed with the Judges, but that they shall very certaynly have their Eers cut off. And this already hath such Good Effects as that all the Booksellers of Worth & Substance about St Pauls be now reduced into a more Obedient Complecion & these do not suffer any Word to be Printed but what hath first bin Licensed by Mr Secretary his Office. And a Speciall Jury is got ready & Minute Inquiry by Spyes made into each Jurors Affecions so that no surly Puritan Fellows be there.

*

Homeward riding I met with my Neighbour Yeoman Russett. He hath this Yeer four Acres in their Prime of a Wondrous
Plumb yclept the Glostershire Drooper — althow that be just
a Gloster Bragg as it was Farmer Bransford in Woostershire
that graffed it first as I have often heard my Father say.
These be of a full rich Golden Fruit & Yeoman Russett saith
there hath never bin seen a finer Crop. But all, saith he, must
rott on the Grownde for the Dealers will not Haggle. And he
hath thrown open his Orcharding to the Poor who come on
Asses & on Foot to carry em away, onely leaving a *d*. or two
for Charitye. And he hath Determined to cutt all downe &
break up those Lands & put em under Barley. And the City
Folk must buy the stale & sour Fruit of France or else they
must want. As for his great Field of Hoppes betwixt the Ings
and the Lynchetts, there is no selling em at all, for the great
Brewers have brot into their Imploy cunnyng Apothecaries
who wth certayne Salts can so Disguise Pond Water as to
make it pass for Ale. Wch Salts, saith Farmer Russett, he hath
bin assured by a Dr of Physicke in Bromyard be Poysons &
do breed Distempers of the Brain & Raging Melancolys by
wch the Nacions Counsels be brot into Ruine.

*

At my Gate I was accosted by Master Giles, Wheelwright
of Powicke, he that is said to be of a new Puritan persuason
& to be a great Reader by Candlelight & to have strange
Lecturers to visitt at his House. He greeted me uncouthly &
wthout doffing his Hatt & he said that the State ran in Ill
Courses & that the Queen had bad Advisors & that he and
some mean Fellows do intend to gett up a Remonstrance to
the Comons House willing em to pass an Act of Attaynder of
the Queens Privy Council & her chief Secretarys of State.
And further he blurted out that as he had alwayes held me to
be an Honest Country Gentleman (thow no great Thinker he
was pleased to add) he had come to Sollicit my Hand in this
Affair.

I raised myself High in my Saddle, the better to bring
down my Whipp upon his Back. But as I turned I saw on every

Side the noble Trees planted by my Forefathers cutt down & Burned & Natures Foison all at Waste, & it came to Mind how the Dealers & the sly Agents of Forrayn Lands & the Privy Contrivers of Silly Peevish Cheeting Tryals of State do bring our Country into Contempt, do lead our Queen into foul & false Courses, & do blight the Labour & the Honor of Men of every Degree.

Come into my Study, Goodman Giles, said I. I will take Counsel with thee. And I do assure thee, I keepe no Mirrours in Episcopi Hall.

Squire Edwd Tomson

The State
versus its 'Enemies'

Let us consider State Trials. I cannot say why these should come into my mind this month, unless it may be that it is in the midst of general public silence that a historian is best able to meditate. Such trials of state as we now have are obscure, infrequent and ill-produced. They do not merit a moment of television news. Indeed, a young lawyer has told me that there is no such thing as a 'State Trial', so that some volumes on my shelves must go off to Sothebys and be auctioned as legal fictions.

This must be true. Certainly, we do not see the Attorney or Solicitor-General driving in his coach through astonished crowds to Westminster Hall to arraign the traitors to the Queen. These great persons are now retiring fellows. They are shy of the applause of the mob. They shun the public camera and order that the camera be turned against the public instead. They do not wish to be the stars of every paltry occasion nor to stand in the light of younger or lesser men. They hire others to do their work.

Indeed, the very hiring is put into other hands, lest it be thought that they might influence in the least particular the whole impartiality of the Law. It may not be supposed that they themselves have the least opinion as to what is treason and what is not. They are a sort of official stamp that is put at the bottom of indictments that others draw. It is now said

This article first appeared in *New Society*, 19 October 1978.

about Whitehall — and I trust that this is not already an Official Secret — that these are the first offices in the cabinet that will be put, very shortly, into the management of microchips, and at a great saving to the public purse. Some say it has already been done.

All is passed over now to a neutral public office, a Director of Public Prosecutions. This is a great personage indeed, and the microchip is still on the design board that will take his place. (The DPP should not be confused with the DPM, or Deputy Prime Minister, whose office is the writing of essays on Hazlitt and the making of speeches on Tom Paine as a screen behind which the DPP may go about his work.)

The present holder of this office is a genial fellow, who hides himself away behind no high park gates. He is the darling of *The Observer* (8 October), from which we learn that he entered the legal service of the state out of no suspect excess of zeal in the public good but 'because I was broke and getting married'.

Others have been broke, and some even have married, but few have gone so far and fast as he. But, for all that, he remains a modest, comfortable sort of fellow: not Baron This nor My Lord That but plain 'Tony' to the readers of the press — 'Tony because as a child he couldn't say Tommy'. By the same childish impediment of speech a man might grow up to know his own Mummy as 'Money' — what lisp could be prettier than that? To prosecute the enemies of the state is for him just one more job. It is a matter of keeping files up-to-date and moving them around from desk to desk. He is the very type of modernized man.

When the Court of Star Chamber was abolished, in a thoughtless riot of modernization, it left a certain vacuum to be filled. In the eighteenth century the Crown could no longer be assured that an ordinary jury would bring in the proper convictions. In cases of treasons, riots and the like, the case could be met by bringing offenders before Special Commissions (whose jurors were made up of the Principal Persons in the county) or by moving trial to high and distant courts, whose procedures of jury selection were elevated and obscure. In 1723 some Hampshire poachers were convicted without difficulty in the Court of King's Bench: 'the trying them in the King's Bench' (the Secretary of State was privately informed) was judged 'rather more effectual, especially now we may depend upon having jurys of men of probity and well enclined towards their Kings and country's service and interest'.

These poachers were duly hanged. But it proved to be more difficult to hang, or even to imprison, seditious libellers and such, whose cases could not be so moved. Hence followed the happy device of the 'special jury', twelve jurors drawn from a limited and scrutinized panel of forty-eight, who became well known to the Crown, were paid for their regular services, and, if any proved to be disaffected, these could be stood down; it was said Horne Tooke, 'like offering a man a basket of rotten oranges, from which he was at liberty to take his choice'. The practice was extended silently, on this pretext or on that, but its true virtues were perceived by the Crown only after the passage of Fox's Libel Act (1790), which ended a century and more of tussles between judges and jurors, and which made the jury at last judges of the libel itself and not of the mere fact of the words being uttered.

Thereafter, no reliance whatsoever could be placed upon an ordinary jury, and especially a London jury, to bring in a conviction for seditious libel, however horrendous the evidence and however implacable the instructions of the judge. At the conclusion to William Hone's second trial in 1817 Lord Ellenborough delivered his solemn opinion 'in obedience to his conscience and his God' and pronounced Hone's parody of the Litany 'to be a most impious and profane libel. Believing and hoping that they (the Jury) were Christians, he had not any doubt but that they would be of the same opinion.' When the jury returned, the foreman 'in a steady voice pronounced a verdict of — NOT GUILTY', to loud shouts of public applause.

It was Hone's three trials which blew the system of special juries. It had, perhaps, been overworked at the end of the Napoleonic wars. The victims were the radical printers, the friends of William Hazlitt and the printers of Tom Paine: the DPM might send a memo to the DPP and OPP (Office of

Public Parks) about that. As Bentham noted in his *Elements in the Art of Packing* (1821) the packing of juries 'is now become a *regular*, a *quietly established*, and *quietly suffered* system. Not only is the yoke already about our necks; but our necks are already *fashioned* to it.'

But the credit for blowing it open lay less with Bentham than with Hone's attorney, Charles Pearson. He had the neck to demand to know how the actual *panel* was drawn up. He marched with his client into the presence of the Master of the Crown Office, and watched him a-pricking of the panel. On his left hand stood the Treasury Solicitor; and the Deputy TS on his right. Peering around these officers as best they could, Pearson and Hone found that the Master's pen kept slipping, and, when it came to rest, he recited a name from memory that was not on the page. It was altogether a Proper and Official sort of Prick.

Thus the special jury fell into discredit. I do not say that in its pristine traditional purity it is now revived. To prick and cull a jury it was never essential to make up a special panel; this was only the most certain and convenient way. Other ways could be found of getting a jury 'well enclined towards their Kings and country's service and interest'. For *exactly* how a jury is empanelled is a matter too nice for many lawyers to be able to explain.

When the famous State Trial of the London reformers, Thomas Hardy, Horne Tooke and Thelwall commenced, William Godwin noted, in some *Cursory Strictures* that 'the Sheriffs, instead of suffering the Jury to be struck at the places where the book of the Freeholders is kept, and by the Officers to whom that care ordinarily falls, sent for the books from the office and took the task upon themselves ... It is very obvious to every person who casts his eye over the lists, that it consists of a most extraordinary assemblage, King's tradesmen, contractors, and persons labouring under every kind of bias and influence.'

Godwin's *Strictures* created a sensation. (We have a better sense of proportion in such matters today.) In the event the jury was challenged into a state of honesty. And that old London jury found true. The jurors were the toast of every tavern in the greatest city in the western world. It is an old story of a certain inconvenience in our legal system. Time and again, when judges and law officers, mounted on high horses, have been riding at breakneck speed towards some convenient despotism, those shadowy figures — not particularly good nor especially true — have risen from the bushes beside the highway and flung a gate across their path. They are known to historians as the Gang of Twelve.

How panels are pricked in London these days I do not know. It is said that, until lately, the job was farmed out, in true eighteenth-century style, to an old firm of city solicitors. If this is so, or was so, then there is no doubt that this is the proper way. I make no objection. The way in which a legal thing is done is, as we know, the proper way to do it. We do not need a fellow in a wig to tell us that. And if we were to contradict that fellow, then he could send us down.

I am allowed to say, however, that Mr Attorney-General, in a recent hand-out to the press (*The Times*, 11 October) has been mixing his traditions. We must put this hand-out to a breathalyser test. It pleads neither for the covert packing and culling of juries nor for the revival of the special jury in its prime. It is a sort of bastard special jury which it pleads for; neither the Sheriff's old muzzle-loader, with a pouch of Treasury powder, nor one of the Home Secretary's modern Armalite bores.

Prior to 1974, we learn, 'a practice had grown up', by which the prosecution privately checked the jury list against the records of the police. Ah yes, such 'practices' which 'grow' unseen by the public eye are of the very stuff of the organic state: 'it is now become a *regular*, a *quietly established*, and *quietly suffered* system'. I had supposed that we elected parliaments to find such matters out. But, no: when all this 'came to light' the Home Secretary, the Attorney-General, and the DPP consulted, and ordained (on our behalf) that the practice *should continue*, 'in the interests of justice'. But there were to be certain 'firm safeguards', and these were communicated, no doubt as an Official Secret, not to the British public, nor even to the legal profession as a whole, but to the police.

'Guidelines' were 'set out' and 'brought to the attention' of the police: the law-abiding citizen may relax. And what were these? First, and as a principle 'generally to be observed', members of a jury should be selected at random from the panel. The police are then advised, through eight more paragraphs, as to the ways in which this principle, which is 'generally to be observed', is *not* to be observed: that is, how it is to be broken.

There are 'certain exceptional types of case of public importance' when 'these principles ... may properly be departed from in the interests both of justice and of the public'. The breaking of what we had supposed to be the common law of the land is to be done 'to ensure the proper administration of justice'. 'It is impossible to define precisely these classes of case.' We scent a difficulty here, but we are quickly reassured. 'Broadly speaking', these cases may be ones 'where strong political motives were involved'. Here 'it may be right to conduct a limited investigation of the panel'.

We relax in our chairs once more. The investigation will be 'limited'. It will be done by proper persons. And what will be these stringent limits? No more than a check of the Criminal Record Office; a check on Special Branch records; and a check with local CID officers 'to ascertain if a potential juror is known to be an associate ... of those known to be sympathetic or antagonistic to his cause'.

By some oversight, the records of MI5, it seems, are to go unchecked. But no matter. The Special Branch is on the best of terms with them. They both may make deposits and draw upon the same great Bank of England, the Police National Computer at Hendon, with a capacity for 40 million records, and an average of 150 bytes at each one of us (*State Research*, November 1977). The PNC has an 'immediate response system' to every police station in the land. And for more refined information as to our potential disaffection, the Special Branch has its own privy computer, a penny bank of its own. We cannot suppose that the prosecution will be ill-informed.

And yet I detect some signs of uneasiness at the back of the hall. Be calm, good friends. The Attorney-General has

anticipated every objection. 'There is no question of telephone intercepts' on potential jurors, nor of 'the institution
of inquiries, by way of surveillance ... into occupations,
family, backgrounds, associates, political views and activities.'
Rest assured, good citizen, the fact that you have been pricked
for a panel does not mean that you are instantly carrion to be
blown upon by every nark in the land. If you are a seditious
kind of person, telephone intercepts and surveillance will
have been done long before. It will be all there, entered in
your statements in the general bank. The Attorney-General
may be faulted for a little lack of candour here. For the
bank's accounting becomes more comprehensive and nicer
every day. There is an entry for your driving offences, I
think, and so, it seems, there is an entry if you are a member
of the Anti-Blood-Sports League (*State Research*, January
1978). By an oversight, parking offences are not yet among
the bytes.

The purpose of this, we recall, is 'to ensure the proper
administration of justice'. It is to ensure that no juror 'might
be influenced, in arriving at a verdict, by extreme political,
racial or similar convictions'. It is to ensure that jurors be
'well enclined towards their Kings and country's service and
interest'. It is to ensure that all runs smoothly and that
proper convictions are found. It is to ensure that jurors are
capable 'of coming to a true verdict'. There is even a little
table to show how in twenty-five cases, since 1974, but without public knowledge, the thing has been comfortably done.
That is a formidable precedent at law. For, as I have said
before, if a thing is done at law, that is sufficient proof that
it is proper so to do. No judge would permit some privy
meddling to go on, between the prosecution and the police,
unknown to the defendant or the court, unless this was the
law of the land.

I am, therefore, so far behind the times that I scarcely
have the strength to rise in my place and object. But object
I do and must. I have searched my old history books and I
cannot find the precedent there. I had thought that the legal
mind was to be distinguished for precision and exact con-
structions. Mr Attorney-General, what precision is to be found

in this public relations botch you have issued to the press? Mr Attorney-General, what precision is there in these 'guide-lines' you served out secretly to the police? What *is* a guide-line? Is it a rule at law or is it a nudge-nudge be-careful-how-you-go? What officers have you appointed to see that these 'guidelines' are observed? What sanctions have you imposed against transgression? How are we to know if a case be of an 'exceptional type' or not? What rule at law may hang upon the phrase 'it is impossible to define precisely' the cases to which it might refer? If law is now to rest upon such nice terms as 'broadly speaking', who is to speak and how broad may that speech be? If a person be deprived of his juror's right (which I had once supposed to be a right and duty inherent in a citizen) because of 'strong political motives' and 'extreme political convictions', who is to determine whether his views be 'strong' or 'extreme'? Yourself? Or Tony the DPP? The prosecution? Or the police? Whichever it may be, you are taking a liberty: the liberty of the people.

There have been lawyers in our history — and I do not say that, even yet, all law is no more than sham — who would have spread those definitions across a courtroom floor and shredded them as finely as the weeders do our public records. Could you have taken those sniffling 'guidelines' and looked Sir Edward Coke or Sir William Blackstone in the face? I leave it to the bar, for I am told that there is yet an honest lawyer or two among them, to ask questions which are closer and even more nice. How far, in recent or in current cases, has 'the principle of equality of information' between spook-eyed prosecution and blindfold defence been scrupu-lously observed? And as for those twenty-five noble prece-dents, how are we now to know that the convictions found have, according to the rules of common law, been just?

What I will do is enter a plain statement of the rules that I have learned from history. These rules are not the same as those to be found in every book of law. There are times when lawyers and historians argue from an opposite set of prece-dents and reports. And both are long.

What my reports declare is that an Englishman is to be tried by his peers. And these peers are to be selected at random, without respect to their beliefs or opinions, and to be subject to no influence of state. That is the common understanding of the common law of this land. I do not say that all is thereby perfect. I do not say that every verdict has been good. I say only that this nation has had a certain custom of conducting its courts in this way, and has even had a habit of becoming angry when that custom was corrupted by the Crown.

It is a custom that has served us to a little purpose, and I have not yet seen the argument to show that it must now be set aside. When the jurors enter the box, they enter also upon a role which has certain inherited expectations; and these expectations are inherited as much from our culture and our history as from books of law. I do not say that jurors have always justified the expectations placed upon them. A heavy influence can be brought to bear: the influence of the court. 'A timid jury', said Burke, 'will give way to an awful Judge, delivering oracularly the law, and charging them to beware of their oaths.' Beside this awful influence, other — and external — influences are likely to be slight. I am told that the courts now face new and unprecedented emergencies, and I am no defender of terrorism nor of the Provisional IRA. But history is a long record of emergencies: Gunpowder Plots, Jacobites and Jacobins, Fenian outrages when Irish and English fought in the streets. I do not recall the Attorney-General, in Fenian times, who said that therefore all juries in all cases of 'public importance' (which cases it was 'impossible to define'), must first be screened by prosecution and police.

I say only that there have been occasions in our history — and these occasions more precious to our whole existence than can be set down in a few lines — when that anonymous Gang of Twelve has withstood the whole awful pressure of both court and Crown. Bad lawyers and bad judges have always been found to cry this custom down. It has always been their argument that juries should find their verdicts on the narrowest view of facts: justice is not their concern. The highest Court of Appeal will say, no doubt, that this is the law as found in their reports.

But it is not so in my reports. Jurors have found, again and again, and at critical moments, according to what is their sense of the rational and the just. If their sense of justice has gone one way, and the case another, they have found 'against the evidence'. When capital offences abounded, they found repeatedly a fraction beneath the line at which offence was capital. For, in my books, the English common law rests upon a bargain between the Law and the people. The jury box is where the people come into the court: the judge watches them and the jury watches back. A jury is the place where the bargain is struck. The jury attends in judgement, not only upon the accused, but also upon the justice and humanity of the Law.

It is necessary therefore to repeat today the instructions of William Godwin (*Morning Chronicle*. 30 March 1793) 'to Such Persons as May Be Appointed to Serve upon Juries'. 'I know that the persons who are concerned in the selection of juries are anxious to avoid all obnoxious and disaffected characters. But the character required in the present case, is so simple and moderate, that the most shameless Government would scarcely venture to proscribe it. He need not be the enemy, but on the contrary, may be the warmest friend of the English Constitution. He has only to bear in mind one plain principle, and to say, "This man, though he differs from me, may yet be honest".'

The quarrel between our laws and our liberties has always come to issue at this point. If the Attorney-General's 'guide-lines' had been laid down four centuries ago, how much bother the Crown would have been saved! How many rogues we have had in our history whose political motives and views the King's Messengers and Bow Street Runners could at once have found to be 'strong' and 'extreme'! Think of all those 'associates' of Pym and of Lilburne, of Thelwall and of Paine, of Hone and of Feargus O'Connor, who could have been barred from the jury box! Yet the Attorney-General, with his desire to mix special juries with old-fashioned Pricking, must be something of an antiquarian at heart. It comes through in the authentic tone of an ancient ruling class: jurors must be fixed '*to ensure the proper administration of Justice*'. Justice is there, on high, in the hands of Them: it must be administered (efficiently, and by 'guidelines' issued in secret) to Us. The jury (if we must still have it) is to be geared more sweetly into the administrative machine. It is not there to see, as my books say, that *justice be done*.

Justice is not a set of rules to be 'administered' *to* a people. Verdicts are not 'administered': they are *found*. And the finding, in matters of 'public importance', cannot yet be done by microchip. Men and women must consult their reason and their consciences, their precedents and their sense of who we are and who we have been.

The jury is, I think, the last place in our institutions where the people — *any* people — take a hand in 'administering' *themselves*. What kind of people are we now, that after all these centuries we are to go in fear of our neighbours' judgement? And are to be told by the state who is to have a juror's right and who is not? What kind of people are we, that the state should have an indefinite power to pry furtively into our most private affairs, while the state screens its own affairs from us as Official Secrets? What kind of government that holds us in such contempt? And if times are so changed that it is indeed necessary to provide for new rules at law, to safeguard against racial, sexual, or other bias, or to ensure, in certain difficult cases, that we have jurors with literate or numerate skills, may we not have such rules debated openly by judges, Parliament and the public, and exactly declared? Are our liberties to rest on 'guidelines' privately delivered — and delivered *to the police*? Is the whole of our history to hang on 'broadly speaking'? This to break the bargain made between the people and the Law: all that is left is the matter of how we are to be 'administered'. And administration *of* a people *by* the Crown (speaking 'broadly' and behind its hand to the police) is what, in my old books, was known as 'despotism'.

Well, I have torn a passion into tatters, and half the audience is now asleep. What a futile, out-moded trade mine is: I must see if the Job Creation Project can find a place for an ageing man of letters. I could offer myself as an Ideas Man. I could conform to the standards of the age. In the case of juries, for example, if these *must* be kept, cannot we find a system more rational, more open, and infinitely more certain than Mr Silkin's innovations? We know what is required. We need twelve persons who express unhesitatingly the Public Consensus, not one of whom is 'extreme', and not one of whom has been an associate of the Anti-Blood-Sports League: twelve persons *moyen intellectuel*. The answer comes at once to mind. In future, let all trials of state be solemnly performed in Westminster Hall, before twelve clones of Mr Robin Day. Indeed, this would scarcely be an innovation at all. It would simply bring the Law into line with the BBC.

A historian — as Professor Hoskins has told us — is no good unless he gets his boots on and tramps about the fields. I went down to London last week to see if any State Trials were still showing in these latter days. It was a poor business and not worth my fare. No cavalry in the streets, no press of angry crowds, not even a head to be seen on a pike by Temple Bar. The theatre of the thing is wholly gone.

The best I could do was to lurk about the Old Bailey and attend at Case 771968. It was a paltry affair, a business beneath the interest of the state. Nor could it even be said that Public Examples were being made. On my first attendance the court was *in camera*, arguing whether some commonplace might be named. It might not. On my second attendance the court was in recess so that the jurors' papers might be renumbered. On my third attendance the petty public gallery was full. I am not sure that I may not be entitled to claim my expenses from Tony Hetherington's account.

As I queued on the first day, I fell into conversation with an earnest young woman from Denmark. She had come, she said, to observe 'British justice'. Good God, sir, do we realize the opportunities we are letting go by? Each year the growing throng presses more heavily upon London's tourist attractions. The British Museum can take in no more. And what could be more simple than to offer to them, as a permanent alternative, successive grand and grave Trials of State? Let there be robes and full wigs; let there be frequent changing of the guards; let there be papers seized in Green Bags and Committees of Secrecy! And let the ancient nobility of the realm come to the nation's service once again; let Earls and Colonels and great Editors take their trial, and not mere corporals and such mean fellows.

Ancient traditions, as the case of Warwick Castle shows, may still with careful management be turned in for cash. And why, if we are to save the Warwick Vase, should not a few historians also be listed among the nation's assets? I understand that the Directors of Madame Tussauds have not yet settled on a use for every one of the castle's rooms. Let Mr Christopher Hill and Professor Rodney Hilton be seated behind glass in little alcoves, the one with an old black-letter folio of Magna Carta, the other with John Lilburne's *Just Defence* upon his knee. And then we might go further yet. What of the castle's grounds? Amidst the *son et lumière*, let us have morris dancing on the lawn, jousting beside the moat, and in a secluded spot the re-enactment of a Tryal by Jurye by Twelve Good Men and True.

But my audience is now all gone. My subject has been the antique customs of yesteryear. I find, on a review of the press, that the subject excites only boredom. I do not know where in all England I could place this piece, save that the Editor of this journal bears me an old friendship. He is too soft-hearted a fellow to see me, in my dotage, turned away. 'We have heard the chimes at midnight, Master Barker. Jesu, Jesu, the mad days that we have spent when Jane Liberty was yet alive! And to see how many of our old acquaintance are dead!'

A State of Blackmail

Mr Chapman Pincher has been employed by the *Daily Express* for over thirty years as a sort of common conduit through which 'government ministers, defence chiefs, directors of security and Intelligence, senior civil servants and others' have leaked their official secrets, scandals and innuendos to the readers and to each other. He has now published an account of this commerce, called *Inside Story*. I have examined this work, less with an eye to the subject-matter (mainly Westminster and Whitehall trivia) than to Mr Pincher's style of operation.

Pincher is coy about identifying his informants, unless these were Labour Ministers. Among those who seemingly passed him information in breach of the Official Secrets Act are: 'an official from Government Communications Headquarters (GCHQ), the highly secret network of eavesdropping and decoding stations based at Cheltenham' (p. 18); a girl in the MI5 registry at Curzon Street (p. 26); 'a prime MI6 'source' (p. 39); 'a former MI5 officer' (p. 114); Sir Frederick Brundrett, once Chief Scientist at the Air Ministry (pp. 150, 176, 297); a Deputy-Director of MI6 (p. 165); the permanent secretaries at several Ministries (e.g. p. 212); assorted 'service chiefs' (e.g. p. 228); an attender at the Defence and Overseas Policy Committee (p. 313); 'a very

First published in the *New Statesman*, 10 November 1978.

senior member of MI6' (p. 376), and so on.

Also, we are given the names of persons who are variously described as 'contacts' or 'close friends', who briefed him privately on secret matters in their official capacities, or who perhaps planted 'disinformation' through him. One notes: Lords George-Brown, Wigg and Watkinson; Admiral Sir Ray Lygo, one-time Vice-Chief of the Naval Staff (p. 57); the head of the legal department of MI5 (p. 76); Sir Richard Way, one-time Permanent Secretary at the War Office (p. 125); Air-Chief Marshal Sir David Evans of Strike Command (p. 295); Sir Ronald Ellis, head of Defence Sales (p. 317); Air-Chief Marshal Sir Peter Fletcher, former RAF 'chief planner' (p. 318); Sir Ray Brown, government arms salesman (p. 234). The work has been arduous, involving Mr Pincher in much slumming about Westminster and Whitehall: endless meals in the Ecu de France, Rules, Kettner's, the Savoy, the Dorchester; tedious parties in embassies and at country houses; the slaughter of much game and the filling-up of the boot of his car with bloody hares. He has had to sip tea from silver tumblers with the Shah ('he expressed dismay at the kid-glove way the British Army was dealing with terrorists in Northern Ireland'), followed by the 'briefing' by Mr Pincher of the British Ambassador (' "I shall have to warn London right away", he said as we took tea in the splendid Embassy garden, while parakeets flitted in and out from the Russian Embassy across the road, equipped, so Ramsbotham joked, with eavesdropping bugs', p. 264). Pincher's life has been much like that of a parakeet, and we must look to see his name in the Honours List.

It is not directly suggested that any in this last paragraph broke the Official Secrets Act, although it is directly suggested that Lord George-Brown broke his Privy Councillor's oath (pp. 94-5). The operational style is displayed most clearly in Chapter 33, which describes how (in 1975?) 'a naval contact in the Ministry of Defence' told Mr Pincher that an unarmed naval auxiliary vessel carrying Polaris nuclear warheads between Portsmouth and Falane had apparently gone missing in the Irish Sea. There is a regular ferry service, because the fuses and trigger mechanisms have

to be checked against corrosion every few weeks at the
Royal Ordnance Factory at Burghfield near Reading.

This, which could hardly be more 'secret', Pincher leaked
in fictionalized form, serializing *The Eye of the Tornado* in
the *Sunday Express* (1976):

> In a brief forward I acknowledged my indebtedness to 'senior
> officials present and past, in the Defence Ministry, Royal Navy,
> the Secret Intelligence Service, and others'.
>
> Inevitably the Prime Minister, James Callaghan, was asked in
> Parliament what assistance of this nature I had in fact been given.
> Also inevitably he replied, 'None that I know of.'
>
> He could not have inquired very deeply. Not only was I given
> technical assistance as stated but the text was read and corrected
> by very senior government officials. The only concession I was asked
> to make was to omit reference to Burghfield and name the nearby
> Atomic Weapons Research Station at Aldermaston as the main-
> tenance depot. This was not a security measure, for it was known
> that Soviet bloc Intelligence was well aware of Burghfield's function.
> It was to avoid anti-nuclear demonstrations outside the factory.
> [pp. 308-9.]

What is one to make of all this? There are three possible
views. First, that Chapman Pincher is merely romancing: no
one has broken the Official Secrets Act with him, Lord
George-Brown did not break his Privy Council oath, and all
the 'close friends' and 'private briefings' are empty brags.
This seems to me improbable. There is far too much circum-
stantial detail in the book; far too many of Pincher's leaks
were subsequently confirmed, and anyway this book would
not have gone to press without scrutiny by an expensive
libel lawyer.

Second, we may suppose that Mr Pincher has been less an
operator than the tool of other operators. In this view, we
must suppose that no one has leaked Official Secrets improperly. All the leaking has been contrived and wholly proper.
It has been an exercise by our superiors in the management
of news: in which proper persons decide not only when an
Official Secret becomes an Unsecret, but how it becomes
an Unsecret for some, while it remains defended by criminal
sanctions if published by others. This might be justified as
an exercise in confusing and 'disinforming' the KGB, although

in fact — as in the case of Burghfield — the real objective is to confuse, disinform and manage opinion in Britain.

In this view, the columns of the *Express* may be seen as a kind of official urinal in which, side by side, high officials of MI5 and MI6, Sea Lords, Permanent Under-Secretaries, Lord George-Brown, Chiefs of the Air Staff, nuclear scientists, Lord Wigg, and others, stand patiently leaking in the public interest. One can only admire their resolute attention to these distasteful duties.

But although this view explains many episodes (especially during the premiership of Macmillan and Heath, who would appear to have had some sense of propriety, and to have kept the security services in a state of low visibility) it is not a sufficient one. For what Pincher's text suggests, again and again, is private enterprise in leaking Official Secrets, some-times by persons in pursuit of private or political vendettas, sometimes in the course of lobbying by service chiefs (for this missile, or against that aircraft carrier), but most parti-cularly in pursuit of extreme right-wing objectives: the aim being to defame the Parliamentary Labour Party, particular Cabinet ministers, and the Left generally throughout the country.

This leads us, then, to a third view: most of Pincher's book is true. The Acts were repeatedly broken in these ways, many leaks coming through private or quasi-official enterprise. Of course, many episodes fall within the second explanation: Mr Pincher is too self-important and light-witted a fellow to realize how often he has been used. He sees himself always in virile posture ('the years when my penetration of the defence departments was particularly deep', p. 100). But for most of the time he was simply being paid for receiving the normal secretions of the state. Nevertheless, we can suppose that this book gives us a true, if misty, record of this commerce. This is the view which we must accept as most probable.

What then follows? It is instructive that this platterful of 'secret' excreta, some of it still warm from the bowels of the state, should have been served up to the public at exactly the same time as the state, with the apparent active insistence of the security services, the armed services and the Foreign

Office — the friends, one might say, of Chapman Pincher — should have brought to trial — upon charges which have in large part had to be dropped, because the judge regarded them as 'very oppressive' — two journalists and a long-retired lance-corporal, for having discussed in private things of infinitely less moment, several of which are openly discussed in Pincher's pages.

We may suppose that Mr Pincher and his publishers timed *Inside Story* to coincide with a General Election. In view of certain of his 'disclosures', this was like launching a leaking oil-tanker upon troubled waters, in the hope of further polluting the polluted electoral beaches.

Whoever master-minded this operation is, anyway, so arrogant as to suppose that no one would notice the flagrant double-standards displayed. Or perhaps he, or they (for may we not assume that the text of this book also was 'read and corrected by very senior government officials'?) hoped that we *would* notice and take the point? Anticipating a favourable conclusion to the ABC trial, Pincher's book might drive home the point that double standards are of *the very essence* of the Act. Pincher reminds us (p. 209) of the Normanbrook ruling, still in force, under which 'any information arising in a government department is officially secret until it is officially released'. It may therefore follow that any information released (or leaked) by any official who is influential enough cannot be construed as a secret, since it has been released by an official. The question is whether the leakage is in the 'public interest', and we have 'officials' who alone can decide this for us. Thus everything to do with the state is secret until officials decide to tell us, or to leak it to favoured places, or to disinform us. Anything we find out for ourselves is against the public interest and may bring us within the Acts. This is, of course, the old class war continued by other means.

The point of interest is whether this war is more one-sided and malevolent lately. On the evidence of this book it certainly is. In the last few years senior officials of the security services have taken to leaking like a wardful of incontinents, daily sheets from Fleet Street wrapped between their legs as nappies.

Twenty years ago, MI5, MI6, etc., were deployed with some circumspection. In 1961, according to Pincher, Lord George-Brown approached him on behalf of a 'secret committee' comprising Brown, Gaitskell and Patrick Gordon Walker, with the request to be put in touch with the heads of MI5 and MI6, and with the intention of gathering from these sources material on the activities of 'crypto-Communists' within the Parliamentary Labour Party, as evidence for expelling these MPs from the party. This genial move was blocked, not by the head of MI5 (who was glad to gossip with Brown) but by Harold Macmillan (pp. 21-6).

In this case, the initiative came from morally defective politicians who — some readers may yet remember — were under extreme pressure when the demand for unilateral nuclear disarmament was carried by Labour's Conference. If we are to credit Pincher's account, the initiative in the seventies has passed wholly into the hands of the security services. 'The links between some left-wing Labour MPs and foreign revolutionaries like Chilean Marxists, not only allowed to settle in Britain but encouraged to do so, have been investigated by the CIA' (p. 159). The inter-operation and exchange of information, intercepts, etc., between British and US security services (CIA, NSA, etc.) is total: as one 'prime MI6 source' told Pincher, 'anything and everything would be possible if it was considered necessary to protect the Anglo-American joint Intelligence arrangement' (pp. 38-9). One 'anything' was the deportation of Agee and Hosenball in 1977, on evidence 'partly based on telephone-taps' (p. 147), and also, presumably, the decision to put Aubrey, Berry and Campbell on trial. Pincher makes a mysterious pudding out of whether Sir Harold Wilson was bugged or not, but he leaves us to infer that this was done by the CIA or NSA, and that MI5 and MI6 then covered up for these (p. 38). He directly alleges, though, that there was some native surveillance of Wilson (in 1974) and he refers to a document 'in the registry of MI6' and gives a précis of its contents (pp. 30-1).

With respect to more notorious subversives, the tale is plainer yet. In 1976 Mr Pincher took part in an operation (during which he had dealings with the head of MI6) which resulted in the naming, under parliamentary privilege, of Jack Jones, Ernie Roberts, Hugh Scanlon and Lord Briginshaw as 'prime targets for Soviet bloc Intelligence' (pp. 138-9). He also alleges that 'certain ministers' in the Cabinet are denied access to intelligence information on security grounds (p. 19). He further tells us — and was permitted to inform the nation on television — that (in 1975?) certain officials in M15, serving and retired, tried to bring down the government, making preparations to publicize the activities of Labour MPs (from evidence derived from 'undercover surveillance') including two serving and one retired Cabinet minister (p. 17).

There are also two steaming turds *from the last two years' excretions* which deserve fuller quotation:

> As regards those crypto-Communists still sitting in Westminister, I can quote from a 1978 Intelligence report in my possession which states that 'at least 59 serving Labour MPs ... have current or recent connections with Communist, Trotskyist or other Marxist organisations ...' A list attached to this report ... includes five ministers and four junior ministers. [p. 28.]

And this one. George Young, a former deputy-director of MI6, wrote in 1977 to David Yorck, formerly of the American Office of Strategic Services (OSS, forerunner of the CIA):

> At one point under Wilson there were five ministers of the Crown whose membership of the Communist Party of Great Britain is not known to have been renounced and overlapping with them other ministers whose ultimate allegiance is outside Britain. [p. 28.]

The first thing which a historian must remark on all this is that a government (or a House of Commons) ceases to have any credibility if it tolerates these kinds of repeated 'disclosure', with the alleged complicity of its own security services, without calling them to full public inquiry and account. In the absence of this there is no longer any government. Government has ceased to govern, and Members of Parliament have ceased to have any regard for their political honour.

If Mr Pincher has evidence in his possession as to the covert surveillance of a Prime Minister, or a 1978 Intelligence Report naming fifty-nine MPs and nine ministers of the Crown, then he should be called to produce his evidence, and if he cannot do so he should be exposed. For offences far more trivial than this, calumniators have been hauled before the Bar of the House and made to substantiate their allegations.

If there is any honour left in that House, this crescendo of allegations must lead to inquiry on the scale of Congressional and Senate inquiries into the CIA. If the allegations are sustained in any part, then there must be dismissals, and total reorganization of the security services under new forms of public accountability.

But the unpleasant truth is that this inquiry cannot and will not be made. It is becoming evident that the reason why the Prime Minister, the Government, the Parliamentary Labour Party, and the House of Commons, will do nothing whatsoever about the situation is that they lie under a state of blackmail to the security services.

I know of *no* historical precedent for this. It is beginning to appear that MI5, MI6, etc., have accumulated in their dossiers enough unpleasant-seeming material on enough MPs, including senior politicians, to make it impossible for MPs, collectively, to break and run. If the blackmail was called, it might not amount — except in a few cases — to much more than scandal. But the scandals would be numerous. For several years, the political air would be fouled up, and there would be some terminal casualties in political life.

If a person is in public life for some years, and subject to 'undercover surveillance', it may be hard not to commit some indiscretion (sexual? receipt of a gift?) or some act which can be made to look worse (East-West trade? helping a government contract along?). MPs, casting their minds back over the past, don't know exactly what 'they' may have got on them, or on their colleagues, and as the profile of the security services rises more and more ominously above its undercover waters, they fall victim to a collective unease.

The blackmail falls, of course, much more heavily on a Labour administration than a Tory, since the security services appear to operate on a Midwest college kid's definition of 'Marxist organizations' (the Institute for Workers' Control? The Royal Arsenal Co-Op?), and for whom solidarity with Chilean refugees constitutes 'allegiance ... outside Britain'. This explains why the present and recent Labour administrations have dealt more weakly with the security services than previous administrations, why the profile of these services rises higher every month, why Mr Pincher's book can appear in the midst of the ABC trial, why Labour Home Secretaries and Attorney-Generals dance to their advisers' nods, and why there is worse to come.

It is not clear whether such pressures were involved in Sir Harold Wilson's sudden resignation: Pincher's chapter on this appears to fall into the category of 'disinformation', and it concludes with a distinct warning-off. 'A very senior member of MI6' warned him that 'I would be wasting my time trying to find out why Wilson resigned because there was something of a mystery there' (p. 376). A 'most eminent Oxford Professor' has written to Mr Pincher to tell him that Sir Harold Wilson said, last year, that MI5 'plotted against him, tried to secure his downfall'. (Which eminent Oxford Professors act as Pincher's informers?)

One might imagine, in a Thatcherite administration, the Tories attempting to benefit from their close ideological accord with the security chiefs, by selective unloosing of dossiers at the Labour benches in a McCarthyite climax. I think this unlikely. First, it might cause even the most abject of Labour politicians to stand and fight. Even Mr Rees and Mr Sam Silkin would arch their backs and utter a terrific treble mew. Second, it would destroy the threadbare but still serviceable myth of security 'neutrality'.

And there is a third reason. I do not see why we are always *bound* to take a charitable view of MI5, MI6, etc. Mr Pincher's memoirs suggest that every corporal in the security services nourishes fantasies that he carries in his knapsack the baton of General Pinochet.

The present situation is wholly satisfactory to senior

security chiefs. The black widow has bitten its parliamentary victim: eyes are glazed, limbs paralysed. MPs and ministers are keeping their heads down, and are abjectly compliant to each piece of 'advice'. But there may be younger, rising men within security for whom all this is not enough. They will wish to move in and eat their prey. This eating will be presented in full colour to the British public, perhaps as the formation of a National Government in the public's own interest.

Mr Pincher's book has one cheery piece of disinformation:

As recently as the summer of 1978, I have been assured by a most senior British Intelligence official that the secret services, which are active in checking on all subversive movements, have no evidence whatever of any right-wing group aimed at disturbing the elected government in any way. [p. 136.]

Now, while this is inaccurate — there are certainly right-wing groups which *aim*, however ineptly, at disturbing the government — I think it may have historical truth. It is like a bank robber who has achieved a high position in Securicor assuring the bank manager that there are no robbers planning to break in and blast open his safes. The bank will be entered in full uniform, and the safes opened from within by those already officially apprised of the combinations.

I don't discount the significance of neo-fascist bodies, nor underestimate their contribution to polluting the atmosphere. But my sense of history suggests that any Rightist take-over in Britain will come, not through the agency of the Mosleys or Websters, but by steady, vegetable pressures from within the state itself: the management of news, the black-mailing of politicians, the political 'vetting' of civil servants, the clipping of the coinage of civil liberties, the enlargement of police powers, the dissemination of calumny against dissenters, the corruption of the jury system, the surveillance and intimidation of radicals, the management of state trials, the orchestration through the media of a 'law and order' *grande peur* — and the cry of 'national interest'. The strategic centre for this pressure will lie with the security services, armed services, and police. But it will be ably supported by a vociferous lobby of Tory MPs, captive editors, 'neutral' television commentators, under-secretaries at Whitehall, some judges, and the odd 'eminent Oxford professor'. My sense of politics suggests that this take-over is already under way. As John Berry said in the dock on 27 October: 'There is a state within the state, a secret state about which questions should not be asked.' Against such a take-over this country is provided with few constitutional defences.

The secret state moves forward and occupies the public state from within, leaving most of the latter's rhetoric, and most of its electoral legitimacy intact. What better 'cover' for 'M' than a Labour Prime Minister?

I might leave it there, but I have some personal accounting to do. Pincher provides, with an equable hand, some low-level information, as well as disinformation, about the security services themselves.

The silliest piece of disinformation, passed on with a sceptical shrug, is that 'the highest official figure for the number of telephones tapped in one year is 242' (p. 145). Some of us could tot up that number fairly easily by running through our own associates and friends, starting with the offices of the National Council for Civil Liberties, *Peace News*, the Bertrand Russell Peace Foundation, and so on.

'Most of the telephones tapped in Britain', Mr Pincher hastens to reassure us, 'belong to suspected spies, criminals, subversives, customs evaders, Communists, the New Left, Fascists, National Front leaders and journalists' (p. 147). Since we are also informed — the truth? or more disinformation to frighten us? — that there are two million dossiers in the registries of MI5 and MI6 (p. 143), an unexpectedly large percentage of the British population fall within these categories.

I am not vain enough to suppose that my own file bulks large among these. Our phone was probably tapped in the early 1950s, when my wife and I were active in our opposition to the Korean War, since in those technically immature days our calls sometimes got snarled up with the Halifax police station. Just possibly we might have been under

lukewarm surveillance at the time of CND and the early New Left.

But our efforts to overthrow the state did not meet with success, and I suspect that the spooks lost interest. Perhaps the file was got out and dusted at the time of the 'troubles' at Warwick University. Since that time I imagine that it has been collecting dust once more in one of the 'Wendy Houses' of the MI registries (which Pincher so lovingly describes), perhaps marked: 'File inactive. Query — Gone to earth? Query — Dead?' The last time I was aware of being under rather heavy surveillance was in India, during the last months of Mrs Gandhi's Emergency — as a consequence of my reck-lessness in assuring shocked academic audiences that Mr Michael Foot's endorsement of that unpleasant police state did not carry the approval of the entire British labour movement.

My dossier may have been got out again, rather sharply, when I began to take an interest in the ABC Defence Committee. At least, I have good reason to suppose that my mail is now being 'surveilled'. The background makes too long a story, but in short I have an interest in opening the archives of the Special Operations Executive from the last war — records which I consider to be at present improperly held beyond even the reach of the Deputy Keeper of Public Records.

My interest is personal. For the records should include full evidence as to the British Mission sent in support of the Bulgarian partisans (1943-4), which my brother Major Frank Thompson, at one time commanded, and in the course of which he was captured on Bulgarian soil, brutally interro-gated, and shot. To my knowledge, no official statement has ever been made as to the existence of this Mission, nor as to my brother's death, so that the matter remains an Official Secret — to the British public at least, since in Bulgaria the work of the Mission is acknowledged, a railway station has been named after my brother, and he is a National Hero of that country.

I have recently taken up again my rather long and wholly fruitless attempts to look into these archives, and have

exchanged some letters with others who have a public interest
in the matter. A few days ago an important letter, from an
extremely distinguished officer of the last war, disappeared
from a packet in the post. The letter (no more than a courteous response to one of my own) was of no possible 'subversive' character, though the writer mentioned his own
difficulties with the custodians of SOE papers. The sender
is certain that it was in the packet when sent, and I am
equally certain it did not arrive.

Compared with any page of Pincher's memoirs, this is
very small beer. I was amused, however, to note one of the
last 'official' statements on the interception of communications, in the Report of the Birkett Committee (October
1957), in which Parliament was told that such powers are
used only against 'wrong-doers' and are

> used with the greatest care and circumspection . . . and never with-
> out the personal considered approval of the Secretary of State.

So I must ask why Mr Merlyn Rees may recently have
given his 'personal considered opinion' that an inoffensive
social historian and member of the General Management
Committee of the Kidderminster CLP should rank as a
'wrong-doer' meriting this attention?

Mr Pincher, who knows much more about it than did that
committee of Privy Councillors, is able to deflect this question from Mr Rees. For he tells us that he has established, 'by
questioning security officials', that the Home Secretary is
very rarely troubled with these matters. The duty is delegated
to underlings: moreover, any of fifteen Secretaries of State
(and their underlings also?) can approve warrants for tapping
of telephones (p. 145). I suspect that by now the notion of
ministerial delegation is only a fiction. So I may continue to
regard Mr Rees as a jolly good liberal fellow.

Such surveillance is age-old: one should keep one's cool and
reflect what a service is being done for historians in the
75-year future. But for spies, narks and letter-copiers, the
history of the English working class would be unknown. The
archives of the Library of National Security in 2078 will be

infinitely grander than anything now in the Public Record
Office, complete with tape, film, and computerized retrieval
systems.

What was different, in the naive nineteenth century, was
that citizens had not yet come to a mature view of these
things. When each informer or letter-opener showed his
sticky marks, they squalled and ranted, and at least made
them keep their heads down. When it transpired that, on the
authorization of the Home Secretary, Sir James Graham,
letters passing between Mazzini and William Lovett and
W.J. Linton had been opened, and information passed to the
Austrian ambassador as a result of which (as it then appeared)
nine bandieras were ambushed and killed in Calabria, there
was a quite ridiculous fuss.

Graham was in fact acting as the cat's-paw of the Foreign
Secretary, a condition not unknown to contemporary Home
Secretaries and Attorney-Generals: this was not accepted by
the public as an adequate explanation. Indignation meetings
were held, and people franked their letters: 'Not to be
Grahamed'. Should our friends who are in correspondence
with dissidents in the Soviet Union, East Europe, Iran, Latin
America or South Africa mark their letters: 'Not to be
Reesed'?

It is enough for me to invite the Postmaster-General to
inquire into the route taken by Recorded Delivery No.
V.678007: if we fall within Mr Pincher's generous categories
of 'subversives', we will be surveilled; let them card-index
and compute our efforts if they wish. I am not yet aware
that the spooks have touched me in any sensitive point:
threatened my family or close friends, stolen my notes on
the Muggletonian Church, or tampered with the whiskers of
my favourite cat. We do not have a Prussian or a Russian
state.

Yet, after reading Pincher, I must understand that the
state has powers not only to survey me, but to void the
contents of their survey into the Fleet Street urinals. If I
surmise my mail may have been opened since late 1977,
when I indicated support for the ABC Defence Committee,
then I must reflect upon what may have passed before

GENTLEMEN'S CONVENIENCE

security's eyes. Amid all the chores, to which they are welcome, I can think of one quite deadly and compromising leak, an admirable Fleet Street pee, which perhaps I should save them the trouble of writing:

HISTORIAN LINKED TO BULGARIAN EMBASSY

Exclusive by Filchbag Peeper

Commentators have been at a loss to explain the motives which led E.P. Thompson, a historian with long Marxist associations, to write a bitter attack on Sam Silkin, the Attorney-General, in *New Society* last month.

Thompson, who left Warwick University a few years ago after being detected giving aid to student extremists, has no overt political ambitions. Why then should he have intervened so vociferously in a matter of security in which he had no direct interest, thereby giving comfort only to the KGB?

I am now able to give exclusive information to readers, as a result of conversation with prime sources in MI5 and MI6, that Thompson has been under surveillance for some time as a contact with the security and defence forces of an Iron Curtain country.

On more than one occasion, a high-ranking Bulgarian officer has driven to his Worcester home. The purpose of these visits has not been disclosed . . .

There is nothing in Filchbag Peeper's report which I could deny. My own contacts with Bulgaria dried up after the particularly foul trial of Traicho Kostov in 1949, and the subsequent disgrace of many ex-partisans as 'Titoites'. (My brother ceased, for a time, to be a National Hero, and became an 'agent of Anglo-American imperialism'.) But in the past year I have been in touch with General Slavcho Transky, one of the most heroic of the surviving partisans, who fought alongside my brother, and who survived the years of jail and disgrace. I consider it my right to welcome to our table one of my brother's comrades-in-arms, despite my publicly-expressed distaste for the Bulgarian regime. I cannot expect Filchbag Peeper, or his informants, or Mr Rees to understand or condone such behaviour. But I do not intend to change it.

There is one further point, one not easily made without committing the deadly sin of being 'heavy'. I have been wondering all week what was the sweet smell that entered my mind whenever I opened *Inside Story*. At first I thought it was only the sweet smell of Mr Pincher, who (on one report) is receiving £25,000 for serialization in the *Express* of material gathered in that paper's employment. Next, I thought it might be the whiff of the Fleet Street urinals. But now I recollect the smell more clearly: I encountered it first on the battlefield of Cassino, when I stumbled upon some blackened six-day-old corpses of soldiers and mules. It is the smell of animal decomposition. I suppose the decaying body must be that of British Imperialism.

Mr Pincher never ceases to remind us of his 'wartime background', which brought him colleagues who 'went to the top in Whitehall'. He is always on about his own exceeding patriotism and loyalty:

> I have spent a large slice of my life investigating and trying to expose the machinations of the extreme Left against the interests of the country I love.

A good part of the biography on the dust jacket is given over to his war service. He was 'commissioned in 1941 in the 6th Armoured Division', but was transferred in 1943 to the Military College of Science, and spent the rest of the war researching into such matters as anti-tank weapons. I think we must take it that he did not see any active service, since if he had, the biography would have entered into all the details.

As it happens, I also was commissioned, a little later, in the 6th Armoured Division, and my own researches into anti-tank weapons were conducted at the receiving end. This argues no particular merit or patriotism in me. It was how the chips fell. I am not even clear what I am trying to say, except that it has to do with the betrayal of the past and the calumny of the dead.

One is not permitted to speak of one's wartime reminiscences today, nor is one under any impulse to do so. It is an area of general reticence: an unmentionable subject among younger friends, and perhaps of mild ridicule among those of radical opinions. All this is understood. And one understands also why it is so.

It is so, in part, because Chapman Pincher and his like have
made an uncontested take-over of all the moral assets of that
period; have coined the war into Hollywood blockbusters and
spooky paperbacks and television tedia; have attributed all
the values of that moment to the mythic virtues of an authoritarian Right which is now, supposedly, the proper inheritor
and guardian of the present nation's interests.

I walk in my garden, or stand cooking at the stove, and
muse on how this came about. My memories of that war are
very different. I recall a resolute and ingenious civilian army,
increasingly hostile to the conventional military virtues,
which became — far more than any of my younger friends
will begin to credit — an anti-fascist and consciously anti-
imperialist army. Its members voted Labour in 1945: knowing why, as did the civilian workers at home. Many were
infused with socialist ideas and expectations wildly in advance
of the tepid rhetoric of today's Labour leaders. Give us that
army back today, and half its members, and their girlfriends
and wives, would have to go onto the dossiers in the Wendy
Houses of MI5: Left Book Club readers, supporters of the
Labour Party, the CP, ILP, Commonwealth — subversives
everywhere. Our expectations may have been shallow, but
this was because we were overly utopian, and ill-prepared
for the betrayals at our backs.

But we were not Pincher's People! And I refuse, also, to
borrow Pincher's strategies. The merits of that moment did
not lie alone with the Left, and the demerits alone with the
Right. Conservative soldiers were brave and effective, not
only through an inherited patriotic code of class: many
acquired a more democratic code as well, a settled anti-
fascist commitment. These were not Pincher's People either.
If any moral assets from that moment are left, let's not
haggle over portions. Let us leave it at evens.

But yes, I do now remember, Pincher's People were already
around. They were to be found thickest in Whitehall, in
Baker Street, in Shepheard's in Cairo: a few, it seems, may
have been at the Military College of Science. These were
the people who intrigued ceaselessly to restore 'British

interests' in the East and Near East, and capitalist enterprise in Europe; who sent Missions into exposed positions in the field, and who then failed to give them support, or double-crossed them when in action; who tried to prevent even Churchill from knowing the truth about the Yugoslav partisans, and who then tried to prevent his personal representative to Tito, Sir Fitzroy Maclean, from carrying out his mission.

These are the people who shattered the anti-fascist consensus, by engineering the sending of our reluctant forces to Athens, at Christmas 1944, to crush the Greek partisans. These are the people, few in number but deeply concealed within the strategic centres of the state, who became with Stalin the joint-architects of the Cold War; who became the eager accessories of the CIA; who trained their clones and multiplied them within the state's secret organs; who now lay claim to the whole inheritance of that war as their private asset, and who today hold the public state and the private citizen in their blackmail.

It is difficult to explain how memories affect one in middle life. For months, the past stretches behind one, as an inert record of events. Then, without forewarning, the past seems suddenly to open itself up inside one — with a more palpable emotional force than the vague present — in the gesture of a long-dead friend, or in the recall of some 'spot of time' imbued with incommunicable significance. One is astonished to find oneself, while working in the garden or pottering about the kitchen, with tears on one's cheeks.

I have found myself like this more than once since reading Mr Pincher's book. I have no notion what the tears are about. They are certainly not those of self-pity. There may be something in them of shame, that we should have let that world be degraded into this. There is also fury — that younger people, and among these some whom I most approve or admire, should have had this foul historical con passed upon them — should suppose that this is all that that generation was . . . Pincher's sort of people!

I can now see what was wrong with that generation. It was too bloody innocent by half, and some of them were too open to the world, and too loyal to each other to live. But may we be saved from this last obscenity — the lie that it is in 'loyalty' to their memory that we must now submit to pre-packaged juries, tapped phones, a compliant press, a managed television, the gross suppression of public truth: to the blackmailing of the nation by Chapman Pincher's patriotic, but anonymous friends!

'Pah, pah! Give me an ounce of civet, good apothecary, to sweeten my imagination!'

The Nehru Tradition

Early in January 1977 I paid a courtesy visit to the palatial Jawaharlal Nehru Memorial Museum in New Delhi. My business was to exchange copies of letters which passed between my father, Edward John Thompson, and Nehru in the years 1936 to 1946.

The place was like a vast, modernized shrine. I was received not only with courtesy but with unction. My 'reminiscences' (as a fourteen-year-old) of the great Founder of the Nation were reverently put on tape. As was proper.

For no one, in those last months of the Emergency, was allowed to forget for a moment the awe due to the Dynasty of Nehrus — Jawaharlal, Indira, Sanjay. In the tourist traps of New Delhi, shop windows were decorated with posters: 'In support of Prime Minister Indira Gandhi's 20-point programme, we offer 10% discount.' (Most of these shopkeepers had been Jan Sangh — Hindu communalist — supporters until the Emergency turned them sharply around.)

My business was serious. I welcomed the exchange of manuscripts. But I also had another matter on my mind — to find out how the Emergency was biting and how it was being resisted — and I wanted to shake off any possible surveillance.

After a month of moving around India, from one university to another, I was perhaps a little paranoid. At one

---

Part of this essay appeared in the *Guardian*, 16 November 1978.

university an outspoken member of the seminar was arrested immediately afterwards: perhaps a coincidence, but my friends were not sure. At another, where my wife and I held a three-day faculty seminar, we were told that two silent members of the seminar were intruders who could not be identified as university staff. And so on. We were not worried for ourselves — but might we be carriers of the plague of police attention to our friends?

That afternoon I had agreed to attend a secret meeting of opponents to the Emergency from the new Jawaharlal Nehru University in New Delhi. I must taxi here: walk there: get another taxi: meet someone by a cinema: and then (ludicrously conspicuous with my European complexion, grey hair and briefcase) slide into the upstairs room of a villa where about twenty young women and men, mainly graduate students, were packed on the floor.

If the meeting had been 'blown', every one of them could have disappeared indefinitely into India's overcrowded and insanitary prisons — and I, presumably, could have gone on waffling around the sub-continent unscathed. There followed three hours of the most heartening, intense, undogmatic and searching political discussion I have ever taken part in.

The group had survived the first onset of the Emergency by luck and then by excellent tactics and security. At that university the Emergency had been inaugurated with a splendid coup of theatre. The campus was encircled by police at 2 a.m. and hundreds of students were thrown out of bed and paraded before a masked man (a student informer) who pointed out suspects to the police. In the following days some four hundred were interviewed at the police station. Only a score were arrested then: but interrogations and a trickle of arrests went on through the ensuing months. At the University all open politics ceased.

This group could do nothing in public and I was not silly enough to ask them what went on underground. What amazed me was the extent of their knowledge not only of India but of the world. They talked familiarly (usually ironically) about the theories and policies (or non-policies) of little sectarian groups in Britain; about Althusser (they shared my dislike); about whether it was the CIA or KGB, or both, which were advising Mrs Gandhi's security services in the latest techniques.

When a car stopped outside in the street, the look-out would draw back the blind an inch and conversation stopped. 'O.K. — only a neighbour.' Then we got going again, every now and then being reminded to hush our voices. Eventually the conversation came round to the point which it always did — in Delhi, Aligarh, Calcutta, Kerala, Bombay, Baroda — 'Why has the British labour movement abandoned us like this? Don't people know? Why did Michael Foot support the Emergency?'

Twenty pairs of pained, angry, estranged, and brave eyes waited for my answer. I did not have one to give.

The excuse (for there can be no possible answer) lies in the fact that Mrs Gandhi is Nehru's daughter; and some senior Labour politicians held him in high respect, and did something — although, in most cases, not very much — to help the cause of Indian independence along.

Many times during those weeks I reflected upon a visit paid by my father to India some thirty-seven years before. The visit, in October 1939, was in fact a peculiar political mission. Two months before it had been announced to this huge and startled nation that it was at war. Despite the fact that much of India was then ruled by Congress ministries, India was 'declared a belligerent' by Britain, without any pretence of consultation with the Indian people. It was simply announced to those who had radios in a Viceregal statement. In the fury which ensued, a Congress declaration of 'civil disobedience', and the consequent internment of many thousands of Congress leaders and activists, was expected daily.

My father was known to the Indian press as a 'friend of India', and that is in fact what he was. He commenced in the 1910s as an educational missionary in Bengal; was educated by Tagore and Bengali poets (whom he presented to the

West); and was further acculturated to the point of leaving the Methodist Church — one of his last novels was about the Buddha. In politics he was a fluid liberal (with a small 'L') and, in his last years, staunchly pro-Congress. His late-flowering friendship with Nehru was both cause and consequence of this.

He had a gift for friendship and a passion for Indian history and culture. As a child I had no doubt that Indians were our most important visitors: the sideboard loaded with grapes and dates was testimony of this. A little older, I would cadge postage stamps from poets and political agitators. Older again, I stood in awe before the gracious Jawaharlal, as he asked me about my batting technique.

My father and Nehru had other bonds: they were both staunch anti-fascists and opponents of appeasement. Nehru, fresh from a British prison, passing through Rome, turned his back on a request to attend on Mussolini. Writing to my father from Prague (August 1938) he predicted the outcome: 'War can be avoided if only England and France made it clear that they would not tolerate any German aggression in Czechoslovakia.' In October (after Munich) 'the outlook is about as evil as it could well be. It is a little difficult, even for me, to rouse up enthusiasm for this wretched world. Still I suppose one has to go on and fight the monster . . . Visit us in Allahabad when you come east. And remember that the Himalayas are always there as a refuge, for a while at least, from fascism and its friends.'

In October 1939 my father flew to India with an unofficial brief to act as a kind of go-between — to visit all sections of Indian opinion (and some British), to talk , carry messages between people who had been carried beyond talking-distance with each other: the Viceroy, Jinnah, Sapru, Ambedkar, the Congress Working Committee. My father hoped that civil disobedience could be called off or at least postponed; and that, as *quid pro quo*, the British would make an explicit declaration of intent as to Indian independence after the war.

In the midst of this crisis Nehru somehow found time to write to a schoolboy in England: 'Your father suddenly turned up here . . . We had long talks into the night. We met

not only in Allahabad but all over the place in India — in
Wardha, Bombay, and Delhi.'

The meeting in Wardha was with Gandhi and the Congress
Working Committee. The atmosphere throughout India was
cracking with tension: everyone expected arrests to commence. I find this among my father's notes:

> I travelled down to Wardha in distress of mind. I had seen the
> decency of both sides and felt the tragedy of what was coming, a
> clash that would be far fiercer than the three previous civil dis-
> obediences. On the long journey through those heavenly Central
> Indian jungles I was the only Englishman on the train. From first
> to last everyone showed me the most perfect courtesy and friendli-
> ness. There is no nation whose common people are more naturally
> 'gentle' than Indians are . . .
>
> I reached Wardha in the evening. It was the *Vijaya Dasami*, a day
> of good omen. Congress that morning had decided to pull out its
> Ministries.
>
> A small child, not more than about five years old, greeted me on
> the threshold with an offering of *sami* leaves: a young man and then
> a young woman came, and did the same. This is the custom towards
> elders on this day. Mr Gandhi had postponed his weekly Day of
> Silence by three hours, and came to me at once, Nehru with him.
> Gandhi began talking about *Vijaya Dasami*, and the offering of *sami*
> leaves, then checked himself: 'I forgot. You understand our customs.'
> He was friendlier and gentler than I had ever known him . . .

Next day my father was invited to meet the full Congress
Working Committee — an honour which (I have been told)
was extended to only one other Englishman, C.F. Andrews:

> It was a charming experience, abounding in kindliness and goodwill
> . . . On my right sprawled Kripilani, the All India Congress Secretary.
> He is a Sindi, a man of strikingly handsome appearance; with his
> black hair and clear-cut features and spare athletic body he looks
> like the hero of one of Byron's wilder romances, as if he had just
> arrived leading a horde of Tartar bandits. Then came Rajagopalachari,
> Premier of Madras. To his right was the Maulana Abul Kalam Azad,
> the only one seated on a chair, because of a recent illness . . . In a
> corner sat Pattabi Sitaramayya . . . with his bristling whiskers and
> upright carriage, looking like an extremely fierce Struwelpeter hare,
> but with a mischievous twinkle that took away all the fierceness . . .
> To my left sat Sarojini Naidu, the poetess, a brilliant orator and
> brilliant and witty woman — somewhat apart and critical of her
> brethren, coming in with disconcerting reminders and disrespectful
> thrusts at 'the Oracle' (Mr Gandhi), and next to her Jawaharlal

Nehru, more cheerful than he had any right to be. From time to time he guided our talk, saying perhaps: 'Could you give the Working Committee some idea of war conditions in London . . .?' The Working Committee, unlike British circles, believed the war was going to turn into a distinctly nasty war, and their interest in world affairs was profound and alert.

It turned into a war far nastier than even Nehru or my father supposed. Civil disobedience, postponed for a while, was eventually declared, and the great British round-up took place. That Working Committee was split up into a dozen jails. My father, back in England, busied himself with the chores of solidarity — meetings, letters and articles, more meetings.

At first the meetings were small. As he used to say in the thirties, 'the mere mention of the word "India" is enough to empty the smallest hall in Oxford'. But, for once, this proved untrue. As the war went on, the meetings grew. Labour politicians were not, as I recall, prominent in this: they were co-partners in the repression of Congress. It was the socialist, liberal and communist fringe which acted: the India League, the Majlis, student societies. The speakers I recall were journalists and writers (H.N. Brailsford, Kingsley Martin, my father), S.O. Davies (whom the Labour Party expelled as its eightieth birthday present), Harry Pollitt (of the CP), Sir Richard Acland (of Commonwealth), Sir Geoffrey Mander (Liberal), Fenner Brockway (ILP), and everywhere, indefatigable and uncompromising, the saturnine Krishna Menon: 'We are not asking you to "give us freedom". We will take it when we want to. I am not here to ask you for your help but to remind you of your duty.'

Communication was not easy. Few of my father's letters got through, and, if there were replies, these must avoid all public topics. In January 1941 Padmaja Naidu, the daughter of Sarojini, was able to send out a little news, gathered from Mrs Pandit (Nehru's sister), then jailed near Allahabad. Nehru then was in Dehra Dun jail, sharing with Ranjit Pandit (his brother-in-law) 'very cramped quarters in what used to be at the time of the Mutiny the gallows house of the jail . . . which Mr Amery [India Secretary] gaily described as his "private quarters" '.

It was at this time, strangely, that the friendship between my father and Nehru took on a more personal tone. My father sent books — histories, poems — some of which got through. 'Ranjit left me yesterday after a full year', Nehru wrote in December 1941:

> A year together in jail means something much more than outside. We are together all the time, night and day, within a few feet of each other. Ranjit looked after our little garden and I was his willing but inefficient assistant. He used to spot out and tell me the names of new birds that passed Dehra Dun. Often, when the seasons changed, we would watch the migratory flights of geese to or from Tibet. And then he would talk about ancient history or Sanskrit literature and drama or Kashmir or the Marathas. Now that he is gone I am alone and I have to support the burden of the garden he made. But I am not unused to being alone. Here in this jail I once spent 7 or 8 months all by myself with no companion.

'Remember,' my father wrote, 'I am your friend, and when I say that I say it without reservations. My sword, such as it is is at your service.' Then letters were forbidden altogether. My father was banned, on the orders of Mr Amery, from visiting India again 'for the duration'. Between 1942 and 1945 I can find nothing, except a brisk note from Indira, December 1943, saying that her father had received his books, and passing on a message: 'Tell him that I often think of him and of the bond of friendship that ties us. Such bonds have helped me greatly not to allow "black thinking", as they call it in the language of prison, to find a home in my mind.'

It was not until February 1945 that Lord Wavell, going out to India as Viceroy, visited Nehru in prison and told him of my brother's death. He promised to transmit a personal letter from Nehru back to England, but, despite the Viceroy's authority, some India Office nark impounded it. But (Nehru later wrote) 'suspecting that letters from prison often go astray I had kept a copy'. The letter had the warmth of a physical embrace, and it ended:

> I do not think death frightens me much. What terrifies me is the fearful load of bitterness and hatred that we accumulate all over the world and leave as a legacy to those who come after us. And so the

old cycle goes on. In this barren desert the oases of friendship and understanding are few but very precious, and more and more I come to realise how much they mean to me and to others. The books that you sent me have been my companions here ... Often I have felt that physical companionship is only just one way, and not always the closest, of meeting together. We can understand the lack of it and understand each other even more sometimes at a distance ...

The war ended. Nehru, released from his 'private quarters', was plunged into the complex agitational and diplomatic tasks of ensuring the transition to independence. I returned to England to find my father, furious at his enforced inactivity, dying with hideous slowness from cancer. As his sixtieth birthday came up, in April 1946, I knew that he had only a few weeks to live. I asked him if I should let Jawaharlal know. He told me to mind my own business, Nehru had far more important matters to attend to. But I thought this *was* my business, so I sent an air-letter to India.

Sooner than I conceived possible, a letter came back. My father read it, propped on his pillows, in the evening hours when his mind was cleared of drugs. It was a letter with the warmth of an Indian wind, thanking him for his work for India. My father let the letter drop onto the sheet: 'Oh Lord, now let thy servant depart in peace!' Several days later he died.

There was a letter also for me, in the same generous terms. From this moment, I suppose, stemmed my 'deviation'.

I have often been told, at that time and subsequently, by British and by Indian friends, that Nehru was a patrician, and, worse, a representative of 'bourgeois nationalism'. In his last years, as excellent historians like Professors Gopal and Barun De have shown, he became more autocratic, distanced from reality, dreamy, and arbitrary in his measures.

In India in December 1976 it was scarcely possible to mention Nehru's name with approval, among opponents to the Emergency, without calling down instant suspicion. Had it been safe to talk to me after all? The Nehru name had been confiscated by Indira and Sanjay. Sanjay was flying into provincial airports to be fêted and garlanded: if the garlands weren't on time, then the provincial government would be overthrown. (This happened at Orissa, where the Chief Minister was surrounded in her home by Youth Congress thugs, her phone cut off, and she was starved into 'resignation'.) Or, in Rajasthan, he was heading a cavalcade of jeeps, elephants, camels and tractors, and proclaiming an ideology much like Mussolini's ('Talk less, work more'). Mrs Gandhi and her son were teaching the Indian people to turn their backs on Nehru's name.

But I was unable to turn my back on that past. Nehru remained for me much as my father described him in those notes of 1939:

> Sarojini Naidu probed me as to why I cared for Nehru so much. I said, 'He calls out my maternal instincts.' She was very struck by this. She said, 'He does that with the whole of India. Everyone wants to help him . . .'
> Everyone who gets close to Nehru is attracted by him. You see men's eyes following him: as he runs in that boyish manner of his: and as his face lights up with that smile. He is desperately lonely; 'the poor fellow has no family life', Sapru keeps saying.

I have even meditated upon the heresy that if Nehru was a representative of the 'progressive national bourgeoisie', then there is something to be said for that article. We might even order a small quantity of it one day for ourselves. One would have to go rather far back in British history to find an article of that quality: to find persons willing to undergo years of imprisonment, and to emerge with unflagging intellectual vitality and with so little bitterness.

What annoys me is the condescension of the West towards India. It takes many forms, but all share a certain cultural relativism. On the Right the same people that support the Shah of Iran were eager to see Mrs Gandhi's point of view. The point of view is much like that of the Westernized jet-setting businessmen, who sat beside me as I flew over the parched countryside, and who, peering down, would say (in terms expected to ingratiate themselves to any Englishman):

'What these people need is discipline' — supporters of Sanjay to a man. That is one point of view: too many people, too little surplus value.

On the far Left some Westerners take one glance at the Indian muddle and decide, in an instant, that what is needed is 'revolution'. That might certainly solve the population problem. But they are unclear as to who would revolt against whom; they have scarcely inquired into the Naxalite tragedy; and as for the extremely complex problems (and the small successes) of the present democratic Marxist (CPM) government in West Bengal — swept into power with an overwhelming popular vote in 1977 — these only make them yawn.

In between there is a soft academic blur: development theory, modernization theory, etc. But India is not just *a* 'developing country', to be assimilated to other abstract and distancing categories, among 'traditional societies' which must pass through aeons of historical time before they are civilized like us.

India is a country with very old intellectual and cultural traditions; with long working-class and peasant histories, in which generations of activists have struggled and suffered; a country which engaged in an extraordinary, protracted and self-disciplined struggle for independence and identity, using every tactic known to democratic politics — and inventing some new ones; whose national leadership (whether bourgeois or not) was of a personal and political stature to compare with any other nation whatsoever.

India is also a country which has adopted deeply within its life notions of democratic practice and participation. Nor can I agree that this happened *despite* Nehru and that Congress Working Committee. Late in 1939 the British authorities would gladly have purchased Indian support for the war by trading any kind of spurious, multi-cameral, quasi-democratic solution: so many seats for Sikhs, Parsees, Christians, Muslems, Princes: perhaps a literacy qualification here, and a veto there.

Nehru conveyed the flat negative of Congress in a letter to my father (11 November 1939) which he intended to be for the public record:

We are deadly in earnest and we mean exactly what we say — indeed we mean a little more than we say . . . So long as we suspect that the aims of the war are imperialistic, we shall keep far away from it, and we shall thus serve not only ourselves but others who want to pull out this war from the old ruts. In India it is essential that real power passes to the people. We do not want it. The Congress can be ignored. Let there be an election for this purpose. And a Constituent Assembly to be summoned later to draw up India's constitution. This must come from the widest mass franchise.

This was the ticket that took the Working Committee to their separate jails.

That meeting in New Delhi was one of a score of such experiences (with individuals or with groups) that my wife and I met with in the winter of 1976/7. Wherever we went, our generous hosts, of many political persuasions, sooner or later managed to convey to us their profound concern. In Calcutta, which had managed to keep Sanjay at a distance, the atmosphere was more relaxed: not even Mrs Gandhi could silence the discourse of that Paris of the East. Here also we met prisoners on provisional release from jail. They told us about the high mortality rates, worst of all in the women's block. They told us also about the way in which political opponents — Christian Socialists, followers of J.P. Narayan, CPM, Naxalites — had discovered in jail a common solidarity and compassion.

Not for the first time, we were given this message: 'I was imprisoned for nine years under the British', said a Praja Socialist MP, just released, yet again, from jail. 'I never thought I would have a word to say for your people. But the situation today is ten times worse than in those British Emergencies. People disappear in silence; no one can defend them or ask about them; they die without record. When you get back, tell your Prime Minister . . . Tell Mr Foot . . .'

No doubt the Prime Minister and Mr Foot had their diplomatic difficulties. No doubt 'private representations' were made. The fact remains that through the length and breadth of Emergency India the media pumped out the devastating news that Michael Foot had endorsed Mrs Gandhi's regime. He may have been misreported. If so, has he made a full, public, plain apology to the Indian people for this error?

Meanwhile a claque of public relations operators imposed on a section of the British public the story that Mrs Gandhi, in the face of CIA-promoted 'de-stabilization', was upholding the best traditions of Congress and of Nehru. The only people to pretend to believe that story were the leaders of the CPI, perhaps the most slavish and unreconstructed Stalinist CP in the world, which acted until the last month or two of the Emergency as Mrs Gandhi's jackal. (The members of the CPI — the trade unionists beaten by *lathis* and the intellectuals whose presses were shut down — at last called their own leaders to order.)

The story could never stand up. For those who took a leading part in throwing the Emergency off were, exactly, the veterans of Congress in its years of greatest combat — J.P. Narayan (Nehru's chosen successor), Desai, even Nehru's sister, Mrs Vijayalakshmi Pandit (the widow of Ranjit Pandit, Nehru's gardening companion in Dehra Dan), speaking out from her retirement.

In January 1977 a small event took place, which perhaps passed unnoticed in the British press. A ninety-year-old veteran, long in retirement, abruptly announced (in advance of the election announcement) that he intended, on his own if need be, to address meetings throughout South India against the Emergency. He was unwell, and a friend tried to reassure him: 'You have a strong constitution, surely you'll pull through.' 'My constitution is gone,' the veteran replied. 'All that is left is amendments.' But he, and India, did pull through.

The name? Acharya Kripilani — former All India Congress Secretary, although no longer the handsome man whom my father had seen sprawled on the floor at Wardha in 1939. But a man still strong enough to carry out to the end the agenda of that fateful Working Committee.

An hour before I left for the airport, in January 1977, Indira Gandhi came on the radio to announce that an election would be held. The taxi driver had not yet heard. 'Ah, good,' he said, 'ah, *good*.'

I supposed that it would be an exercise in public relations, a rigged election controlled by Youth Congress thugs. My Indian friends had warned me to expect exactly this. The opposition would be tempted to show themselves, and then, after the 'election', the doors of the jails would close on them again.

Then, cautiously, people began to lift their heads. And another small, but remarkable, event took place. Mrs Gandhi sallied out, in New Delhi, to hold the first great open-air meeting of a triumphant campaign. The attendance was poorer than she had been given to expect. And then, when she was in mid-speech, some hundreds, and then thousands, in her audience simply turned around and offered her their backs. The news got around India, by train, and car, and bullock-cart. From that moment, the election was fought in earnest.

The story in the condescending West is that the outcome was all due to sterilization: the religious susceptibilities of a profoundly 'traditional' people had been upset. That is one part of the story. But the democratic convictions and the national pride of Indians had been offended even more. Trade unionists were offended by *lathis* and prisons. Town dwellers were offended by bull-dozing mass evictions. Poor villagers were offended by corrupt Congress bosses, 'land reform' which never happened, 'aid' which went always to the rich. All were offended in their most cherished democratic rights, which, despite the notions of some Western academics, even the poor know a thing or two about.

Oh, yes, Janata India is a mess. I don't know what my friends in Delhi or Aligarh or Calcutta are fighting for now, nor against what difficulties. Yes, the *lathis* have been out again, and there have been murderous attacks on crowds in the UP and Bihar. Yes, that temporary alliance will soon fall apart.

But the shedding of Emergency remains a hopeful and

momentous episode of our time. India is not *an* important, but perhaps *the* most important country for the future of the world. Here is a country that merits no one's condescension. All the convergent influences of the world run through this society: Hindu, Moslem, Christian, secular: Stalinist, liberal, Maoist, democratic socialist, Gandhian. There is not a thought that is being thought in the West or East which is not active in some Indian mind.

If that sub-continent should be rolled up into authoritarianism — if that varied intelligence and creativity should disappear into conformist darkness — then it would be one of the greatest defeats in the human record, sealing the defeat of a penumbra of other Asiatic nations. If the society remains open to the active mind and to the self-organization of the working people — then things will be difficult, very difficult, but they will be unpredictable and creative things.

That is what the true Nehru tradition is about. Mrs Gandhi, may I offer you my back?

The Secret State

In the informative and carefully researched papers which
follow, the authors have been at care not to intrude upon
the text with their opinions. In this, one part of the value of
State Research is to be found.

The task which the authors have set themselves is both
difficult and hazardous, for they are concerned with disclosing the mode of operation of some of the most secretive and
arrogant 'servants' (in practice often *masters*) among modern
bureaucratic states. It is difficult to disclose these operations,
because these are generally defined by the operators themselves as 'Official Secrets'; what the operators themselves
wish to secrete from public view they are empowered to
classify as forbidden materials, and to defend from publicity
by a number of sanctions — not only, as a final resort, the
implementation of the Official Secrets Act, but also the
recourse to 'D Notices', pressure (or favours) towards journalists and editors, the deportation of insubordinate aliens
(such as Agee and Hosenball), the disciplining of civil servants
(who have already been passed through the screens of 'positive vetting'), and so on. And if, by the careful accumulation
of evidence from public sources, independent investigators
are able to reconstruct these operations with some accuracy,

First published as the Introduction to the *Review of Security and the
State 1976*, the corrected edition of *State Research* Bulletins 1977-8,
published by Julian Friedmann Books, 1978.

then they instantly become possessed of an 'Official Secret' which they publish at their own hazard.

This is the double-bind within which the British public has been held, for many years, by its own security services, and increasingly in recent years by the police and other agencies of Government. It has worked so well that, whereas the CIA is now a household word, many people have only the haziest notion as to the character and functions of MI5, MI6 or the Special Branch of the police. Indeed, for a large part of the public, these organizations might not exist; or, if they do, they are thought of as either counter-espionage agencies, playing a John Le Carré game of spooks with the Russians, or as emergency flying squads brought into being, on an *ad hoc* basis, to counter evident threats from hi-jackers, bombers, or alien terrorists. It would amaze many British citizens to learn that these and other organizations are only at the end of a long historical line of ruling-class institutions, with agents or informants in trade unions, educational institutes, and political organizations (especially of the Left), and with direct access to the postal and telephone systems of the country; that they are larger and more powerful, and less subject to ministerial or parliamentary control than they have ever been; and that a large part of their function has always been to invigilate the British people themselves.

The most satisfactory conditions for the effective operation of these organs of the state — and also for the operation of private information-gathering organs such as the Economic League — are ones in which they can lie low, beneath the threshold of public consciousness and concern. When Mr Merlyn Rees, the Home Secretary, introduced the pitiful Government White Paper on the 'reform' of the Official Secrets Act, he retorted to one of his own critical back-benchers that 'he doubted whether more than two or three of his constituents care about the issue' (*The Times*, 20 July 1978). That is certainly the situation which he and his advisors *hope* to be the case. One objective of *State Research* is to ensure that no Home Secretary will dare in the future to address such an insult to the House of Commons and to the British public. If Government refuses to enlighten the people, then such private initiatives as *State Research* must supply that want.

The authors of this work are of the view that their purposes can best be served by scrupulous objectivity and the painstaking accumulation, from public records, of factual accounts. They do not offer any general theory of the State, and still less any wholesale invective against all organs of power. But they have invited me, as an independent reader, to offer a more general comment on their enterprise. I approve warmly of this enterprise, and I am honoured by the invitation. But I must make it clear that my comments are of a personal nature — and they come from a person committed, as a historian and as a citizen, to the libertarian traditions of the radical and working-class movements of this country. My comments do not carry the authors' assent or endorsement. Indeed, I have not met the authors, and we have not discussed the issues together. It is probable that, in this or that particular, we may disagree.

I have already said that the operators of the British security services are 'some of the most secretive and arrogant' to be found in modern bureaucratic states. My words were chosen with care, and are intended to be neither complacent nor alarmist. I am insisting upon a peculiar combination of invisibility, lack of accountability, and the consequent composure of an antique ruling group which has been bred to govern from behind a wall of silence. The situation could, very certainly, be worse, and, if we are not alert, it will become worse. The German security organs are blatant and massively visible, in an old Prussian statist tradition; and they have seized gratefully upon the opportunity provided by Baader-Meinhof to enlarge their brutal presence in civil life. In Russia and in several parts of Eastern Europe it is never possible to disentangle the motives of administration from those of 'security' and control, and in significant areas it is not possible to speak of civil rights or of a rule of law at all. In the United States we have witnessed three decades of the frightening enlargement of agencies of 'security' (including massive espionage, provocation, 'dirty tricks', and possibly even assassinations, committed against their own citizens); but this has at length been met, by the American liberal tradition, in a very vigorous counter-attack, in which some journalists and lawyers have played an honourable part. Without this counter-attack, which included the massive 'leakage' and then the legally enforced disclosure of 'secret' documents and tapes, the mountain of official excreta known as 'Watergate' would never have been exposed to public view. And it is now possible, under the US Freedom of Information Act, for victims of these organs (such as Alger Hiss or the sons of the Rosenbergs) to gain access to some part of the documentation necessary for their vindication.

Thus the United States security organs are more powerful and more intrusive, but they have suffered a public check, are disgraced in the eyes of many American citizens, and are at last subject to some legal accountability. In this area at least, the American liberal tradition has turned out to be much tougher than the British. It is now a platitude — but one which bears repeating — that in Britain a 'Watergate' could not have occurred exactly in that way; but if it had occurred, in a more 'British' way, the British press would neither have been able nor have dared to disclose the facts about it, and the British public would have been told only so much as certain 'wise men' of the Establishment thought it safe to allow them to know.

Thus British security operations are distinguished by their invisibility and their lack of accountability. (This is so much the case that even sections of the British Left customarily denounce — as they should — the conspiracies of 'the CIA', overlooking the fact that for decades the invisible British counterparts have collaborated unreservedly with United States agents, fed them with information on British subjects, and shielded them from exposure behind the same screen that protects themselves.) They are also distinguished by a peculiar quality of ruling-class composure and arrogance.

A historian is bound to reflect upon the particular route which led us into this situation. Not much more than one hundred years ago, the British people were distinguished throughout the world for their resistance — at least on their

own home ground — to the pretentions of the state. This
resistance stemmed not only from 'Radical' but also from
'Tory' sources. The settlement of 1688 had been marked,
above all, by jealousy of the Crown, and, hence, of the central powers of the state. The gentry emerged as the rulers of
England, and (more selectively) of Scotland and Wales also.
In the eighteenth century, as the limited resources of parliamentary democracy became obstructed and corrupted, and
as the aristocracy and great gentry enlarged their lands and
wealth and their purchase upon interest and patronage, so
both Whig and Tory magnates enlarged their hostility to a
bureaucratized and rationalized state: they wished to be left
free to govern in their own way within their own spheres of
influence. This was very far from being a democratic impulse;
but it did, in the Whig tradition, afford shelter for libertarian
modes of thought, in continued jealousy of central power
and in vigorous resistance to the examples of absolutism
provided by continental monarchies.

By the end of the eighteenth century, this was an all-
pervasive Whiggish rhetoric, shared by Tories, Whigs and
Radicals alike. Moreover, it was a rhetoric taken over and
applied to greatly more democratic ends, by the rising
popular reform movement. The parliamentary oligarchs
wished to contain their debates within the privacy of the
walls of Parliament; they did not wish the British people to
overhear how their governors talked, in private, about them.
Wilkes and the printers defied 'the law' and breached this
privacy; we owe *Hansard* to this defiance. In area after area,
the 'common people' insisted that the civil rights of the
'freeborn Englishman' were not the privileges of an elite but
were the common inheritance of all: freedom of press, speech
and conscience, rights of assembly, inhibitions upon the
actions of military or police against crowds, freedom from
arbitrary imprisonment or unwarranted arrest and entry upon
private premises. The insurgent British working-class movement took over for its own the old Whiggish bloody-mindedness of the citizen in the face of the pretentions of power.
Even when labouring under the manifest class discrimination
of the Combination Acts, the secretary of an illegal trade-

union branch of framework knitters in Mansfield in 1812 was able to protest against a clause in a Bill proposed by the workers' representatives themselves, which authorized the search for shoddy goods in the houses of manufacturers: 'if iver that bullwark is broke down of every english mans hous being his Castil then that strong barrer is for iver broke that so many of our ancesters have bled for and in vain'. The workers had appropriated the democratic precedents and practices of past generations for their own; the ancestors were not 'theirs' but 'ours'.

And this was how matters continued for at least one hundred years. The Chartist, Radical Liberal, Irish Nationalist, and formative labour movements were distinguished by their sensitivity to libertarian issues, and their suspicion of the polity of statism. When the police forces were enlarged and rationalized (or as some would have it today, 'modernized') in the mid nineteenth century, this was a victory for bourgeois utilitarian bureaucratic policy in the face of intense resistance extending from old Tory localism through Radical Liberalism to outright Chartist opposition — for Chartists and trade unionists very well understood what kind of imperatives dictated Government policies. As a consequence of this opposition, the presence of the police in British public life remained unusually subdued. They must be seen as 'servants' of . . . either the gentry or 'the public', and they must in no circumstances exhibit a brash public presence. And, as a more concrete evidence of the old libertarian tradition, which endures to this day, the British police (at least in Britain) must usually go about the streets unarmed.

There were some anticipations of the statism of the twentieth century in the increasingly intrusive and punitive presence of the police in Britain in the 1880s. This was a natural reaction of the propertied classes, who reacted to the rumour that there were now socialist agitators in the streets (making speeches against *their property*!) with seemly terror. In general the police were impartial, attempting to sweep off the streets with an equable hand street-traders, beggars, prostitutes, buskers, pickets, children playing football, and free-thinking and socialist speakers alike. The pretext, very often, was that a complaint of interruption of trade had been received from a shopkeeper. William Morris remarked on the impatience of 'the more luxurious part of society' to 'clear the streets of costermongers, organs, processions, and lecturers of all kinds, and make them a sort of decent prison corridors, with people just trudging to and from their work'.

Less evidently impartial were the statements and actions of Sir Charles Warren, who, in the face of mounting demonstrations by unemployed, Radicals, Socialists and Irish Nationalists, was appointed Chief Commissioner of the London Metropolitan Police in 1886. Here he engaged in exercises of 'public relations' quite as vigorous as any subsequently set in motion by Sir Robert Mark or Sir David McNee. He presided over the processionals which culminated in his banning all meetings in Trafalgar Square (on the grounds that it was Crown property) and the subsequent episode of 'Bloody Sunday' when demonstrators were scattered by massive police and military forces, and with a violence which, in any accounting, was unnecessary and inexpedient. But Warren had overplayed his hand, the Liberal Party was shocked and riven down the middle. The general dislike of his methods was fueled by the public's dislike of the police's treatment of women, and by the conspicuous failure of Warren's forces to solve the 'Jack the Ripper' murders. When Warren refused outright to accept the instructions of the Home Secretary, he was forced, with the *douceur* of a KCB, to exchange the command of London for the command of Singapore (1889).

I do not mind about the KCB. I am perfectly willing for all over-mighty security officers and police to be given KCBs, so long as they are dismissed. I have introduced the case of Sir Charles Warren for two other reasons. First, it is a reminder — and an important reminder, in the face of a certain pessimistic determinism which is in fashion on the Left — that it is not absolutely foreclosed and prescribed that ordinary people will lose every contest with power. The history of the past ninety years is not an unrelieved record of the enlargement of the powers of the state, and of the impudence of its officers. Because people made enough row, Warren was sacked;

Trafalgar Square was re-opened and in the main has stayed open (apart from demonstrations about Ireland); the battle for free speech in the streets was, largely, won, for the Radicals and Socialists at least.

The second reason, however, is less comforting. Sir Charles Warren signals the feedback of imperialism — its experience and its consequences — to the streets of the imperial capital itself. Glancing at the DNB I see that, before serving as Metropolitan Police Commissioner, he had gained military experience in Gibraltar and Griqualand West; had commanded the Diamond Fields Horse in the Kaffir War (1877-8); and had been military and civil administrator of the Bechuanaland protectorate. He came from Suakin to London, and departed thence to Singapore; he served with distinction in the Boer War ('he cleared the country between the Orange River and the Vaal'), and was a founder-member of the Boy Scouts. He was, in short, a representative figure of the imperialist climax; and he reminds us of the inter-recruitment, cross-posting, and exchange of both ideology and experience between those who learned to handle crowds, invigilate subversives, and engage in measures of 'pacification' in the external Empire, and those who struggled with the Labour Problem, the Unemployed Question, the Women Problem, and sometimes just the People Problem, at home.

We are entering the world of a John Buchan novel — British imperial interests are endangered by alien agents and by subversive rotters at home (perhaps even by milksops in the Cabinet?), but our hero knows that he can rely upon a few absolutely trustworthy people — men who went to the same privileged school, served together on the North-West Frontier or between the Orange River and the Vaal, and who bump up against each other in select London clubs or deerstalking on the Scottish moors. These people know better than 'the politicians', and very much better than the public, what British interests are. They accept, with a grimace of resignation, the duty to save Britain from herself.

That is the novelettish way of seeing it. But in fact it remains true that the growth of an unrepresentative and unaccountable state within the state has been a product of the twentieth century. Its growth was, paradoxically, actually aided by the unpopularity of security and policing agencies; forced by this into the lowest possible visibility, they learned to develop techniques of invisible influence and control. It was also aided by the British tradition of Civil Service neutrality; this sheltered senior civil servants from replacement or investigation when administrations changed, and afforded to their policies the legitimation of 'impartial, non-political' intent. Ministers, and Prime Ministers, increasingly became putty, on questions of 'security', in their senior advisers' hands. They were handed their briefs, and — often, in the press of business, with the haziest understanding of these — they knew that it was their first business in the House to defend their own advisers or Departments. And it must be admitted that Labour Ministers have shown the greatest eagerness to learn the same lessons of loyalty to their 'servants', and no one has been more eager than Mr Merlyn Rees.

A complex of forces has impelled the increasing statism of the past decades, and I will only mention two or three. Very obviously, two world wars have not only habituated people to uniform and to the arguments of national interest, but have also facilitated such lesser (but significant) perquisites as the busy exchanges between Oxford and Cambridge colleges and Whitehall, as scholars have done their bit in Intelligence. The rapid erosion of Empire had perforce retracted the imperial ideology, has brought it back home, into the security services, the army, and the police, where experience gained in Ireland, India, or Rhodesia, looks restively for new fields of application — these services are the last refuges of imperialism, within which a ghostly imperial ideology survives its former host.

There is also the very substantial, and very seldom mentioned, legacy of the British phase of 'McCarthyism' in the high Cold War. This resulted in extensive 'positive vetting' procedures in the public services, which were subjected to an opaque and pusillanimous inquiry, under the chairmanship of the late Lord Radcliffe, in 1961-2. The brief of this committee was to inquire into the measures of safeguarding information in the Civil Service against the Intelligence services of foreign powers — although not, it seems, of the CIA — and against 'subversive organizations in this country, of which in current conditions the most formidable is the Communist Party of Great Britain, with its fringe of associated bodies and sympathizers'. This was a flexible definition, for 'current conditions' may change, and in the past fifteen years, as the Communist Party has become increasingly less 'formidable', one wonders what other organizations, fringes and sympathizers have been added to the subversive list. In any case, the Radcliffe committee proceeded on the assumption that any sound security man would know, instantly, what was subversive and what was not, remarking at one point: 'We have followed the common practice of using the phrase "communist" throughout to include fascists.' The point is that *any* term would have been as good as any other — anarchist, situationist, rapist, or agronomist — provided that it signified to the proper people opinions and associations which, in current conditions, proper people disapprove.

There are two further points. First, liberal-minded opinion in Britain today is very properly angered by the loud and intrusive measures (*Berufsverbot*, etc.) of the West German authorities against political dissenters of the Left. I am glad that this solidarity is being shown. But it is not always remembered that the *Berufsverbot* of 'positive vetting' goes on in the British public services every day, in ways that are certainly less intrusive and that are very certainly less loud. What goes on, in the screening of applicants, in the promotion of public servants and in their allocation to different departments, we do not know; nor do we know what criteria are employed; and we would not be told even if we (or the House of Commons) asked. All that we do know is that men and women are passed through screens which select, for the most privileged and influential positions, those whose records appear to be most 'moderate', conservative and orthodox. It is perhaps time that a Russell Tribunal sat in Whitehall. Where — and this is my second point — it could take no evidence, since evidence would be, by definition, an 'Official

Secret'.

This is to return once more to the John Buchan theme. The ruling group within the state in Britain has a kind of arrogance about it which may be historically unique. It has a settled habit of power, a composure of power, inherited from generations of rule, renewed by imperial authority, and refreshed perennially from the springs of the best public schools. It is a group which does not bother, or need to bother, to get itself elected. It knows what 'British interests' are, and defends these through every change of political weather. It decides whether you or I are subversive, and whether our actions should be watched. It does not have to justify its decisions in any public arena. It rules, unobtrusively, from within.

What it does is an 'Official Secret'. For example, do the security services simply invigilate 'subversives', and pass on information promptly to appropriate authorities, or do they also engage in provocations and 'dirty tricks'? A historian is well aware of the latter in the longer record. At one time, in the Napoleonic Wars, the main centre of underground English 'Jacobinism' was, with some difficulty, kept in being only by the unremitting efforts of several Government spies, as a kind of honey-pot in London which might attract to it unwary reformers. In the next decades, the official papers in the Public Record Office are abundantly covered in the slime left behind by Oliver, Castles, and successive spies and provocateurs within the Chartist and Irish movements. In later decades the trail is less evident, because it has been more effectively obscured. Not only are matters of 'security' covered by a thirty-year rule prohibiting disclosure, but even where the records are opened one may sometimes detect where the hand of a 'weeder' has been at work. (A 'weeder' is a scrupulous civil servant trained as an *anti*-historian, whose business it is to remove from the files obnoxious materials.)

The innocent might suppose that such practices will have been curbed by the rise of Labour to political influence, and (purportedly) to power. If any such innocents still exist, they should read and reflect upon Sir Harold Wilson's account of his handling of the national seamen's strike in 1966, in

Chapter 4 of *The Labour Government, 1964-1970: a Personal Record*. The seamen's union, which for decades had been reduced to little more than a servile 'company' shop, had at length, in response to the pressures of its own membership, proclaimed a strike in furtherance of a series of demands for improved wages and conditions. As ship after ship tied up in British ports, the crews joined the strike with enthusiasm. And also with unusual militancy — partly because conditions of work were bad, partly because a long record of union torpor had at last been broken, but particularly because a national strike of seamen is one of the most difficult industrial encounters to organize, and once it has been launched the seamen *must* hold firm until they obtain the optimum settlement. The usual mechanisms for fobbing-off such crises — for example, a minor concession, on condition that the strike is called off, followed by some committee of inquiry, and the distant hope of further concessions — can never be acceptable to seamen. For once the ships are untied and have put to sea again, for a hundred disparate destinations, they cannot be abruptly recalled again to muscle the union's negotiations: to strike on the high seas, or to turn back to port, is mutiny. Thus in 1966 even the union's very moderate leaders acted — and, for a time, actually were — very tough. They must stand out for the maximum settlement, since it might be many years before they were in so strong a bargaining position again.

That was the seamen's side of the matter. The other side of the matter is so familiar that I scarcely need to rehearse it, since it is the background of 'national interests in danger' against which, for fifteen years, *every* strike has been enacted. The livelihood of 'the nation' was endangered; the national economic crisis was acute; the pound was falling; the Government's policies of wage restraint must not be breached. The Minister of Labour at that time, Mr Ray Gunter, was a well-known 'Red-baiter', who was eventually to find that even Harold Wilson's Labour Party was too red for him to continue as a member. But Wilson and Gunter acted smoothly together in setting in motion the familiar and grossly inequitable repertoire of power. A State of Emergency was declared. The armed services were called upon, but only for limited purposes ('I announced the use of RAF Transport Command planes for help with urgent export shipments'). The TUC and a Court of Inquiry were brought in to bully the seamen's leaders. Wilson broadcast to the nation on television. Finally, in the House of Commons, the Prime Minister placed full responsibility for the strike upon a 'tightly knit group of politically motivated men'. As he recounts in his reminiscences, 'I did not use the word "Communist", though no one in the House or in the press, which next morning headlined my words as a sensation, had any doubts whom I had in mind.'

'The fact was', his account continues, 'that the moderate members of the seamen's executive were virtually terrorised by a small group of professional Communists or near-Communists . . .' But there was one trouble with this story: as every informed member of the trade union movement knew, there was *not one single Communist* on the executive of the National Union of Seamen. (If the 'moderates' were terrorized by anyone, apart from Wilson and Gunter, they were terrorized by the militancy of their own members.) Hence, eight days later, Wilson was forced into an unusual predicament in which he raised, for a brief instant, the veil of political lies and half-truths which is normally held between the public and the state within the state. 'From various sources we began to receive undeniable evidence of what was going on,' he tells us. (These sources may have been as 'various' as MI this or that, the Special Branch, and the Economic League.) Addressing the House once more, he itemized the (pathetically small) resources of Bert Ramelson, the Communist Party's industrial organizer: 'He has three full-time officials on his staff' — i.e. rather fewer than the staff of a firm making bicycle-clips, and very much fewer than the Merseyside Special Branch. More than this, he was able to report in detail upon the travels of militant members of the seamen's union, where they had been, whom they had visited, at which flats they had stayed overnight, and who had visited them there. It added up to a chilling James Bond scenario; or, if one was even moderately informed, to the normal lobbying accompanying any industrial dispute.

There was, however, one very curious episode within this drama, which is well to remember lest we fall into the error of assuming that 'the state' always operates as a well-oiled and synchronized ruling-class conspiracy. The Leader of the Opposition, Mr Edward Heath, saw through Wilson's rhetoric, and thought that Wilson and Gunter had mishandled the situation and provoked the seamen into stubbornness. Knowing that there were no Communists on the seamen's executive, he pressed Wilson to disclose his evidence and substantiate his charges. Wilson complied by arranging for Heath a highly secret meeting, 'on Privy Counsellor terms', to which meeting he brought not only the 'senior people responsible for these matters' but also *one of the operators "in the field"*'. Despite all these remarkable favours, Heath, to his credit, remained unconvinced. But Wilson pursued his cloak-and-dagger script to the bitter end. Unprecedented measures were taken to split the seamen's executive, Wilson personally bullied their general secretary (giving him 'a sealed envelope' with information from the 'operators in the field'), and the strike was smashed.

I have run through this narrative because, while it should be familiar, it is not: people have short memories, and official mythologies seek to make them shorter. We are rarely allowed as much information as to the operation of the state as we have in this episode, since few senior politicians have as large and loose a mouth as Sir Harold Wilson. We will note only three points. The first is that it should not be assumed that Tories are always more active in their capitulation to the state within the state than Labour ministers. A certain kind of Labour politician may have a malice against 'militants' and, above all, a deeply engrained reflex of deference towards the 'real' guardians of British interests (whether in the Treasury or in the security services) which a certain kind of Tory — who meets these operators as class equals — need not always have.

Second, this episode illustrates not only how information is gathered upon subversives, but how it may be *put to use*. In 'normal' conditions of industrial and social peace, it is very rarely necessary for the 'operators in the field' to disclose their operations. And this leads to a certain complacency in the public. After all, if all that these people are doing is observing and invigilating us, but putting all this information to no use (unless against terrorists, spies, etc.), then let them have their fun — and let them have the most advanced, computerized data-bank as well. What harm is there in that? But the point about the seamen's strike is that it demonstrates that we remain safe from intervention, blackmail and state-suborned calumny only so long as we remain good and quiet. The state within the state only becomes, briefly, visible during a State of Emergency; and a State of Emergency is a moment when any group of people with economic or social power stand up vigorously for their own rights. When the immediate crisis is over, the pall of invisibility settles down once more.

Third, I have recited this episode because, in its general outlines, it is now so familiar. The national crisis — the State of Emergency — the deployment of armed forces — the attempts to induce panic on the national media — the identification of some out-group as a 'threat to security' — all these are becoming part of the *normal* repertoire of power. Of course, there are historical precedents for all these things; but never before, since 1816, has government been able to employ this repertoire without inflaming the nerves of outrage and resistance in a minority — a minority which, by patient agitation and political education, has often been able to influence the majority, and, in the long run, secure some reversal of the pretentions of power. What is new, in the last two decades, is the dulling of the nerve of resistance and of outrage. Familiarity has bred contempt — not contempt for the state and for the specious alarms and rationalizations of power, but contempt for any possible alternative. And in this moment a new danger appears. For once the libertarian responses of the British people have been brought under sedation, then the reasons for the invisibility of the state within the state begin to lose their force. And so we see the evidence, in the present decade, of the police, the army, the security services, the quasi-official and the pseudo-private agencies of control, becoming *more* public, engaging in active 'public relations', lobbying for new curbs on civil rights and for 'simplified' legal process, and attempting to familiarize the public with their intrusive presence. And in face of this new danger, the ancient historical nerve begins to throb once more. *State Research* is one of the evidences of that.

I will conclude by advancing some arguments which are, in part, addressed to my friends on the Left. In doing so, I am bound to tread on corns, left, right, and centre. So that I must insist, once again, that these comments are personal, and need carry no assent from the authors of this work.

A large part of the blame for the dulling of the nerve of outrage lies with the Left itself. I do not make this as a wholesale accusation. There have been honourable centres of resistance, as in the long and dogged record of the National Council for Civil Liberties. We owe more than is often supposed to the vigilance of a few Labour and Liberal MPs, and even occasional questions from crusty Tory back-benchers. More recently, some journalists have been alerted to the dangers. And there are many others, among the splinters further to the Left. But the resistance has been inadequate, and, if we are now faced with the need for a massive campaign of political re-education of the people, one reason is that Liberal, Labour, Communist, and Marxist-intellectual opinion, has, for different reasons, never fought the earlier campaign with conviction.

The reasons for the capitulation of much *official* Liberal and Labour resistance have already been rehearsed. The episode of the breaking of the seamen's strike encapsulates them all. The uniformed — and sometimes actively democratic — national consensus of the last war was protracted into a kind of populist celebration of the servants of the state. A former leader of the Young Communist League, Lord 'Ted' Willis, was the creator of that homely neighbour and universal uncle, *Dixon of Dock Green* — the precursor of the somewhat less homely and more truthfully observed heroes of *Z Cars*. 'Positive vetting' in the public service was tightened up, as a 'non-party issue', during the panic of the high Cold War, and confirmed in the aftermath of the cases of Philby, Vassall *et al*. The bureaucratic statism towards which Labour politicians increasingly drifted carried with it a rhetoric in which the state, in *all* its aspects, was seen as a public good, a defence of working people, or of the little man, against private vested interests. The dividing line bet-ween the Welfare State and the Police State became obscure, and bureaucracy, in every form, waxed fat in this obscurity. Labour politicians were anxious to prove that they were fit to 'govern'; and they, quite as much as the Tories, habituated the public mind to the normality of these enlarged resources of government.

I will not delay over the Communist Party. No doubt its members have, here and there, fought sharp and significant skirmishes on behalf of their own or others' rights. But the Party's association, in the public mind and often in its own mind, with the obscene record of Soviet statism has weakened the credibility of any libertarian professions.

One would have supposed, in these circumstances, that the libertarian tradition would have migrated to that archipelago to the Left and outside of the official parties — New Left, socialist sects and splinters, unorganized 'Radicals', the women's movement, the movements of ethnic minorities, and so on. Fitfully this may have happened, and potentially it may yet prove to be so. But in fact no very coherent, impassioned or consistent agitation or education in civil rights or in libertarian traditions has come from this quarter. To diagnose this failure is to touch on sensitive issues and to provoke furious counter-polemics; but since I believe that 'the nerve of outrage' has always in our history been carried, in the first place, by minorities; and since I also believe that the failure of our present minorities to react with sufficient clarity and consistency to the present threats of statism constitutes a significant contributory element in that threat — that the ambivalence *within the 'Left'* towards civil liberties is the most alarming evidence of all that the libertarian nerve has become dulled, and carries with it a premonition of defeat — then it becomes necessary to touch these sensitive points.

There has been around, for a decade or more, on the unofficial Left a general rhetoric which passes itself off as a 'Marxism'. Sometimes this is expressed in sophisticated intellectual form, sometimes as an old-style Leninism, sometimes just as an unexamined vocabulary coexisting with other vocabularies. I will not address here the question as to whether this rhetoric is derivative from an authentic Marxist tradition or not; I have recently had my say on this at length elsewhere. But what are very often found, as common elements, in this rhetoric are some of the following: first, there is a platonic notion of the true, the ideal capitalist State, to which any actual case is only an approximation, but to which all cases must inevitably tend. This State is inherently profoundly authoritarian, as a direct organ of capitalist exploitation and control, and any inhibitions upon its powers are seen as 'masks', or disguises, or as tricks to provide it with ideological legitimation and to enforce its hegemony. It may (but need not) follow that any symptoms of authoritarianism are seen as disclosing a 'crisis of hegemony', and they may even be welcomed as unmasking the 'true' (i.e. platonic) character of the State, and as signalling the 'conjuncture' in which a final class confrontation will take place. This may easily consort with a profoundly pessimistic determinism, in which that kind of authoritarian state can be seen as the necessary concomitant 'structure' of the 'capitalist formation'. And this may, and often does, consort with a loose rhetoric in which civil rights and democratic practices are discounted as camouflage, or as the relics of 'bourgeois liberalism'. And, to cut short the list, this very often goes along with a wholesale dismissal of *all* law and *all* police, and sometimes with a soppy notion that *all* crime is some kind of displaced revolutionary activity.

This is not the place to engage in a philosophical wrangle. I will simply say that, to a historian in a libertarian Marxist tradition, these are all half-truths which have a continual tendency to degenerate into rubbish, and, moreover, into rubbish which has a particular appeal to a certain kind of elitist bourgeois intellectual. If we survey advanced capitalist societies today, we may certainly find common tendencies at work, but we will find an immense variety of forms of state power, traditions of law and of civil rights, and of popular expectations and resistance. If we extend our overview, and scrutinize post-capitalist societies which have attained to a situation in which there is no law, no police, and no crime, then our survey will come to an abrupt halt.

What is more to the point is that this rhetoric can be seen to unbend the springs of action, and to discount the importance of any struggle for civil rights. Pessimism is cherished, and then it is varnished over with revolutionary adjectives. If *all* law and *all* police are utterly abhorrent, then it cannot matter much what *kind* of law, or what *place* the police are held within; and yet the most immediate and consequent struggles to maintain liberty are, exactly, about kinds and places, cases and precedents, and the bringing of power to particular account.

If I may cite one case, I was first alerted to the extreme danger into which the Left can be led by such rhetoric when I noted the pitiful absence of concern displayed towards the recent modification in jury procedure, which allows for a majority verdict. Very clearly, the powerful lobby behind that 'reform' was motivated by intense hostility to the jury system as such. Many of the police, and some judges and lawyers, saw the jury system as an antique survival and an impediment to more 'efficient' executive action, in which judges and magistrates themselves, or perhaps some kind of 'expert' trained assessors, should determine questions of guilt. Sir David McNee, in his recently highly publicized package of proposals to 'simplify' legal procedures and to facilitate the labours of the police, does not directly ask for the abolition of the jury. But it is not difficult to guess that this proposal will be in the next or the next-but-one package to come.

In the last few years I have sounded out friends of mine on the Left about this question, and have met with some support. But I have met with more cynicism, and even with some abuse. I have been told (predictably) that the jury system is a relic of bourgeois liberalism, although it is in fact

'Members of the jury, have you anything to say before
I pass sentence on you?'

a very remarkable survival from a time when the bourgeoisie was not even a glint in feudalism's eye. I have been told that all juries (on *class* issues) are 'rigged', and this not as an occasion for outrage and reform, but as an inexorable fact of capitalist life. I have been told that juries make everything worse, by cementing the hegemony of the ruling class, and by legitimating its rule through co-opting the people into being the instruments of their own oppression. I have been told, most of all, that juries are middle class, stupid, bigoted and racist, although I cannot see to what this argument tends, unless towards a revolutionary clerisy who govern the people in their true interests and in spite of the people's ineradicable false consciousness.

The trouble with all such arguments is that they presume to contrast sordid reality with some pure alternative which exists only in an intellectual's abstracted utopian noddle. As a historian, I am competent to put together a substantial list of bad verdicts by bigoted, confused, or intimidated juries. I can also put together a much smaller list of good verdicts by independent-minded juries, a number of which were found in the full face of Government pressure, and which were of critical significance in the defence or enlargement of the citizen's liberties. The jury system is not a product of 'bourgeois democracy' (to which it owes nothing) but a stubbornly maintained democratic *practice*. It has never been a perfect practice; its practice can never have risen higher than the common sense and integrity of the jurors; but it has provided, repeatedly, a salutary inhibition — especially in matters of conscience and political behaviour — upon executive power. And, if we are to be purists, what other arrangement would revolutionaries propose? The notion of democracy as 'self-activity', as being — not the rule over the people by bureaucrats, 'experts', or a substitutionist vanguard, but — the rotation among all ordinary citizens of public responsibilities and roles, would appear to be uncommonly well fulfilled in this curious survival, in which everyman or everywoman must take upon themselves the serious role of judgement of their peers. I can imagine better laws, and I can imagine better jurors, but I cannot imagine a better system. I would like to think of the jury system as a lingering paradigm of an alternative mode of participatory self-government, a nucleus around which analogous modes might grow in our town halls, factories and streets.

The jury system will certainly not survive this century, unless 'the Left' regains its libertarian memory. Those on the Right who seek its end, or its savage delimitation into some segregated area of justice, do so on the grounds of its inconvenience: it is slow, costly, unpredictable, and (in the view of lawyers and police, but not of jurors) it gives rise to too many acquittals — and some of these 'bad' acquittals. Few on the Right are far-sighted enough to envisage the situation in which the absence of a jury might deliver critical democratic rights into their hand. They share, rather, an impatience with messy, uncertain procedures, and a desire to 'rationalize' and 'modernize'. And they adduce no general theory of justice but hard-seeming, practical arguments. For example, some sectors of crime are now Big Business, and offenders command the wealth to suborn members of the jury.

It becomes important, then, to distinguish between genuine arguments — which, in their own terms, may have force — and the use of these arguments as pretexts to stampede the public into false conclusions. For we may be absolutely certain that no curbs will be proposed upon our democratic rights, and no extensions will be made in the resources of the organs of security, without our being offered 'practical' reasons and pretexts enough. Just now, the pretexts which will be flourished again and again will be two: the threat of terrorism and the increase in crime.

These both commence as genuine arguments, which are then taken over and manipulated by those who wish to employ them as pretexts to deliver us into authoritarian solutions. The Left, and in particular the intellectual Left, stands in need of greater clarity upon both problems. It is no good pretending that the state, or the 'capitalist formation', has *invented* or somehow engendered these problems, as an excuse for clapping the working class in irons.

Terrorism, kidnapping, bombing, etc., are abhorrent to me, as they are to most of the Left. I am an old soldier, and

consequently I was forcibly disabused before my twenty-first
birthday of any notion that violence is more 'real' than other
modes of dispute. Armed violence is the empire in which
contingency and accident reign supreme. Of course, in conditions of extreme repression, democrats and socialists may
be forced to take arms in self-defence or in a strategy of
insurrection. And in such conditions they merit our solidarity.
But where other measures of organization and agitation
remain open, the recourse to terrorism is at best romantic,
self-defeating and profoundly elitist (people who cannot be
moved by arguments must be terrorized by guns), and at
worst merely sick and villainous.

In terms of mere expediency, the matter is self-evident.
Terrorist organizations are notoriously easy to penetrate with
agents and provocateurs (the Weathermen in the United
States, or the Naxalites). They are notorious also for their
savage sectarian internecine warfare (Provisional and Official
IRA, the present Palestinian disasters). They generally provoke both fear and hostility among the very people whom
they are supposedly 'liberating'. (If any among the Baader-
Meinhof gang or the Italian Red Brigade supposed that they
were acting for the 'Left', then they must know by now
that they have driven ball after ball through the goal of their
own side.) Above all, they provide in superfluity the perfect
pretexts for authoritarianism to rehearse its methods and to
enlarge its repertoire.

This is clear enough to all, although some sections of the
British Left have been slow to see it, and, through misplaced
notions of solidarity, have been slowest to see it in the case
of the Provisional IRA. I will therefore allow myself to state
what has long been obvious to most of the people of Eire as
well as of Northern Ireland. The methods of the Provisionals
constitute an absolute degeneration from the earlier Civil
Rights movement. Provisional terrorism, and its Loyalist
counterpart, are a symptom of the present malaise and point
towards no kind of solution. And, whatever aggravations
have been afforded by British policies and by the British
military presence, the source of the malaise is not to be
found in contemporary 'British imperialism' ('Britain's back-

yard Vietnam') but in a historic conflict within Ireland itself, and *within the Irish working class*. In such circumstances, the duties of internationalism should be met, not by giving equivocal rhetorical support, from positions of English safety, to the Provisionals, but by throwing our arguments, and if need be our bodies, in between.

Not all readers will agree with me — although I find that many Irish friends do. But we may agree that terrorism in Northern Ireland — and its sporadic threat in English cities — provides a superb training-ground for the security services, as well as pretexts in abundance. I hope we may also agree that abstract intellectualist apologetics on behalf of such outfits as the Red Brigades utterly discredit the Left in its struggle for libertarian objectives.

It now seems that hi-jacking, kidnapping, and terrorism are among the permanent benefits of modernization; in one form or another, we are likely to continue to experience episodes of these in coming decades, if only because the suffering of the most exploited parts of the former colonial world are now being re-exported back to the imperial powers. And it is futile to pretend that this will *not* present an argument for greater security — the security of particular threatened persons, the security of aircraft, on occasion the security of the underground and of the public house. Are we really to suppose that any state would do nothing? So that the struggle to contain the security forces — to keep them in a place appropriate to the actual threat, and to resist the transformation of real arguments into pretexts — will become increasingly complex and close. Just as those who, like myself, find the methods of the Provisionals abhorrent, must also support unreservedly the vigilant scrutiny which *State Research* keeps upon the Prevention of Terrorism Act, and the growing employment of its powers of detention and exclusion, so we must equally station ourselves to watch every twist and turn in the coming game. A blanket denunciation of all law and all police will do no good at all, since both will continue undisturbed, and a great part of the public will support them, saying: 'Well, *something* has got to be done.' So that exactly *what* is done becomes of prime importance: screening of all

air passengers, *yes*: introduction of identity cards, *no*: colla-
boration with the Iranian security forces in the shadowing of
Iranian students, *no*: data-banks on all citizens, spies in our
unions and universities, *NO*!

Spies, data-bank, identity cards, more expeditious legal
procedures — no doubt all these things would make the
legitimate work of security easier. It would also open the
door to every kind of illegitimate work as well. So that the
maximum efficiency of operation of legitimate security (or
crime-prevention) can never be accepted as the supreme
priority. Civil rights will always place obstructions in the way
of speedy executive action, and they should do so. The
policing of Britain has been, and should continue to be, a
difficult and ungrateful operation. But what about the other
half-argument, half-pretext, the growth in crime?

Here, also, the Left must clear up its mind. In secure and
secluded places, some marvellously abstract notions are
afloat. It might even be supposed that the increase in crime
was wholly fictional, a pretext orchestrated by the media to
legitimate ruling-class and racialist measures, or was of
interest only as a symptom of the crisis of the 'capitalist
formation' in this 'overdetermined conjuncture'. But whatever conclusions are reached as to the actual increment of
offences; whatever diagnosis is made as to the social and
economic predicament of offenders; whatever objections are
upheld against the punitive ('exemplary') measures of the
courts — there remains an objective record of suffering, loss
and fear. For example, even if women are more ready to
report rape and sexual assault than before, thus inflating the
number of recorded offences, it does appear that there are
parts of our cities in which women are afraid to walk alone,
when they were not afraid before. And if this is so, then it is
an intolerable offence against civilized life and personal
liberty. 'Something must be done', and that something must
be deep and extensive, and involve the active co-operation of
all citizens, male and female. Meanwhile, in the short run,
something must be done with the aid of the protection
afforded by the law. I do not suppose that the matter will be
set right by a few 'exemplary' sentences. But, equally, I do

not suppose that it will be improved without the aid of the police.

Each one of us, who has not lived an utterly retired life, can offer examples. But there are some who refuse to acknowledge the obvious. It is apparent from some recent pronouncements, that there are exalted theorists who suppose that cat's-eyes are placed in the roads by fairies, that missing persons materialize of their own accord, and that the police are nothing but an organ of the state with the function of repressing the proletariat. That the police are called upon to fulfil this function, on occasions, is manifest; but, once again, we are being offered a plausible half-truth on its way to degenerating into implausible rubbish.

The police are daily subject to the pressures of the most conservative ('law and order') ideology; those special sections of the force which are particularly trained in crowd control and in security operations (such as the Special Branch) have, notoriously, in the past been found to be permeated by extreme Rightist, or fascist — and today, perhaps, National Front or racist — ideas and connections; and the means of democratic control over the police are wholly inadequate. But this has never been the whole story. In any known society, some of the functions of the police are as necessary and legitimate as those of firemen and of ambulance-men; and these legitimate functions include not only helping old ladies across the road (which I do not often notice them doing today) but enforcing the law and protecting citizens against offenders. In these respects, as the Socialist pioneers always insisted, the police are in a particularly ambiguous social space: they are not only called upon, on occasion, *against* the actions of the working class, they are also, like firemen and ambulance-men, a section *of* the working class. As such, they are open to organization, argument and persuasion; and historians can point to many successful examples of this taking place. On many occasions over the past thirty years, as I have shambled along in some street demonstration, I have fallen into conversation with the policeman shambling at our side — not, of course, the 'special' or the mounted 'officer' (these always behave like pigs), but the member of a local force drafted in for extra, Sunday duties. And after the first grumpy exchanges, when the policeman complains at the duty when he wanted to dig his back garden, I have often found my companion to be seriously interested in the issues of the march — nuclear disarmament, or the Vietnam war, or even racialism itself.

That is a sentimental picture. Grunwick showed the police in a less endearing light. But a wholly indiscriminate attitude of 'bash the fuzz' is very much more sentimental, more self-indulgent, and counter-productive. It is not only that, with the modern technologies of crowd control, the crowd will nearly always get the worst of the bashing. Nor is it even that such infantile emoting must drive the police directly into the Rightist ideology of which they are accused, in one single self-fulfilling motion. It is even more that if we are wholly serious in our libertarian intentions — if we mean to keep the British police unarmed, to limit them to legitimate activities in a legitimate place, and to enforce upon them democratic controls — then we must fairly acknowledge that some part of their work is both proper and difficult, that the controls which we seek to place upon them will certainly add to the difficulties in the way of smooth 'executive' action, and that the police are entitled to expect, in return, some assistance from citizens in their legitimate business.

These proposals will not meet with universal acceptance. I may wish to revise my judgement, in this or that particular, in the future.* At a certain point, a Police State can pass a point of no return, where such considerations become irrelevant. But I do not think that we have got close to passing that point in Britain yet, and this is why the libertarian Left must clear up its mind on the issues. For we can be absolutely certain that, in the next few years, each and every attempt to limit our liberties will be supported by plausible pretexts: the growth of violent crime, the threat of terrorism. If journalists and others find it necessary to disclose, in the public interest, 'Official Secrets' as to the invigilation of citizens, then we will *always* be told that the disclosure of these secrets will give aid to the Provisional IRA or to desperate criminals; and since

*And have done so, in 'The State of the Nation'.

the true state of affairs will remain an 'Official Secret' beyond public inquiry, it will always be impossible to disprove the prosecution case. One natural reaction then will be to denounce all pretexts in advance, to abuse the police and the law without discrimination, and to discount both crime and terrorism as if they did not exist. But the public will not accept those arguments. And then libertarians will be driven into a small and ineffectual minority.

It will now seem to some readers that I have been trapped in the double-bind against which I have myself given warning. What, indeed, can we do? One answer, which itself can become a double-bind of a different kind, is to reform the law. This is certainly important. It is especially important in the struggle to reform negative and punitive laws. The struggle to dismantle the provisions of the Official Secrets Act (Section 1 quite as much as Section 2) is important, not only in its own right, but because of the public airing which it gives to the issues and the education of the public mind.

It is equally important to struggle to bring the police under much stricter democratic controls, and to strip the security services of their invisibility. And it is of the utmost importance to fight such individual cases as may arise, and to give them all possible publicity. A historian knows that the governed can very rarely manufacture cases exactly to their own requirements — the governors are in charge of that. But it is, exactly, around particular cases that the motives and methods of the governors become disclosed. That is why the cases of Agee and Hosenball, and of Aubrey, Berry and Campbell, are of first significance, and concern us all.

Beyond this, and as part of the campaign to educate the public, there is a strong case for new affirmative laws. But this is where the other double-bind begins. I will leave aside the oddity of those who are against all law but who call for stronger laws against rapists and racialists: that is their problem. The difficulty is, first, that when any affirmative measure, such as a Freedom of Information Act, is being drafted, the entire invisible establishment of 'public servants' is alerted, and immense pains will be taken to offer some innocuous concessions (to journalists, etc.) while at the same time actually strengthening the hard-core security provisions, which are then offered with a new legitimacy. This is exactly what is taking place inside the Government's White Paper on the Official Secrets Act. If we are alert enough, such manoeuvres may be spotted and exposed, but then the second difficulty arises. It has been admirably expressed by Mr Merlyn Rees himself, in the image of the 'self-sealing tank' (*The Times*, 20 July 1978). That is, if some Freedom of Information Act commands that there shall be public access to this and that category of document, then the state within the state will simply seal off this information in new ways: they will either assume, in their obscurity, the right to 'weed' the papers, or they will take care that certain decisions never appear in documents at all, or they will find an even more simple recourse. Thus the White Paper on the Official Secrets Act makes immense play upon the question of which categories of classified documents should come within its provisions — should these be TOP SECRET, or SECRET, or DEFENCE — CONFIDENTIAL, or whatever? But of course, whatever decision is come to, this tank will be able to seal itself in the easiest possible way, by a simple motion of reclassification, in which all that top people do not wish the public to know is placed within the inviolable category.

We should certainly campaign for a Freedom of Information Act. The campaign will have educative value. It might secure small gains, and, for historians, significant ones. But we should be under no illusions about it; whatever act is passed, our public servants will find a way around it. And they will probably find a way more effective than that of their cousins in the New York FBI who, several years ago, were caught red-handed in a succession of illegal break-ins into the offices of a small socialist party in New York. Pursuant to a court order (which, in this country, it would have been impossible to get) the party's legal representatives were authorized to inspect the relevant FBI files; here nothing as to their agents' activities was to be found, until, upon a renewed search, the representative chanced upon the letter 'N'. And here he found a very fat file indeed, complete with all the names and addresses of the party's members, tidily put away under the suffix 'Not to be Filed'.

We seem to be reaching pessimistic conclusions. But this need not be so. For there are certain other factors which may be working on our side. One of these I can only describe as a very ancient cultural tradition in Britain of bloody-mindedness towards the intrusion of authority. It has been there for as long as my knowledge extends. In the seventeenth century popular hostility to the apparatus of the summoner, the apparitor, and the moral inquisitors of the Church Courts was a contributory factor leading to Civil War. Agents of the Society for the Reformation of Manners or intrusive Excise inspectors were often targets of the crowds' ebullient resistance in the eighteenth century. I have already mentioned that public resistance to the 'modernization' of the police in Victorian England was immense. Again and again, in an unbroken series of cases, public opinion has eventually come to the side of the rights of the individual against the over-mighty state.

I do not believe that this inheritance of bloody-mindedness is exhausted, and I consider that we should regard it with respect. It is not to be simply equated with this or that kind of approved 'political consciousness', although it has certainly been an active force within the working-class movement. It is more pervasive than that. For example, I do not know the political views of the motorist who, in 1951, refused point-blank to produce his identity card, and hence necessitated a High Court case which resulted in the withdrawal of that system. But my sense of history leads me to suggest that he was unlikely to have been a militant revolutionary, and might equally have been a Conservative or marginal Labour voter, and a bloody-minded 'freeborn Briton'..

The difficulty of calling for affirmative laws to ban these marches and outlaw those organizations is that, while on occasions these measures may be necessary, the measures can very easily be turned to quite opposite purposes; they familiarize the public mind with new accretions of state powers; and they tend to dull the nerve of bloody-minded resistance to the intrusion of authority.

And this is the main point which I have been making all

along. We have to renew the nerve of outrage and we have to
alert the public conscience. For ways of doing this we may
turn to our history for many precedents. One way has been
to break the law. This was the way of Lollards and of
Levellers, of heretics and Puritans; it was the way of Wilkes
and the printers; it was the way of Daniel Isaac Eaton (seven
times in the dock) and of Richard Carlile (for whom prison
became an editorial office), in their fight to publish the
works of Paine; it was the way of Henry Hetherington, and
of the hundreds who took part in the fight of the 'great
unstamped'; it was the way of the Suffragettes. Whenever
the governors of Britain have assumed to know better than
the British people what it was in their 'best interests' to
believe, to read and to know, one proper response has been
to defy the law.

I am suggesting that we can never know (since that will be
an 'Official Secret') when the security forces and the police
are engaged in legitimate or illegitimate business. But there
are plain indications, some of them documented in these
pages, that much of their business is now illegitimate, and
that this is enlarging. We must therefore educate the public
conscience to the point where, on every side, their spies are
surrounded by our 'spies'. If a copy-typist or a filing clerk
falls upon offensive material, if a university assistant registrar
or a civil servant knows that illegitimate invigilation is taking
place, then this information must be 'blown'. What is legitimate and what is illegitimate will always be a difficult question; but I am saying that, increasingly, British people must
become jurors in their own case. And, as public concern and
understanding enlarges, we may hope that at least a few of
the 'public servants' and 'operators in the field' will recollect
their larger civic duties, as has happened in honourable cases
in the United States. We need only one good 'blow' from this
quarter, and it will become at once more easy to estimate the
problem, and to reconstruct the operation of the state within
the state.

This course will be not easy. If successful, it will not
extinguish the danger; but it will make the operators more
guilty, more secretive, more cautious, and this is one way of

containing them and of keeping them in their place. I think it utopian to expect much more. Indeed, I think this would be a notable victory, since it would mean that we had checked the immediate tendency for matters to grow worse.

If the secrets of power are 'blown', then fellow-citizens will be exposed to danger. The British security services will react more vengefully than their American counterparts to any attempt to disclose their operations. They will defend ferociously their invisibility and lack of accountability; and their peculiar style of ruling-class arrogance will leave them genuinely horror-struck at the bare notion that a British citizen might have his or her own view of the 'national interest' and find their actions illegitimate. Home Secretaries will loyally lisp through the briefs that their masters give them. Judges will hurry to the side of the state. A section of the press will slaver after 'exemplary' sentences. This means that, if we support the right to public information, we must be very serious indeed about coming to the defence of those who may expose themselves in this cause.

Nor will difficulties end there. We cannot automatically support every case. We do not want to provide cover for some mercenary spook. And it is possible that provocateurs may seek to 'plant' supposedly secret papers upon some journalist, in the attempt to provide a distraction. And even the 'good' cases may have their own wrinkles. We may need to defend — and I am certainly not referring now to any case which may be before the public eye — cranks, or egotists, or fanatic sectarians, who kick us in the face when we offer them a shoulder, or who seek to enlist us in a sectarian cause of their own. But *there is nothing new about this*. 'History' has never offered to libertarians perfect cases, nor permitted those with nice palates to reject all food that has not been prepared by their own hands. We have to decide where principle lies. And then we have to defend that principle without reserve.

The Great Fear of Marxism

Since British newspapers almost never discuss ideas, I suppose one should welcome Dr O'Brien's article, 'No to a Nauseous Marxist-Methodist Cocktail'.

The article purports to be about Marxism. Anyone who is even casually informed knows that Marxism, as an intellectual system, is in a state of crisis. The term 'Marxism' conceals an immense conflict going on between different claimants to the Marxist tradition. In Russia dissidents like Roy Medvedev are offering, in Marxist terms, scholarly exposures of the Stalin era — analyses which are refused publication by Soviet (Marxist-Leninist) publishing houses. In East Germany Rudolf Bahro, a Marxist, is imprisoned by a Marxist state for his stubborn and honest thought.

If we move from intellectual to political and social movements, the conflict is even more obvious. In Africa the most disparate regimes, from old-fashioned military tyrannies to more open societies with real democratic potential, all invoke the word 'Marxist'. In India one Marxist party supports Mrs Gandhi, another supports Janata (or used to do so), a third supports neither. Last month in Cambodia my friend Malcolm Caldwell, a Marxist, was murdered as a by-product (it seems) of a war between two Marxist states.

Dr O'Brien may suppose that this confirms his simple thesis: Marxism = 'hate'. But he is a good enough historian to

---

This piece first appeared in *The Observer*, 4 February 1979.

know that such mutations and confusions, as ideas and social forces roll over in the mud of actuality together, are not unprecedented. In an island he knows well, scarcely a week goes by without a Christian being murdered in the course of terrorist actions between two groups of Christians. Am I therefore entitled to draw the conclusion: Christianity = hate?

We have to try to understand the national, racial and class struggles of our time. Dr O'Brien simply denounces the Marxist tradition. It offers no solution: it *is* the problem. Marxism 'is dangerous in a society like ours', 'works like alcohol', is 'a contagion'. And so on. And *then*, after more about sheep and 'the lupine Left', he tells us that Marxism must 'be met by intellectual means'. Are these the means he is employing?

The first requirements, if we are to discuss Marxism as an intellectual tradition today, are information and discrimination. To suggest that Marxists 'in and around the academies' can be explained away as 'aggressive personalities' in search of licences is scarcely an intellectual means of debate. There may be some such people. Perhaps there are. There are also some such Christians and Conservatives.

But many academics are interested in intellectual values. And those interested in Marxism are more likely to have been moved by the intellectual authority of Marxist practitioners: by the history of Georges Lefebvre or Christopher Hill or D.D. Kosambi or Eugene Genovese: the criticism of Lukács or Benjamin or Goldmann or Raymond Williams: the substantial Marxist contribution to economic thought and to the understanding of imperialism and developing countries. They may have been moved by the indomitable intellectual vitality of Gramsci in his prison notebooks or by the dogged intellectual independence displayed by the *Monthly Review* in America.

To mention only these few names, in a few fields of work, is to return to the theme of conflict. It can be argued that very ancient philosophical, ethical and political arguments are now being conducted within a common Marxist vocabulary, and that incompatible positions (from terrorists to statist bureaucrats to determined libertarians) have got entangled in a common network of categories and terms.

If this is so, then two things follow . First, Marxism is one of the most universal vocabularies of thought today, in which critical issues of human destiny are being argued out. Younger British intellectuals who monitor, or take part in, this dialogue today have sensed that this is so. To denounce this as 'contagion' is to retreat into an impossible insularity.

Second, the Marxist tradition is in the process of splitting apart into several traditions and fragments. I think that it has already done so. These new traditions are very sharply opposed to one another; some have rejected certain 'Marxist' concepts and have greatly restructured their thought; they may be critical of much of Marx's work; but none would repudiate the powerful formative influence of Marx. And what competent thinker today (Marxist or anti-Marxist) would accept Dr O'Brien's lampoons, in which Marx 'had no use for an analytical tool' unless as a 'cosh or jemmy', or in which 'Wesley's teaching was one of love; Marx's of hate'?

All this is souped up with talk of Marxism luring 'the worker towards the abyss', Mr Tony Benn with his 'nauseous cocktail', 'the present disorders on the industrial front', and the 'aggression' of pickets. It would be pleasant to discuss all these matters, not as noises but as facts.

All I have room to say is that it has been very cold this past few weeks, and the great British public (as presented to us by the media) has been going through one of its regular moralistic spasms. There has been a lot of inconvenience, some of it (in the shops) self-induced, and a few cases of real suffering.

There have been some rough passages on the lorry pickets, fully publicized in every possible way by the media, but the culprits have not identified themselves as readers of Lukács or Althusser. The only recorded fatality of that strike has been a picket. The other 'disorders on the industrial front' (the 'front' where most people happen to live and work) seem to me, as an historian of such matters, to be very much like those that have gone before. There has been a legitimate withdrawal of labour by groups of workers who found

SECONDARY PICKET

themselves to be disadvantaged, in good order and with surprising good humour and self-control.

If I were in the business of sniffing around for wreckers who create 'maximum disorder and break-down' I would look first at Mr Callaghan, Mr Healey and their Treasury advisers who committed the blunder of imposing 5 per cent in the face of a peak Bank Rate, dear money, rising mortgages, fares and prices. I am not aware that *all* of these wreckers are Marxists, although Mr Healey once was. In any case, I have not noticed any 'abyss', but a society in which those at the bottom are, in general, a good deal more humane and tolerant than those at the top.

One has come to expect these spasms, although the media are now recycling them with increasing frequency. But how can a writer with Dr O'Brien's knowledge of history compose a sentence like this: 'Excessive, insistent, competing pay demands are likely to close factories, put people out of jobs, send prices soaring, and generally lead to ruin.' One might copy this *exactly*, word for word, out of any tract of Political Economy since 1820. Always, *always*, when we come to 'crisis', the working people are the real threat (to 'us', to 'society'), and their wages 'lead to ruin' and the 'abyss'.

As a Marxist (or a Marxist-fragment) in the Labour Party, I have always tried to envisage a politics that will enable us, in this country, to effect a transition to a socialist society — and a society a great deal more democratic, in work as well as in government, than our present one — without rupturing the humane and tolerant disposition for which our working class has often been distinguished, in this country, if not abroad.

I do not know by what right or office Dr O'Brien presumes to advise the Labour Party on its need to purge itself of Marxists like myself who by service and by democratic commitment are wholly entitled to be members. Nor do I know by what authority he chastises Mr Benn for making the wholly accurate observation that Marxism (from the days of William Morris and Eleanor Marx) is among the traditions that have fed that party. But I know that when a writer of distinction allows rancour to overwhelm his judgement and to vulgarize his style — as Edmund Burke's virulent Anti-

Jacobinism did in his last years — then we are indeed at the edge of a crisis. It is the crisis of a culture that cannot adjust, in which reason is being overwhelmed by a kind of class panic or hysteria.

I find in Dr O'Brien's lampoons against undefined Marxists, his tabloid style, his roads to ruin and his abyss, the tell-tale signs of an oncoming *grande peur*. Historians have not invented the *grande peur*: this is a real event, a psycho-social class spasm of irrationality, analogous to the displaced sense of 'threat' in the neurotic personality. When it comes it can claim many victims, but the first victim of its formless passions is always the reason. And this would indeed lead us to an 'abyss' in which the humane restraints of our society would not survive.

Law Report

The People of Britain v. the Judges, Ex. parte Peach.

Before Lord Muggery, Lord Dunnem, Lord Void of Tax, Lord Shortshrift and Lord Vox of Populi.

Four out of five Lords of Appeal upheld the decision of the Lord Chief Justice (The Times, Law Report, November 15 1979) that the possibility that a member of the public might have been killed by a severe blow on the head from a weapon wielded by a police officer did not amount to "circumstances" the "continuance or possible recurrence" of which was prejudicial to the safety of the public.

Their Lordships refused an appeal by the People of Britain, on application by the relatives of Mr Clement Blair Peach, to order the coroner, Mr John Burton, to summon a jury of inquest.

LORD MUGGERY said he regarded the matter as straightforward and raising no question of public interest. If the British people had been killed by a blow from a weapon wielded by a police officer, it might have cause for complaint. But what were the facts in this case? Not the British people but a foreigner, a New Zealander, was the deceased. It appeared that the deceased had brought himself into a position of danger by entering a precinct where police officers, in the course of their duty, were wielding weapons. Was it probable that such circumstances would now recur? One might be confident, after the example given to Mr Peach, that New Zealanders would keep out of public precincts.

His Lordship said that the relevant statute admitted of one interpretation only. Section 13 (2) of the Coroners Amendment Act 1926 provides:

If it appears to the coroner . . . that there is reason to suspect . . . (e) that the death occurred in circumstances the continuance or possible recurrence of which is prejudicial to the health or safety of the public . . . he shall proceed to summon a jury.

The relevant words of the statute are *"appears to the coroner"*. It does not say "appears to the British people". That would be an extraordinary construction. Was public opinion to be placed above the coroner or even above the House of Lords? (Laughter in court.) His Lordship hoped that a jest would be excused.

In any case, how could it be argued that *any* action of the police in due execution of duty could be "prejudicial to the . . . public"? He would invite the Director of Public Prosecutions to institute proceedings against the British people for flagrant barratry.

The Coroners Amendment Act 1926 was passed by the legislature at a time when government had a proper respect for law and order. It is true that this Act by some oversight, explicitly excluded from its provisions cases of death by murder, manslaughter or infanticide. And that in such cases the summoning of a jury had remained mandatory.

However, this was taken care of in that excellent piece of modernization, the Criminal Law Act 1977, section 56 (2) :

Without prejudice to the power of a coroner under subsection (2) of section 13 of the Coroners Amendment Act 1926 to summon a jury if it appears to him that there is any reason for doing so in a case in which he is not requested by that subsection to do so, paragraphs (a) and (d) of that subsection (which require him to do so if it appears to him that the deceased came by his death by murder, manslaughter or infanticide . . .) shall cease to have effect.

This clause was a model of lucidity. His Lordship could not praise the parliamentary drafting enough. Indeed, he had had a small hand in drafting it himself. One might say that in this clause the ancient right of inquest by jury was Mugged. (Laughter.) But he would not take all the credit on himself. The law officers of the Crown, in 1977, disliked the jury system and had helped the measure on. As for MPs, it was no business of this House to inquire into them. His Lordship supposed that they did not know what they were doing. They rarely did. It had perhaps gone through "on the nod". He thought it would be injurious to the public interest to discuss the matter further. He would accordingly dismiss the appeal.

LORD DUNNEM concurred but wished to enter other arguments. Counsel for the British people had cited a long and tedious list of cases and precedents, and had grounded their appeal on the common law and on the antiquity of the custom. His Lordship had not looked far into these cases, but it was true that juries of inquest could be found at very distant times. And what did we find then? In the 13th century an inquest jury was constituted of every male of the age of 12 and above in four or more neighbouring townships (*Stat. of Marlborough*, 1267). What kind of a precedent was that? Were we to assemble every male from Southall and adjacent boroughs as a jury? (Laughter.) Where? How would a verdict be found? How could irresponsible persons, Asians, persons who had also received blows from the police, be excluded? And how would we be able, now, to exclude from the jury persons of the gentle sex? If we were to have 15-year-old schoolboys, might we not have 15-year-old schoolgirls also? (Consternation in court.)

His Lordship went on to look at other precedents. Fourteenth-century juries did not submit to the orders of the coroner, but went out and inquired into matters themselves. In one case (*K.B. 27/476, King's membrane*, no. 31) the sheriff and coroner twice sent the jurors out into the streets to inform themselves before finding a verdict on the third attempt. What kind of a precedent was that? (Great laughter in court.)

His Lordship was aware that there were one or two judges still about who supposed that case law and precedent still had effect and constituted some part of the common law. His learned colleague, Lord Devlin, still argued in this wholly conservative way, but happily his arguments were confined to books which the public was unlikely to read. In these days of modernization it could not be stressed too solemnly that case law was a fetter on the public interest. What common law means is the commonsense of judges, and judges are the only proper persons to determine what is the public interest. He hoped that arguments from antiquity would not be offered to their lordships again. He would dismiss the appeal.

LORD VOID OF TAX was happy to defer to his learned friends. He only understood about money. Was any matter of money involved here? Was it suggested that compensation be offered to Mr Peach? What good would that do him? (Laughter.) He would dismiss the appeal.

LORD SHORTSHRIFT said that he had never heard so much rubbish in his life as had been argued by counsel for the British people. If a police officer had executed his duty on Mr Peach, surely that was an end to the matter of Mr Peach? How could a jury help? A jury would be a waste of time. Appeals were a waste of time. Speaking of time, surely their Lordships were already late for dinner? He would dismiss the appeal.

LORD VOX OF POPULI, in a dissenting judgment adverted to several score of cases in the 18th and 19th centuries in which juries had inquired vigilantly into deaths occasioned by military or police action; as, for example, the case of John Lees, the case of Calthorpe Street, etc. (*New Society*, 8 & 15 November 1979.) He supposed that these cases had established a constitutional principle. He supposed that it was a matter of common law that the British people had established the right of a jury of inquest, a right which had existed in all sensitive cases such as this for 700 years; and that it was a point of constitutional principle that the police were to be placed under the civil power.

His Lordship argued that over-zealous actions by the police were very clearly "prejudicial to the health and safety of the public" and decidedly came within the meaning of the Act; that he did not know why the legislature struck out this ancient right in 1977, but that he supposed that MPs were unaware of the construction that might be put upon the clause; that in view of other pending cases (as *Kelly* v. *Merseyside Police*) there was every reason to anticipate the "continuance or possible recurrence" of such regrettable episodes; that ... (But their other four Lordships had retired to dinner, and his Lordship was taken in charge by the coroner's officer, P.C. Crackem, for contempt of c**rt.)

The State of the Nation

What if the Church and the State
Are the mob that howls at the door!
Wine shall run thick to the end,
Bread taste sour.

                    W.B. Yeats

1 On the New Issue of Postage Stamps

I have been admiring this month's new issue of stamps. I don't refer to the magnificent series of Pioneers of British Liberties, with John Ball (8p), John Lilburne (10p), John Wilkes (11½p), and Feargus O'Connor for the transatlantic airmail. This set is not yet available at my post office. I have been admiring the new series on the British police.

There they are, our splendid public servants, sitting on horses, directing traffic, messing about in boats, and, most touching of all, there is one of the handsome young constable bending solicitously over a little blonde girl with a doll, a jolly darkie toddler in between. For some reason they are standing in the middle of a racetrack, and there is a British elm (miraculously unscathed by elm disease) in the background. Ten pee for that.

The occasion for this new issue is not made evident on the stamps. Of course, since our police are a matter for continuous celebration, year in, year out, in most of the media, there is no need for any particular occasion. But perhaps this series was designed to commemorate the inquest on the body of Mr Blair Peach.

If that is so, then this is even-handed on the part of the Post Office, since Mr Peach's inconsiderate behaviour in becoming the subject of an inquest has made for certain difficulties. An editorial in *The Observer* (7 October) noted

---

'The State of the Nation' was first published, in a somewhat shorter form, in *New Society* between 8 November and 13 December 1979.

that Mr Peach is 'obviously a welcome martyr to many on the extreme Left'.

If we were strict logicians we might argue that the unfortunate police constable who was killed several weeks ago while apprehending a suspect, and whose widow was instantly pressed forward on the media to call for the return of hanging, was 'obviously a welcome martyr' to some editors and chief constables. But I have no wish to be that kind of a logician. The argument is a contemptible one.

We are, however, considering the 'extreme Left', those persons of 'extreme political beliefs' who, in the view of the last Attorney-General and Home Secretary, may be thought, in certain sensitive but undefined cases, to be unsuitable for jury service. It is possible that some thought of this kind occurred to the coroner investigating the death of Mr Peach. 'Dr Burton said that there were good reasons for not having a jury, not least because it would present problems about its selection' (*Guardian*, 12 October).

As Dr Burton will know, he owes the modern definition of the coroner's functions and duties to — more than anyone else — that great coroner, Thomas Wakley, the founder of *The Lancet*, Radical MP for Finsbury and Chartist sympathizer. It was Wakley who insisted that coroners should not be legal hacks but persons with medical qualifications. He carried a great campaign to the public (for coroners were elected by the freeholders in those unmodernized days) and swept the polls for West Middlesex in 1839 — holding the post for more than twenty years.

It should not be supposed that Wakley was a narrow professional, an enemy of legal incompetence and of medical malfeasance only. He was an active democrat, and he instructed one of his first juries that 'the coroner was the *people's* judge, the only judge whom the *people* had the power to appoint, while the office had been specially instituted for the protection of the *people*'. Wakley went on to observe that this circumstance was much disliked by 'certain persons in authority who had been, and wished to continue to be, free from observation and control'.

I am very probably unjust to Dr Burton. The problems in

the 'selection' of a jury which may have come to his mind
were perhaps those of finding a true verdict, in a sensitive
case in which the police are involved, at a time when the
minds of potential jurors are exposed to massive propaganda
as to the superlative merits of the police, the alien habits of
Asians, and the 'strident hatred' (*The Observer*, 7 October) of
the 'extreme Left'; and when the officer responsible for
empanelling a coroner's jury is an officer of the police.

I will allow this difficulty. But I do not think it to be an
argument sufficient to permit an interference with due process. It would be over-zealous in a coroner or Old Bailey
judge to cite the Post Office for contempt of court for
choosing this moment for its new issue of stamps.

For the difficulty is one to which the British people has
become habituated, over some centuries, since well before
the time when Queen Elizabeth learned to 'tune her pulpits'.
It is to be expected that authority, by means of Proclamations,
assize sermons, homilies at the scaffold, manipulation of the
press, and TV chat shows, will always seek to present approv-
ing images of the forces of order. But this has not prevented
juries from fulfilling their difficult duties, considering cases
with responsibility, and finding verdicts which, on occasion,
have been greatly displeasing to authority. The gross manipulation of opinion will always militate against the truth,
but, in a democracy, I think we must take our chance.

I may still be misunderstanding the problem of the jury's
'selection'. For it may possibly have passed through the mind
of some high official somewhere that it would be advisable
for coroner's juries, in 'certain sensitive cases', to be vetted
also. And in that event one could scent a real difficulty. For
it may be that the Police National Computer is not yet perfect enough in its sums to show up instantly all those who are
known to be relatives or associates of Asians, nor even of
persons who had been kicked in their testicles at Southall.

That is indeed a serious consideration for any coroner or
judge. It is their business to ensure that the courts are free
from the least suspicion of bias. And we have it on the
authority of a most experienced retired Old Bailey judge (Sir
Melford Stevenson, giving judgement on BBC's *Man Alive*,

9 October) that no bias has ever been known to enter any jury from the Right.

The extreme Left is another matter. They are everywhere. Your neighbour might be one, or your workmate, or the teacher of your child. And *The Observer* tells us, in the same editorial, that its aim is to 'discredit the whole police force as a crucial part of a wider attack on the institutions of this country'.

This must certainly not be permitted. For what, indeed, are the 'institutions of this country'? They are everything that we hold dear, everything that makes up our consensual world of racetracks, ancient elms, and bobbies leaning down to whisper to little children.

We may not have a written constitution, but these institutions are not the less real for that. One might think of the rule of law, the independence of the judiciary, the even-handedness of justice, the privacy of the citizen, the paramountcy of Parliament, the subjection of military and police to the 'civil power', the accountability of public officials, the integrity of the jury system, the freedom of press and television from overt or covert influence by the state. If extremists should attack these institutions, is it any wonder that they should inflict upon themselves severe injury, by running their heads furiously against the impartial consensual instruments of the Loyal and the Good?

Such persons cannot be permitted to influence the outcome of an inquest. But if we are in search of precedents in this difficulty, these come to hand. There is the case of the Oldham inquest in 1819 upon the body of John Lees who suffered injuries upon the field of Peterloo from which he subsequently died.

The coroner in this case, Mr Farrand (who was not a medical man), handled counsel and witnesses for the deceased's family with commendable firmness. It was obvious to him that Radicals found in John Lees a 'welcome martyr'. The coroner would permit no capital to made of the affair, and the reporters of those strident newspapers, *The Times* and the *Morning Chronicle*, were excluded from the court. A score of whining witnesses were brought forward to describe their confused experiences on the field ('there was whiz this way and whiz that way, and as they were going to strike, I threw myself on my face, so that, if they cut, it should be on my bottom'); and although these witnesses clearly implicated themselves as being actors in the same criminal affray, the forbearing Mr Farrand did not, as in current practice, seek to intimidate them by binding them over.

He did, however, adjourn the inquest for some weeks. Counsel for the deceased's family then applied to the Court of King's Bench for a mandamus to compel the inquest to proceed. But in this high court the learned judges discovered, to their horror, that a grave procedural error had been committed. While the jury had viewed the body of John Lees, and the coroner had viewed it also, the parties had not done so *together*. In view of these most serious 'irregularities' all proceedings were quashed.

It is not to be supposed that the family of John Lees was left without remedy. Mr Justice Best advised the family's counsel that their proper recourse was to apply for an inquest to be heard before the Grand Jury of Lancashire. This was a remedy both proper and in strict accordance with the law. It was also more likely to result in a true verdict. For it transpired that the jury at Oldham had been ill-affected, seven of them writing to the press to say that, if the inquest had been concluded, they had already determined to bring in a verdict of 'Wilful Murder' against the Manchester Yeomanry. As Mr Justice Best pointed out, in recommending his own remedy, 'no failure of justice will occur, because the case will go before the Grand Jury of the country — a body of men much better calculated to examine so complicated a question'. The qualifications of the Grand Jury were enhanced by the fact that, if not Yeomen themselves, they would all be, to a man, relatives of Yeomen and associates of the magistrates who ordered them in.

I mention this case, not only to remind us that the difficulties which we face are not unprecedented, but also to reassure us that, in the past, there have always been coroners, judges, High Courts, and even Lord Chief Justices learned enough to find stratagems to avoid inconveniences in our system and pretexts to upset the layman's sense of natural justice. And are we to say now that such ancient British traditions have utterly died out? I think, at a casual glance at certain events of the past year, that we are not. The stratagems and pretexts are, of course, in every case, in the strictest accordance with the Law, not least because they are judges who think them up, and judges are persons who decide the law. I am sorry to labour the self-evident.

Somewhere within this precedent a solution to current difficulties might be found. I have no doubt that if the case were to be submitted to the strictest judicial examination it will be found that the inquest on the body of Mr Peach ought either to be quashed or removed to a higher court before a jury both Grand and Pricked in particular ways. And as a concession to public opinion, might not the Lord Chancellor devise some way in which the long-abeyed inquest upon John Lees could now be re-opened? The family of Mr Lees has been remiss in letting 160 years go by without seeking the redress afforded to them by Mr Justice Best. It is hard, nay, it is intolerable that the citizens of Oldham should have been kept so long in suspense.

In the matter of the police, I would certainly not wish to associate myself with Left extremists. Indeed, it is to clear my name of any such suspicion that I am writing this article. I am anxious about this point, since, four years ago, while reviewing several books on the history of crime and law, no less a person than the present Lord Chancellor described me as 'the worst offender'. It is no small matter to a private citizen, pursuing his business in humble obscurity, to know that that Awful Eye has taken him within its cognizance.

I have not the least wish to 'discredit the whole police force', and I am sorry that certain parts of it have recently been so active in discrediting themselves. Like most citizens who have lived for fifty years or more, I have had a little experience both of its rough and its beneficient characteristics. I know the value of the police. If I had the power I would close down the Special Patrol Group at once, as well as many of the activities of the Special Branch and of MI5, and I would place the police force as a whole under much stricter democratic discipline and control. I consider that the police would gain in credit thereby, and that its many legitimate functions would be exercised more effectively.

I have had some good experiences of British police as well as bad ones. But my purpose is not autobiography, and readers can supply this absence, with differing results, by consulting themselves. The generalizations which I can offer, as a historian, as to police are few and platitudinous. Thus, it is historically observable that there is an ever-present tendency towards symbiosis between the police and the criminal world, which gives rise to successive crises, in Fielding's England as it does today. That there is a recurrent occupational pressure upon police, who are anxious to catch the eye of their superiors for their zeal, to push people around, as vagrants, or drunks, or buskers, or street-traders, or street-orators, or under 'sus' laws — an easy kind of zeal which enables them to book numerous offenders but which may have an inverse correlation with their activity in the more arduous work of the prevention of serious crime. That police, as defenders of 'law and order', have a vested interest in the status quo, whether the *status* be capitalist or communist, and whether the *quo* be that of Somoza's Nicaragua or of Rakosi's Hungary: that is, the occupation is one which is supportive of statist and authoritarian ideologies. And, more simply, in whatever kind of society, the police will always have good reasons for pressing for more resources, more powers, and more pay.

There is nothing sinister about this, in an alert and democratic society, since, once these things are understood, proper measures will be taken to ensure that the police have adequate resources for their legitimate functions, and to curtail in the strictest way those functions which are not. This is not a new problem. It is a problem which — in relation to military or police — we have lived with in this island for centuries.

I have been reading, with mixed feelings, Sir Robert Mark's *In the Office of Constable*, which is now available in paperback and which should be read. Sir Robert expresses, in a British way, the authoritarian and statist ideology which I have indicated. He has many attitudes which I find odious:

he resents democratic control of the police, is contemptuous of do-gooders and civil libertarians, prefers summary jurisdiction to trial by jury, and he is very proud of the way in which 'an Anglo-Indian running a small business has courageously and successfully stood firm against politically motivated violence on the streets at Grunwick'.

'Politically motivated' is a term which he employs here for any democratic action which arises from 'below', rather than being authorized from 'above', and which is in the least unsettling to the status quo, although his own motivation, in an authoritarian and statist sense, is deeply political. This comes through, not only in particular arguments, but in the tone of everything. In 1973 (he tells us) the Metropolitan Police were under serious strain, 'having to deal with 72,750 burglaries, 2,680 robberies and 450 demonstrations'. Football crowds and traffic accidents go unmentioned, as do lost children or lost dogs. The point is the sequence: burglaries → robberies → demonstrations, and to associate in the readers' minds popular democratic manifestations with crime.

In the months before its self-inflicted closure, *The Times* might have been sub-titled 'The Organ of the Police Federation'. In almost any week one might find a public relations hand-out from the police on its front page, tricked out as 'news'. Thus on Sunday, 25 September 1978, there was a large Anti-Nazi League demonstration at Brixton, and a very small National Front march. Both these affairs passed off in complete peace, and the police may have done something to help in this by keeping the marches apart.

On the next day *The Times* carried three columns on its front page, headed 'Police Presence at Marches Cost £400,000', itemizing the cost of helicopter patrols, extra duties, and sandwiches. Immense suffering had been inflicted, not only on the police, but also on the taxpayer. ' "It is all a question of what value you put on freedom and democracy", a senior Scotland Yard officer said.' It was evident that the value put upon these commodities by the Yard was not high, and certainly very much below the sum of £400,000.

This is all in order. It is not new. The value which Sir Charles Warren, the Metropolitan Commissioner in the 1880s (the decade of the banning of meetings in Trafalgar Square, of 'Bloody Sunday', and of the incessant harassment of socialist street-speakers) might have put on these commodities was probably below the sum of four old pennies. That is why, in the long run, he had to be sacked.

It is even possible for a libertarian to read other parts of Sir Robert Mark's apologia with sympathy — to understand his difficulties with bent cops and pusillanimous politicians — to see how he came to think in that kind of way, and to develop a sort of paternalist trade-union consciousness when defending the interests of 'his' force in the face of actual difficulties. In the matter of demonstrations, these difficulties have been created, first and foremost, by the National Front. And the extreme solicitude with which the police have often treated the Front, even when this has been engaged in manifest and racist provocations, has aroused justifiable anxiety, especially among those who recall that a similar tenderness towards the British Union of Fascists in the 1930s was suspected to have been in certain cases the consequence of actual complicity.

There have also been counter-provocations by a few who suppose themselves to be on the 'Left' and who mistake the drama of a punch-up for serious political agitation. I don't refer to the necessary self-defence of minority communities, if these are left without police protection and are under actual attack (whether Asians today or East End Jews in the 1930s). I refer to those provocative incidents (Red Lion Square, Lewisham, etc.) which have been recited *ad nauseam* in the media, which added grist to every mill on the Right, and which served to advertise the Front. The Anti-Nazi League, when it repudiated such tactics and organized its peaceful pageantry of young people, was much to be congratulated.

It was not, of course, congratulated by the Special Patrol Group, which had perhaps been taught too well by a respected Commissioner that demonstrations belong in the same category as robbery. In *The Times* report which I have cited it was added that 'the police also had to contend with a TUC march for pensioners ... and with a march in the East End

by the National Union of Public Employees about pay'. Since
police are public employees and may even survive to be
pensioners, it is not clear why they regard these marches as
something to 'contend with', nor why 'contending with' old-
age pensioners should require heavy expenditure on heli-
copters, motorized transport and the rest.

For two hundred years the democratic organizations of
this country have been perfectly prepared to provide efficient
stewarding for their own demonstrations and meetings, and if
the police were to ask nicely I have no doubt that we could
do the same again, thus saving the suffering taxpayer (some
of whom are members of NUPE and even of the Anti-Nazi
League) from wasteful expenditure as well as officious dis-
plays of force. The police might then limit themselves to an
abbreviated presence, in pursuance of such legitimate duties
as diverting traffic and photographing demonstrators for the
records of the Special Branch.

The police, however, do not ask nicely. There is less that is
nice about the British police today than at any time I can
remember. I am told by the Post Office that what the handsome bobby is whispering to the blonde little girl and the
darkie toddler on the ten pee stamp is 'sus-sus-sus'.

Yet there is, even in this, no cause for extreme anxiety.
There have been many other times when the British police
have been decidedly un-nice and have alienated public
opinion. In due course they have been put back into something like a proper place. What is alarming today is that the
police are attaining to a position in which they can actually
manufacture what is offered as 'public opinion', and are
offering their occupational needs as a supreme priority
beneath which, not they, but the British public must be put
in place.

That is what is new. There is nothing new about Sir Robert
Mark's or Sir David McNee's illiberal and impatient notions.
What is new is the very powerful public relations operation
which disseminates these notions as an authorized, consensual
view — an operation carried on out of our own taxes; which
presses its spokesmen forward on every occasion upon the

media; which lobbies inquiries and Royal Commissions,
constantly pressing for larger powers; which bullies weak
Home Secretaries (and boos them when they cross their
wishes); which reproves magistrates for lenient sentencing;
which announces unashamedly that the police are in the
regular practice of breaking judges' rules when interrogating
suspects; which slanders unnamed lawyers and lampoons
libertarian organizations; which tells judges how they are to
interpret the law; and which justifies the invasion of the
citizens' privacy and the accumulation of prejudicial and
inaccurate records.

This is new. This is formidable. As a historian I can say
that I know of no period in which the police have had such a
loud and didactic public presence, and when they have offered
themselves as a distinct interest, as one of the great 'institutions' and perhaps the first in the realm. And I know of no
period in which politicians and editors have submitted so
abjectly or ardently to their persuasions. When Mrs Thatcher
came to power it is my impression that she set in motion cuts
in *everything* — schooling, social services, libraries, universities, research, nursery schools, law centres — *except* the pay
of the police and the budget for Defence. She entered our
money in a public subscription in support of the priorities
of the police.

What also is something new to a historian is the notion
that we should be instructed as to what value we are to put
on freedom and democracy, and *be instructed by the police*.
And that the police are to be seen as, somehow, for themselves, rather than as servants to us, so that we are to be
instructed by the police as to what is to be our place. For the
police are the ones who can tune the pulpits now, and there
are fewer pulpits to tune than in the days of Good Queen
Bess. Three television channels and half-a-dozen popular
sheets (titties here and approved police images there) and the
job is done.

The job is not yet done to the perfect satisfaction of every
policeman. There is a very powerful 'institution of this
country' which writers on our Constitution have insufficiently
regarded. This is known as ACPO, or the Association of Chief

Police Officers, in which all those peers of the constabulary realm who are above the rank of chief superintendent assemble and debate. In this high chamber the Duke of the Metropolis, the Baron of Manchester, and the Earl of the Marches of Merseyside consult. Their decisions are sent down by beadles to the Royal Commission on Criminal Procedure and to parliamentary committees. Home Secretaries attend on them, and deliver deferential addresses at the bar. ACPO does not attend on governments; governments attend on it. As one Chief Inspector has said, ACPO 'is the one authoritative body the government will go to to seek views'. (*State Research*, October 1979.)

At a recent Session of ACPO (June 1979) the Chief Constable of Kent, Mr Barry Pain, proposed that the police, like old-time vicars, should be given access to classrooms to run courses in 'citizenship'. Unruly headmasters who obstructed such wholesome provision should be disciplined by the education authorities. My Lord of Kent's decision is not, as yet, Law. What is decided by ACPO does not immediately have effect, as by royal prerogative. They are still at work on an enabling act for that.

But the proposal opens up new vistas. Why stop at schools? Why should not the law be brought into agreement with the fact, and the police be recognized as the spiritual power in the land, the Church of Scotland Yard as by Law Established? Why should not the Metropolitan Commissioner be given a Cardinal's hat in addition to his habitual crook? And why should not this Church be empowered to levy direct taxation? A tenth of one's substance is not too much to lay aside for Law and Order. Let the farmer set aside one lamb in ten to be collected in black marias, and let us all be tithed on PAYE. As for compulsory attendance at divine service, we have that now, each time we turn on the news.

Yet if there should be moral objectors about — a sort of sect of Quakers who, upon their conscience, cannot pay their tithe — then the proper answer to all this is not to seek to 'discredit the whole police force'. Indeed, to put all the blame for this upon the cops is to confuse the symptom with the cause. It can even be a cop-out, which distracts

THE CHURCH BY LAW ESTABLISHED

attention from far worse offenders. It is only to be expected that the police will push for all the power and pay that they can get. What is not to be expected is that every door will be left open and swinging on its hinges to beckon their advance.

If I may revert to the *Observer* editorial, I am not clear as to the sense in which we can speak of the police as an 'institution of this country'. Police are not peculiar to Britain, and if we are thinking of police just *as* police, with large summary powers and a massive and technically expert authoritarian presence, then we might do better to think of a Prussian or a Russian model.

What has been peculiar to Britain, until lately, has not been the fact that we have police but the place into which the police have been put. That is, the police, including those 'in the Office of Constable', have been firmly held in a position subordinate to the elected civil power and have been subjected to certain expectations and rules; and this has been done both by constitutional safeguards and by a continuous running argument turning on precedents and cases, inquests and judgements, in which the public has been one party to the debate.

That is, we are considering not so much an 'institution' as a tradition, as to whose character we must take advice from historians as well as constables. Seventeenth-century yeomen did not give their children into the hands of the parish beadle, nor, in the eighteenth century, did London tradesmen and artisans matriculate beneath the lecterns of the Bow Street Runners. In the matter of citizenship and its rights and duties there is no person *less* competent to give instruction than the average constable; if he is too 'clever' about things like that he will be kept for ever in the deep obscurity of the beat. For what was remarked upon by foreign observers (including those from Prussia, Russia, and Chicago) over some three hundred years was the peculiar jealousy of the British people towards the central powers of the state, their abhorrence of military intervention in civil affairs, their dislike of state espionage and of any form of heavy policing, their indiscipline and their sensitivity as to the citizen's rights of privacy.

I will allow that the 'freeborn Englishman' congratulated himself too far upon his liberties, especially in view of the double standards displayed in his imperial character. I will also allow that these freedoms were qualified by savage hanging laws, and that where they were effectual they were enabled to survive in an unusually favoured and temperate social climate — although the freedoms (and consequent consensual rules and inhibitions upon violence) made this climate temperate in return. What I will not allow is that these liberties created no difficulties for authority, or that 'times have changed', presenting unprecedented dangers and disorders which require unprecedented measures.

In fact, these liberties, which were wrested *from* authority and not granted *by* it, were greatly disliked by governments and created intense difficulties. The angry crowd, in the eighteenth or nineteenth century, could commit depradations — untiling houses, burning down corn-mills and conventicles, carrying off waggon-loads of grain, letting off mill-dams, unhorsing police and military — which make today's rare affrays look petty. When ACPO, in full chamber assembled in 1977, decreed that there should be 'a new Public Order Act giving the police power to control marches and demonstrations, similar to police powers in Ulster', the preamble to this decree, the inasmuch and whereas, being that 'the police can no longer prevent public disorder in the streets', this was so much unhistorical humbug.

I am not saying this as a proponent of 'disorder'. I am simply noting the facts. In a broad, secular view there has never been a time when public disorder in the streets has been less. Neither police nor military have *ever* been able to prevent all public disorder. But from Sacheverell Riots to Tonypandy, from the Priestley Riots of 1791 to the more recent race riots at Notting Hill — and some of the worst disorders have been those in support of 'Church and King' — the fabric of our civil liberties has survived, tattered, patched and bloodied, but still in a single piece. I see no reason why the British people should be sent down to ACPO now, to be measured for a new suit.

In the old days, the management of a crowd required, in *the civil power* (magistrates or mayors), extreme delicacy and tact, and often negotiation. And this the more so, in that any use of force against the crowd, if not in conformity with every provision of the Riot Act, might bring down upon its author a subsequent action in the courts. In the eighteenth and nineteenth centuries juries returned verdicts of 'Wilful Murder' against those who killed members of the crowd, or else were prevented — as in the case of John Lees — by the most dexterous judicial legerdemain from doing so. This is not to say that, when the authorities were the guilty party, justice was done. It is to say, at the least, that a general popular hubbub against tyranny arose — as after Peterloo — and the authorities acted for some while with extreme caution, for fear of stirring up that sleeping beast again.

There was even one famous case, the Calthorpe Street affair in Clerkenwell in 1833, when the jury at an inquest returned a verdict of 'Justifiable Homicide' upon the body of a police constable who had been killed *by* a member of the crowd. It is worth pausing on the case to see how the minds of English jurymen once worked.

At Calthorpe Street some persons associated with the National Union of the Working Classes had called a public meeting, and Lord Melbourne, the Secretary of State, had decided that this was illegal. The organizers of the meeting went ahead, and there is some evidence that it was their intention to start the speeches and then — if the authorities appeared and challenged them — to disperse. There is some evidence also that the Commissioners of Police wanted to administer to the working classes a severe lesson in civics. Attendance at the meeting was not large, the police appeared in great force down every approach road (blocking, as is often their way, all exits), and on the pretext of seizing an American flag, moved without any preamble into a direct attack. In the affray, men, women and children were beaten unmercifully, casual bystanders and newspaper reporters were bludgeoned, and street-traders' barrows and baskets of loaves were strewn across the roads. Somewhere in the middle of the confusion Police Constable Culley was stabbed close to the heart by a dagger. It was said, in evidence, that members of the crowd, standing around the American flag, turned very ugly indeed, shouting out such incitements as: 'Come, Englishmen, are we to be trampled upon by these bloody Peelers?' and 'Is this the way that Englishmen are served?' I think it likely that their language was more blunt.

The coroner's jury was comprised of seventeen small tradesmen from the immediate locality — bakers, an upholsterer, a corn-chandler, a pawnbroker — they were petty bourgeois to a man. The foreman of the jury was a baker. None of them (so far as is known) were sympathizers with the National Union of the Working Classes. Nevertheless, they returned unanimously a remarkable verdict:

> We find a verdict of *justifiable homicide* on these grounds — that no Riot Act was read, nor any proclamation advising the people to disperse; that the Government did not take the proper precautions to prevent the meeting from assembling; and that the conduct of the police was ferocious, brutal and unprovoked by the people; and we moreover, express our anxious hope that the Government will, in future, take better precautions to prevent the recurrence of such disgraceful transactions in the Metropolis.

Some historians have assumed, too easily, that this verdict was 'preposterous' or 'perverse', or that the jury must have been made up of howling Radicals, with a 'strident hatred' of the police. But the ensuing exchanges in the court do not support this. For two hours the coroner bullied the jury, telling them to reconsider or to modify the verdict. The foreman replied that 'there have been conflicting opinions among us, but we have all anxiously compared our opinions and that is the conscientious verdict of us all'.

At length the coroner proposed to accept the verdict of 'Justifiable Homicide', but 'I shall strike out all the rest':

> *Foreman* — I cannot agree to that, Sir.
> *Jurors* — Nor any of us.
> *Foreman* — Before God and our country, on our solemn oaths, we have given the subject all the consideration in our power . . . If you strike out any part of that it is not our verdict . . .
> *Coroner* — Well! So — you did your duty by giving in a verdict to say that a man is justified in stabbing an unoffending man.

Foreman — If proper measures had been taken, either by reading the Riot Act, or a proclamation, or any other means, we would not bring in a verdict to justify the homicide. Therefore, to let that verdict go abroad alone would be very dangerous, and it might be thought that we justified the stabbing of a policeman who was legally employed.

Coroner — I think that is the fact.

Foreman — No, on the contrary, we wish to give the police every protection . . .

Coroner — So you think that a meeting to overturn the Government was a justification of the homicide?

Foreman — No, Sir, far from it. We are all of us men who have families and some stake in the country. Indeed, I think there is none of us but have some little property. We all of us are of one opinion about the impropriety of that meeting and we are far from liking mob meetings. If the police had acted with propriety we would all of us have turned out to assist and protect them at any risk.

'If we say', another juror added, 'that it is justifiable homicide without that rider it would appear that we approved of any brutal fellow stabbing a policeman in the ordinary execution of his duty.' 'We do not traduce the police nor the Government,' the foreman said. 'We trust that our verdict will prevent the negligence and misconduct which has caused the arms and heads of His Majesty's peaceable subjects to be broken.'

The coroner recorded the verdict in the end, and each juror was escorted to his home by torchlight through cheering crowds. What had been at issue were alternative notions of the rule of law. The verdict was quashed, but not in the minds of the London public. The King, in the person of the Solicitor-General, appealed to the Court of King's Bench, to set the verdict aside. The Court, of course, agreed, and decided that the verdict ought to have been one of 'Wilful Murder'. No legal arguments were given. No further inquest was ordered. The people of Clerkenwell, like the people of Oldham, remain today in suspense.

The rule of law has never been seen, from Calthorpe Street or St Peter's Fields, in the same light as it has been seen from the Court of King's Bench. We have never accepted, in this country, that it means the rule of the people by the army or police. It is an argument, a dialectic, between *both* notions of law which make up the 'institutions' or traditions of this country.

Authority survived these crowds, and the loss of face at such verdicts, and the crowd on its part was bound by its own invisible consensual rules and showed an extraordinary respect for human life. What was unusual about the Calthorpe Street affair was that, not one of the crowd, but a policeman was killed. It was a running argument, which tipped now one way and now the other, and what survived also — and was symbolized by an *unarmed* police — was a consensus that the British people put a value on freedom and democracy so high that, at the cost of a little inefficiency and certain difficulties in government, the police and army must be kept in their place.

I am not, of course, saying that nothing has changed. Some forms of violence and disorder — piracy, highway robbery, huge armed smuggling gangs, Gordon rioters — have gone away. There are today new kinds of threat to civil order, and among these racist and fascist organizations which may require particular measures of control. There are vicious, if infrequent, episodes of terrorism, although this is not altogether new. There are also new forms of sophisticated and capital-intensive criminality, one of whose primary techniques is the penetration of the police. There are changes for the better and the worse, and no simple balance-sheet can be struck.

But loose assertions that the problems of order today are without precedent are assertions that policemen and politicians may favour but which historians cannot support. On the contrary, what may today be without precedent is authority's tetchy dislike of any sign of popular turbulence, as well as the quite exceptional resources and public presence of the police.

Nor is one even sure that 'crime' is what this heavy operation is about. James Anderton, the chief constable of Manchester, recently appeared on the Robin Day show (16 October), and was asked what was the greatest threat to the preservation of law and order today? He reassured us that, looking forward 'from a police point of view' to his next ten or fifteen years in the service, he sees no difficulty in dealing with crime, however serious: 'basic crime, as such, theft, burglary, even violent crime, will not be the predominant police feature'. The threat to 'law and order' today comes from 'seditionists', 'political factions whose designed end is to overthrow democracy as we know it' — persons at work 'in the field of public order', in industrial relations and politics, whose aim is to 'subvert the authority of the state and . . . involve themselves in acts of sedition'. That is where he intends, as commander of an 'immense force', to pack his punch.

One is made a little uneasy by this. Even Robin Day's well-behaved audience did not burst into rapturous applause. For the undermining of democracy is certainly going on, and at an inflationary rate. And it is becoming clear from which quarter the wind is blowing. It is blowing from the quarters of ACPO and from the barracks of the law-and-order brigade.

This is perhaps what 'the public' wants; and, if so, then they must have it. For only 49½ pee they can buy the full set of stamps. And I am left with only a technical objection, a quibble about terms. It is that, if we are to speak of the 'institutions of this country' in an informed historical sense, and of the police among these — that is, if we are to speak of the place in British life in which the police have been tradi-tionally held — then they are the libertarians (whether of the 'extreme Left' — or of any other persuasion) who are trying to *uphold these institutions*, whereas it is the police lobby and its numerous supporters who are trying to discredit them. Not the law-and-order brigade but the defenders of civil liberties are attempting to uphold the constitution and the rule of law.

2 The Rule of the Judges

This is the most remarkable fact about the state of the nation today. Politics and ideology have turned arse-over-tit, yet we still go on mouthing the old rhetoric. Libertarians, some of whom suppose themselves to be revolutionaries, are some of the last to defend our traditions, to care about who we are and how we have done things in the past, to search our precedents and to fight to uphold our constitution. And conservatives of all parties, some of whom are proud to think of themselves as reactionaries, are all for tearing down the structures of the past, modernizing the 'machinery' of government, herding us into new identities (Worcestershire-Herefordshirians or euromarketeers), and inculcating amnesia as to our particular traditions.

They wish to push us into a managed society, whose managing director is money and whose production manager is the police. They have got us half-way inside already. But to finally shut the door upon us they must first brutalize the common law.

One should not be too surprised at this. Such inversions occur in history. But one is surprised all the same. For the very vocal law-and-order lobby is made up, precisely, of those who are most determined to break up our laws and constitutional proprieties and to provoke disorder or to cover flagrant disorderly abuses up.

Lest this be thought to be hyperbole, I must invite readers to consider 'the institutions of this country' and to ask themselves from what quarter these are under 'attack'?

It is not as simple as it might be supposed to draw up a list. A visitor from space, who surveyed our media, would deduce that one of the first institutions of our country was the Pope. Yet that is a mistake. If I was asked to give my professional opinion, under oath, I would have to say that the Pope is not an institution of this country. The papacy may be an excellent thing, but it is an institution of Other Countries.

Not everything that the media is always on about is an institution of our country. NATO is not. NATO is an expensive administrative-military Thing that our country is subjected to under a form of treaty. Disorderly ale-houses, on the other hand, are institutions of our country, and of the greatest antiquity. The authorities have issued orders for their suppression from medieval times. Yet the press is not always on about them, except in Huyton, where drinking after hours has lately been made a felony, subject to summary corporal chastisement with boots and knotted towels.

Another institution of this country is the office of the Director of Public Prosecutions. This is an exceedingly eminent office, which grows more lofty every day. Attorney-Generals conspire in private with him; even ACPO regards him as a fellow peer of the realm. The Director (and his Deputy) are given special license to authorize jury vetting, and when judges find themselves in the least difficulty they appeal to his aid and protection. For a full year, as we shall see, the House of Commons was unable to discuss this matter; but the Director need only nod, and display his wand of office, and a Lord Chief Justice goes scurrying to his chambers. Ill-conditioned persons are no longer dealt with by judges for contempt of court, they are referred to the notice of the Director.

The Director is not answerable to Parliament and it is difficult to see in what sense he is answerable to the law. He is withdrawn from any account, like some fictive *primum mobile* in a Kafka novel. Mr Sam Silkin appeared on that television show (*Man Alive*, 9 October 1979), and it was very evident, from the deference with which he mentioned 'the

Director', which had been the master in his term of office and which had been the man.

This office is not under any attack. On the contrary, the present incumbent, Sir Tony Hetherington, was knighted in a recent honours list, although it was not stated whether this was for his services in shelving the Rhodesia sanctions case, in carrying through the ABC Official Secrets case to its triumphant conclusion, or in preparing so expertly the case against Mr Thorpe.

But to a historian this institution is a stripling. It is younger than the TUC. I do not find a Director in my records. The office was instituted a mere hundred years ago, and for some decades its incumbents occupied an inferior place in the body politic. I cannot allow that, in this ancient realm, the office has yet qualified as an 'institution of this country'.

I have been thinking more of those institutions mentioned in my last article — institutions more properly thought of as traditions: the independence of the judiciary, the paramountcy of Parliament, the accountability of public officers and the rest. And we have had, in the past year or two, an astonishing series of breaches of every one of these traditions, and in every case the breach has been made, not by the 'extreme Left', but by persons known and unknown masquerading as the advocates of law and order.

We have had telephones tapped, mail intercepted, and the citizens' privacy invaded by vetters and compilers of files. We have had Official Secrets privily leaked to right-wing columnists by persons in high public office or in the armed services, and we have seen no trace of even-handedness in the application of justice. We have had several persons (in Newcastle, Liverpool, Southall and Glasgow) who appear to have died at the hands of the police, and others who have been severely injured, and we have had neither prosecutions nor public inquiry.

'From a police point of view,' Sir Robert Mark has written, 'nothing could be worse than to appear to have an enquiry imposed upon the force' (*In the Office of Constable*, p. 177). And it is very evident that Home Secretaries, Attorney-

Generals, and, very certainly, Directors, see things from 'a police point of view':

> Hetherington's relationship with the police is probably better than that of any previous DPP and they are especially pleased at the trouble he takes to attend their social functions. 'I like a pint,' he says. [*The Observer*, 8 October 1978.]

In this genial sociability Sir Tony differs a little from the great ACPO, which instructed the Royal Commission on the Police (1962) (with reference to police conduct) that 'it is always dangerous to become on too intimate terms with people to whom at any time he may have to apply the due process of law' (*State Research*, October 1979).

Of course, if one follows such matters as surface casually from time to time, such as the tangled affairs left by the sudden death of the late Sir Eric Miller, it is evident that more than pints have been accepted both by senior police officers and by ministers of the crown. There has been, in the last three decades, an absolute decline in the standards of public life. But matters such as these — Rhodesia sanction-busting, Crown Agents defaulting, the astonishing episodes of police violence at Huyton police station (*New Statesman*, 24 August 1979) — such matters do not raise the faintest blush upon the cheeks of the advocates of law and order. And why should they? For in many cases the most strident advocates of 'short, sharp shocks' are the same persons as the actual breakers of the law (the leakers of Official Secrets, the privy tamperers with the constitution) and the vendors of disorder.

This may be good class war, but it has nothing to do with the rule of law. The British ruling class has always been hazy about the distinction. But it has, at least, held to a legitimating notion that all was in order because, in the last analysis, Parliament was paramount. And since it could generally find ways of managing Parliament, this was at worst an inconvenience.

This rather old 'institution of this country' is also now in question. I do not mean the actual houses. They are still there, by the Thames. But if we are to consider the bringing of public officials to account, in highly sensitive matters, then Parliament is becoming a no-go area.

The powerful security services are, of course, already utterly beyond parliamentary control or even questioning. These are responsible only to the Prime Minister,* who knows next to nothing about what they are doing, unless (as is said to have been the case with Sir Harold Wilson) they are doing it to him. The activities of the Special Branch enjoy the same immunity. For example, it has been decided — by whom and on what pretext I do not know — that only one parliamentary question in each session may be tabled about telephone-tapping. In 1977 the ministerial reply to that sole question (a request for information) was no more than a negative.

Nor is this all. I was exercised one year ago, as readers may remember (see above, pp. 99-111) by the Attorney-General's guidelines on jury vetting. And some members of Parliament were exercised also. There is a group of MPs with an excellent and principled record in the defence of civil liberties, among them Jo Richardson, Robin Cook, Christopher Price, and Dafydd Elis Thomas. In this most sensitive constitutional area one would suppose that Parliament must be judge of the law. Every measure possible was taken by members to bring the matter forward for debate and every measure failed. Recourse was had to libertarians in the House of Lords, and, once again, procedural impediments proved to be insurmountable. No proper debate, in either House, has yet been held.

The reason why the common law of England was broken with impunity (as I consider to have been the case in the matter of jury vetting) is not that Parliament *could* not intervene but that its managers would not permit it to do so. And the dumb and managed majority of members of all

---

*During the Blunt affair, which blew up after this was written, it became clear that MI5 was fictionally responsible to the Home Secretary and MI6 to the Foreign Secretary, but that this 'responsibility' was honoured as much in the breach as in the observance, and was largely a matter of these services manipulating ministers to serve their own occasions.

parties (supporters of law and order to a man) were only too happy to be allowed to hide their confusion from their constituents in silence. The manager of parliamentary time in that session, the Leader of the House, was that noted libertarian, Michael Foot.

If Parliament is incapable of mounting even a debate about such a delicate point of our constitutional liberties, no doubt we may rest secure in the independence of our press? The media are free. There is no question of censorship. Anyone can start a new publication: Sir James Goldsmith has shown us that.

The state can intervene a little by suppressing public records and by exercising selectively the Official Secrets Acts; and the judges may cast their awful eyes upon us, by *sub judice* rulings and actions for contempt. A little tuning of the pulpits can be done. For example, it has been stated (by David Ross in *Tribune*, 9 February 1979) that in the early stages of the ABC Official Secrets case an off-the-record briefing of newspaper editors and such was held by Mr Callaghan at Number 10 Downing Street. At this it was somehow implied that it was not in the 'public interest' to give too much publicity to the case, since (off the record, of course) it was really 'something concerned with the IRA Provisionals and electronic interception of remotely-fired bombs in Ulster'. At the same time it was put out, off the record, by quarters close to the Law Officers that two of the defendants might only be wrong-headed, but that it was well known to 'Security' that the third was a 'spy'.

I do not wish to believe this story, since I dislike the notion that Number 10 Downing Street and the Law Offices of the Crown serve as centres of black propaganda. The prosecution, when presenting its tedious case in that trial, made no attempt whatsoever to suggest either espionage or any 'Irish connection'. And from my own close knowledge of the case and of the defendants I can say with confidence that these stories (which did indeed surface in the popular press in advance of the trial) were direct and malicious lies, whose authors were guilty of the most flagrant contempt of court.

For the protection of the citizen from the malice or mendacity of our rulers, we are able to turn, of course, to the even-handed justice of our courts of law. No doubt we may rest secure in the independence of our judiciary? But, in questions which are delicate, and which touch upon the interests of the state, I fear that we may not. For the extra-ordinary matter of jury vetting came to light, not through the probity of any judge,* but through the vigilance of defence counsel in the ABC case. And the Attorney-General's guidelines were then smoked out, not on the order of any judge, but in response to an inquiry from John Griffith , Professor of Public Law at London University.

The judges in that case, then ruled that — not the issues of the case being tried before them — but the matter of jury vetting should not be discussed in the press. The matter was hushed up *in camera*. Even Sam Silkin was informed, *in camera*, that, in publishing his guidelines he was in contempt of court. He was not, as it happens, punished upon the spot, nor was he referred to the mercies of the Director. Such even-handed justice was reserved for the 'worst offenders', *Peace News* and the *Leveller*.

In recent weeks another judge has been trying to enact the same scenario but he has met with less success. Editors and producers are returning to a more just sense of themselves. The *Guardian* has shown a sense of public duty, and Mr Justice King-Hamilton — even with the aid of the Director — has been unable to prevent Sam Silkin and Sir Melford Stevenson from exposing themselves in public on BBC's *Man Alive*. There will be repercussions from all these things; and all that we can say, when we consider the freedom of the media as among the 'institutions of this country', is that this very ancient struggle has been resumed.

But we can also see that it would be foolhardy to expect any security for our liberties to come from judges. I do not

---

*There is a small point of literary craftsmanship here. I find, as a working writer, in the year 1979, that it is impossible to bring the two words, 'probity' and 'judge', into conjunction, in any context of public rights, without committing irony, whether intentional or not. I leave the point to literary critics to explain.

know whether our judiciary is independent or not, nor what conversations go on between judges and the Director. It would be improper to raise such questions, since when Professor John Griffith suggested in a small book on the judiciary that there might possibly be sociological or political reasons for the conservative bias evident in some recent judgements, he was accused in the *Times Literary Supplement* of being an intellectual accessory to the Baader-Meinhof gang.

I can say, however, that no British liberty has ever arisen from the decision of judges, although there have been occasions when these liberties have been judicially *defined*, and there have even been upright judges who have imposed just and fair rules of procedure upon the courts. Judges are there to interpret the law and to interpret it with justice. Some judges today may suppose that the rule of law means the rule of the people by any old codger in a wig. They confuse the law with their own persons, and suppose that they (and the Director) are those that rule, and who may instruct the BBC and press as to what is an 'authorized view'. But this is a great mistake. Since judges are the agents and the interpreters of law, there are no persons in the realm who should be more subject to the rule of law than themselves.

That this mistake should now be so commonplace may perhaps be not unrelated to certain sociological and even occupational pressures. I do not know. Judges, after all, do not suddenly appear, bewigged and full-blown, *ex nihilo*. They go through a caterpillar stage before, as lawyers. Then they pupate for a while in silk. And finally they blow in ermine.

In the old days the profession of the law attracted many members of an uppish middle class. Lawyers might have Whiggish propensities, as advocates of the people against the Crown. Or they might have propensities which, while Tory, were profoundly paternalist, in which they could posture as fathers and protectors of the poor.

All this has long gone away. There have been in this century, and there still are, outstanding and liberal-minded advocates. But this minority, for the purposes of promotion, put themselves out of court. A few have been permitted to pupate, but scarcely a single one to blow in ermine as a judge.

Yet this is not where I ground my objection. I am willing to accept that judges are political conservatives, if they are learned in the law and their reasons are clear. We have had, in this century, conservative judges who were men of learning; when they went into the robing-room, they made an effort to put off the Tory and put on the judge. What then they offered as a rule was not their persons but the law. My objection is that judges today are bred up in a different course.

It is not to be supposed that our judges, even in the highest courts of appeal, do not show a tenderness towards certain rights. If one follows law reports one gains some notion as to which rights these are, and what our judges are now tender about.

Thus my eye was caught by the law report (*The Times*, 24 November 1979) of a case heard on appeal in the House of Lords before Lord Wilberforce, Viscount Dilhorne, Lord Salmon, Lord Edmund-Davies and Lord Keith of Kinkel. The case was that of Vestey v. Inland Revenue Commissioners, and it concerned (the facts were not in dispute) a little matter of tax avoidance. Baron Vestey and Sir Edmund Vestey had, in 1942, fixed up discretionary trusts outside the United Kingdom and settled on these 'certain specified overseas property which included an annual rental of £960,000'; the very substantial income from these trusts has been paid out as 'capital' from time to time to children, grandchildren and other Vestey descendants (including sums totalling £2,608,000 to six British taxpayers between 1962 and 1966). The Inland Revenue Commissioners, goaded beyond endurance, had come down on these six taxpayers with heavy assessments, and the point of law at issue was whether these beneficiaries of a tax-avoiding arrangement should be penalized (by paying tax) although they themselves had no part in the avoidance which set up the trusts. Their lordships — Lord Wilberforce sounding off first and at length — unanimously upheld the appeal of the taxpayers, and liberated them from the attentions of the Inland

Revenue.

This is all, no doubt, in order, and according to law. The Inland Revenue had, perhaps, been somewhat ham-fisted in its handling of the matter. It may be noted that, in liberating the appellants from tax, their lordships had to take the unusual step of overruling two previous and directly contrary decisions in the House of Lords (1948 and 1955) — decisions which have guided the Inland Revenue in the past thirty years.

But this was not what caught my eye. My eye, which is undisciplined in law, was caught by more marginal matters. I noted, for example, that Baron and Sir Edmund Vestey managed to transport this substantial income out of the United Kingdom and into a tax-haven in *1942*, at a time when our cities were being heavily bombed, when this country was supposedly at the crisis of a titanic struggle with European fascism, and when every resource of citizens was being called for in the struggle. I noted also that an 'annual rental of £960,000', if at 1942 values, must have represented a princely domain — something whose removal from this country would have required more than a Pickford van. Most of all, what caught my eye was the headline to the report: 'ARBITRARY, UNJUST AND FUNDAMENTALLY UNCONSTITUTIONAL'.

To be honest — for I am uncurably optimistic and sentimentally disposed to hope for justice from judges — I had glanced at the headline and had thought: 'Ah! A Daniel — *five* Daniels — come to justice! At *last*, the highest tribunal in the land has turned its eye downward and noted some grave miscarriage of justice, some intrusion by the state upon individual or public rights!' But this was not it at all. I might have known. What made Lord Wilberforce reach for these large comminatory adjectives was not any offence by power to persons. He was on about the Rights of Money. 'It was respect for the fabric of our fiscal law' that persuaded his Lordship that the prior (and contrary) decisions of the House of Lords should be overruled. The grand money-lake established by the Vesteys in 1942 must continue to flow, by some thirty irrigation channels, to its beneficiaries today, as 'capital', free from 'arbitrary' or 'unconstitutional' tax.

I will not make the same mistake again. I must recognize that what the higher regions of the law are now about, when they are not about crime or state prosecutions, is money. And money must find its ways and means. Some of the most eminent barristers are those whose expertise is, exactly, in finding 'loopholes' in the law: that is, in breaking the law by legal means. They are employed in the service of those who are working out means of avoiding tax and estate duties, setting up evasive trusts, engineering property-development and outwitting planning officers, promoting and merging companies in dubious ways, scrutinizing complex legislation to find the pin-hole of unsealed logic through which money can make its leaky way.

This is to say that the law today can be a profoundly corrupting profession, not in Sir Robert Mark's sense of 'bent lawyers' (if these exist they operate at greatly inferior regions and they will never pupate), but in its more rewarded sectors from which some judges are drawn.

Let us hazard a scenario. Let us suppose that one day one of these expert legal law-breakers catches the eye of the Lord Chancellor's office. Lo and behold, he pupates, he blows, he is a judge! Are we to suppose that he is instantly transformed, as by a wand? That he becomes overnight the scrupulous custodian of the people's liberties, deeply learned in all manner of precedents as to public rights? No, it is more difficult than that. For his mind is still far away, pondering how Parnassus Carparks Incorporated might block up an ancient right of way and enhance the value of its site, or how certain insurers might evade their payments to a client.

I mention this only so that we should learn some patience and charity towards our judges. No doubt at all, each judge will seek to perform his duty according to the law and his own conscience. But it will be no easy matter for a professional law-breaker to mend his habits overnight. His knowledge of the law may commence with the Limited Liability Act of 1862. Whether bred up in the civil or criminal law, employed by the Director or by private offenders, he will have had little occasion to leaf through precedents as to public rights. As for his conscience, he may not recall where he put that down a decade or two before. Even if he should succeed in making over his nature anew, there will always be the danger of recidivism.

I have no particular judge in mind. I am pointing to a general difficulty. I know less about judges than I should, and so do we all. Nor have I any wish to incur contempt of court. The *sub judice* rule protecting cases under process is proper.

But I cannot allow that judges have the power to place the most sensitive liberties of a nation *sub judice*, nor to pretend that there is an 'authorized view' of a matter like jury vetting and that this view may only be given by a judge. We have seen, on two occasions in the past fourteen months, a judge stopping a trial and ordering a new jury panel, not because the first panel was improperly vetted, but (as it seems to a layman) because *it had become known to the public and the jury* that it had been so vetted, with some of the details of this fact.

We are not to have this kind of thing, and then to be told that it is law. We are not to have judges and Directors telling editors what they may publish, when it concerns the most sensitive customs of a nation. We are not to have the integrity of the jury, and the gross invasion of the privacy of citizens by the police, treated as 'confidential matters' to be tampered with behind *in camera* screens, and their public discussion to be referred to the Director as 'an outrageous intrusion' under laws unnamed.

We are not to have judges attending on producers at the BBC, under some new doctrine of the pre-emptive judicial strike, to tell them at what point a programme must be faded out.* We are not to have judges' robing-rooms beside every TV studio.

*It is perhaps not generally known that Mr Justice King-Hamilton, who was then presiding over the trial of 'anarchists' at the Old Bailey, attended in person at a preview of BBC TV *Man Alive* programme on jury vetting (9 October, 1979), vetoed certain items in that programme, and dictated when one panel discussant (from the National Council of Civil Liberties) should be faded out.

There are worse offences to the body politic than contempt of court, and these are contempt of our constitutional history and contempt of the people of this country.

3 Trial by Jury

As I was saying, I know less about judges than I should. I have known only one judge who has taken his ease and taken me into his confidence on public matters, and he was a retired judge of the old school, chatting away on *Man Alive* (9 October 1979). It would be unfair to suppose that Sir Melford Stevenson was giving us an 'authorized view' of jury vetting. His first duty was to entertain the viewers, and he improvised a splendid period act.

I do not have an exact note, but it *appeared* that Sir Melford was saying that the Attorney-General's guidelines were a lot of flannel (some parts of which 'might have been written by the Salvation Army'), and that all experienced Old Bailey judges, court officials and jury bailiffs knew a great deal more about these age-old practices than has yet come before the public eye; and, further, that any outcry about vetting was stirred up by self-interested exhibitionists, and that, since all responsible persons know that there are irresponsible and undesirable persons who are best kept off juries, and that there are privy ways and means of ensuring this, it would be much better to let matters lie.

Letting matters lie, or lying, has been the mode through-out this affair. Two successive Lord Chancellors have also let the matter lie. Lord Hailsham has let it be understood that he cannot intervene in the matter of vetting, since the guidelines are in the province of the Attorney-General and the Home Secretary is in the province of the police. Turn the wheel of justice as you will, it will always come to rest upon an orotund negative:

> The Law is the true embodiment
> Of everything that's excellent.
> It has no kind of fault or flaw,
> And I, my Lords, embody the Law.

As it happens, I have no wish to quarrel with Lord Hailsham on this point of law. The Attorney-General's ill-drawn guidelines were instructions to the prosecution and the police as to their procedures. Since they set to work the powers of the state to poke into the affairs of citizens, and perhaps to manipulate justice, they deeply concerned Parliament and the public. But they could not be supposed to concern a Lord Chancellor. They had, and have, no force at law whatsoever, being administrative instructions to one party only. This lets Lord Hailsham off the hook.

This does not, however, let judges off the hook, since if a judge observes any practice creeping into the courts which gives improper advantage to either party, it is his business to bring that practice to an end. From the start of this affair it has been in the power of any judge to forbid the practice in the case before him, and to refer it to higher places for judgement or redress.

One would suppose that the distinction between the rules of a prosecutor's office and the rules of a court of law was one which could be understood by even a judicial mind. That judges cannot always see such nice distinctions may be the result of the current drift of things, by which they are encouraged to see themselves, along with the A-G and the DPP and ACPO and NATO, as part of an undifferentiated clump, an integrated law-and-order *bloc*.

The pitiful judicial excuse, which has been identified as a new theory of 'negative law' (*Guardian* correspondence, 15 October 1979), by which anything may be done (at least by the state) which is not explicitly prohibited by statute, is not a theory of justice but a large name for a hole.

And it is not altogether clear that the Lord Chancellor is off the hook. The Courts Act (1971) provided that the Lord

Chancellor's office should have overall control of jury panels. It is not to be supposed that the present incumbent, Lord Hailsham, is uninterested in the question of the jury. On other occasions he has been able to act with resolution.

My old law books show that it was always the custom to draw up jury-panel lists, with the names and places of abode of jurors 'with their titles and additions'. 'Additions' indicated status or style and it passed into the custom of citing occupation, or trade. This was for centuries regarded as a necessary safeguard for both parties in a court, and a safeguard upon which was grounded the equally ancient right of challenge. For a juror's occupation might, as any social historian can confirm, predispose that juror to particular bias: for example, a juror might hold an office of profit under the crown, or under Securicor or the like. In 1973, in the law vacation, without consulting Parliament, Lord Hailsham struck this ancient custom out.

In 1977 there was enacted by a Labour ministry the Criminal Law Act, in pursuance of the recommendations of the James committee, a committee pricked by Lord Hailsham and Mr Robert Carr, and whose recommendations pursued, in their turn, the recommendations of ACPO and Sir Robert Mark. ('Everything that he writes about crime, policemen and policing needs to be taken extremely seriously,' Lord Hailsham has noted of Sir Robert's recent book.)

What the Criminal Law Act did was to remove, with a single sweep of the scythe, whole categories of offences from the crown courts to summary jurisdiction, extinguishing in the same swift motion the right of the accused to opt for trial by jury. Sir Robert Mark and ACPO had been offended by the high rate of acquittals by jury trial following upon the Notting Hill carnival of 1976. It was not directly stated that the verdicts found were false or perverse. The term used by the police is 'too high a failure rate'.

Efficient universities and training colleges will qualify all but a handful of drop-outs, and an efficient administration of justice will have the highest possible rate of success. It will move the accused smoothly through its process and graduate every one at the end as guilty. Anything short of this is not only time-wasting but costly. And, next to law and order, the highest priority of civilized society is the saving of tax.

The efficacy of an efficient administration of justice was at once demonstrated in cases arising from the Grunwick picketing. And it has also been demonstrated, week after week, by stipendiaries deciding cases which arose from the Southall affair, where the satisfactory overall success rate of 87 per cent convictions has been found. For public order offences — obstruction, conduct conducive to breaches of the peace, assault on constables, along with night poaching, etcetera, etcetera (*Criminal Law Act*, 1977, Section 16) — were among the categories removed from optional jury trial in 1977. It is now only necessary for a responsible policeman to read through his old notes and — no matter the number and quality of witnesses for the defence — a responsible stipendiary magistrate can ensure that justice is done.

Lord Hailsham has not yet announced his intention to repeal the Criminal Law Act. It is to be supposed that he is well satisfied with the course of innovation. He has never been a hidebound man. He gets around, and addresses comfortable audiences on heavier sentencing. He rides a bicycle to work.

I remember him well, as the first politician who swam into my boyish notice when, under the name of Hogg, he fought a famous by-election in my constituency of Oxford as a zealous supporter of Neville Chamberlain and of his diplomatic triumph at Munich. Hogg was no respecter of persons, and certainly not of the person of his respected opponent, A.D. Lindsay, the Master of Balliol. He had a reputation for being flamboyant and intemperate, a sort of dummy run for Mr Heseltine.

Public life is enriched by the colour of such characters. I make no objection to them. I prefer them to dry, retiring fellows, such as conduct their business privily and issue guidelines in secret. What bothers me is that fellows of this order — indeed, of *both* orders — come forward before the public and offer themselves as advocates of 'law and order', and even of *Tradition*! For there has never been such a bonfire of our ancient laws and customs as has taken place in the last decade, and dancing around the leaping flames like dervishes we find, not the raging revolutionaries of the 'extreme Left', but Lord Hailsham, Mr Silkin, the judges in their ermine, the peers of the realm of ACPO, the bankers and suburban Tory housewives, and all the law-and-order brigade.

This is the change that has come over things. In my old history books it had been the custom that the accused might submit to the jurisdiction of magistrates, or he might 'put himself upon his country'. That is, the accused might opt for trial by his peers in a higher court, thus risking the chance of a heavier sentence in the event of a conviction. Lord Hailsham may suppose that by 'peers' was intended trial by himself and his fellow Lords, but it is not so.

The innocent, the aggrieved, the optimistic, the cunning, and the rich often opted for such trial. But that — or half of that — is now all blown away. You may be a lady member of Parliament who remonstrates with a policeman who is thumping a fellow picket, and you may be thumped and dragged by your hair into a police van in your turn, but you may not now opt to put yourself upon your country. You may be an innocent bystander, a British citizen of Asian origin and a naive admirer of British justice and the British police, who is caught up in an indiscriminate police sally and is swept by happenstance into the courts, but you may not put yourself upon what you had thought had become your country. Your country, in any case, had yawned throughout the passage of the Criminal Law Act and it is yawning still.

The other half of our customs is still half there. Juries survive, for restricted categories of 'serious crimes', although the Criminal Law Act (section 16) has invented elaborate procedures to dissuade the accused from opting for jury trial. And ACPO has recently sent its messenger to the Royal Commission on Criminal Procedure to demand majority verdicts in juries at the rate of 2:1 or 3:2 and 'a closer control of the selection of juries' to remove all persons who are 'irresponsible or criminally dishonest'.

I am sorry if the question of the jury may seem to have become my King Charles's head. For it is rather older than that: and juries of presentment or inquest may perhaps go back to the verge of Domesday. Readers must put my obsession down as an occupational disorder attendant upon my trade. At every side of my desk there are old books in which I may discover reminders of a different kind of law and a different notation of order.

If I turn to an eighteenth-century compendium of the laws which was placed by the desk at every JP at that time, and turn up the entry under 'Jurors', I find that the normally businesslike author suddenly breaks into eloquence:

> Trial by juries is the *Englishman's* birth right, and it is that happy way of trial, which notwithstanding all revolutions of the times, hath been continued beyond all memory to this present day; the beginning whereof no history specifies, it being contemporary with the foundations of this state, and one of the pillars of it, both as to age and consequence. [Richard Burn, *The Justice of the Peace*, 1754.]

And there follow some thirty pages of precedents, rules and provisos, as to the manner of challenging and the safeguarding of the jury's integrity and rights.

I am not so silly as to suppose that an institution is good just because it is old. Hanging is old but it never was much good. I am not opposed to innovation, when it follows upon due deliberation and public debate. I would even be willing, after this long time of argument, to assent to the abolition of the House of Lords. I will not stand in the way of change.

But, equally, I do not think that each generation is well advised to act as if it had never had a past. I would not give it a clean slate and a piece of chalk and invite it to design its institutions from nothing. I would remind the ideologues of the Rights of Money, the wholesale modernizers, and those who are impatient to submit our constitution to a general euromassacre, of the words of Burke: 'By their violent haste and their defiance of the process of nature, they are delivered blindly to every projector and adventurer, to every alchymist and empiric.' Today we have a projector on every bench and an alchymist upon the woolsack.

It is a matter of striking a balance. Not every institution that is old is of equal value. There have been reasons for most of them, but not every reason holds equal force with the passage of time. Some have been supported only by the reasons of privilege and class, and in a democracy these should be put away.

But there are others which are of a different order. Around them have accreted precedents of a different kind. That is, they have been the locus of intense historic struggles, the swaying to-and-fro motions of the contest between social classes. Each precedent signifies a contest between privilege and liberty, lost, gained, or held in the balance; and certain precedents have been signed in blood. Such institutions have proved to be flexible, capable of modification through centuries of conflict, and even, after protracted struggles, of reform.

These are not just any 'institutions' but traditions of a particular kind. They are institutions of a defining kind. They define who we are. They are rules which may sometimes seem to trammel and limit us, but at the same time they limit the powers of those who would rule us and push us about. They are at one and the same time rules of conduct and the places where we fight about those rules.

Each new generation will interrogate these inherited rules. It will be ruled by them only if they command assent. There is no such abstract entity as the Rule of Law, if by this is meant some ideal presence aloof from the ruck of history, which it is the business of judges to 'administer' and of policemen to 'enforce'. That is all ideology. It used to be the ideology of kings and despots. It is now the ideology of the authoritarian state. South Africa and Russia have a Rule of Law of that kind, and no doubt it is well administered and enforced.

If I have argued elsewhere that the rule of law is an 'unqualified human good' (*Whigs and Hunters*, p. 266) I have done so as a historian and a materialist. The rule of law, in this sense, must always be historically, culturally, and, in general, nationally specific. It concerns the conduct of social life, and the regulation of conflicts, according to rules of law which are exactly defined and have palpable and material evidences — which rules attain towards consensual assent and are subject to interrogation and reform. That this itself is an ideal definition, which takes little account of social and ideological determinants of property and class, and which has never been matched by social reality, does not mean that the aspiration towards that state is not a human good.

In this specific sense, there are certain institutions and traditions of each nation which must carry an exceptional sensitivity. They are those little places of account into which a prodigious sum of the capital of liberty has been invested. In British history the jury is exactly such a place of account.

It is chilling to read a former Attorney-General (Sam Silkin in *The Observer*, 11 November 1979) instructing the public that random selection of juries 'is neither in principle nor in practice inviolable. It is merely one of many methods of ensuring as fair a trial as possible.' As to *practice*, he may well know more than does the public: as to the *principle*, it may be 'one of many methods' but it happens to be the method which has lodged in our constitution and been sanctioned by our customs 'beyond all memory to this present day'. I suppose that Mr Silkin has more convenient methods in mind . . . such as Diplock Courts?

Silkin's is only one in a chorus of strident, modernizing voices which are heard today. These often instruct us that the only point at issue is whether, in general, juries find 'true' verdicts — or whether cheaper and swifter methods might be found.

The point is an interesting one, although the answer must be that we do not know, since only a particular jury knows why, in a case which others find 'questionable', it has found its verdict to be true. Recent empirical studies give divergent results; and they are unanimous only in showing that the sensational accusations against juries raised by ACPO and Sir Robert Mark — that 'perverse' acquittal rates were soaring, that professional criminals were escaping conviction, etc. — that these accusations, which stampeded Home Secretaries, Royal Commissions and the James Committee, were without reputable scholarly foundation. In one of the most careful recent studies (J. Baldwin and M. McConville, *Jury Trials*, 1979) it is shown that a percentage of verdicts are, in the view of judges, counsel and police, questionable or capricious.

That has always been so. In my own view the juries of today appear to be *less* capricious and prejudiced, on certain matters, than the 'middle-class, middle-minded' juries of the past. But the place of the jury in our constitutional history does not rest on a naive belief that every jury verdict must be true, rational and humane.

It rests upon a total view of the relation between the legislature, judiciary and the people; upon a notion of justice in which the law must be made to seem rational and even humane to lay jurors (hence inhibiting a thousand oppressive processes before they are even commenced, through the knowledge that no jury would convict); and upon a particular national history of contests between 'the people' and the Crown or state, in which the jury has won and reserved for itself, in its verdict, a final power.

I cannot go over that history once again. Nor is there need to do so, since it has been rehearsed with lucidity by Lord Devlin, some years ago, in *Trial by Jury* (1956). And this same Lord Devlin, to whom I offer an unreserved apology for my general aspersions against the judiciary, has now issued from his retirement a formidable restatement of all these points, and an unqualified warning that, if things go on as they are going now, the jury has only 'another half-century or so of life to be spent in the sort of comfortable reservation which conquerors, bringing with them a new civilization, assign to the natives whom they are displacing' (Patrick Devlin, *The Judge*, Chapter 5).

When we learn, from Lord Devlin in 1956, that trial by jury is 'the lamp that shows that freedom lives'; or from a textbook which JPs consulted over 200 years ago that trial by juries was 'the Englishman's birthright', and it has 'survived all revolutions of times', and that it is 'contemporary with the foundations of this state', I am unable to turn away and hide a snigger in my hand. I must ask myself, what is the revolution of the times which struck us suddenly ten years or so ago, like a typhoon, and swept seven hundred years of practice and of precedent away?

Over this long time the persons qualified for jury service has undergone change, and in general this has been as part of the wider struggle for democratic practice. Householders, some women, and eventually nearly all electors have been admitted to the jury box, inheriting both the 'birthright' and the expectations of the past. This has not been done without public debate. Indeed, it has taken at times immense pressure and a generation of agitation to overcome the resistance of the judiciary and the legislature. This has not been the work of 'projectors and adventurers'.

But what of the work of the last few years? Since the 'foundations of this state' until 1967 it had been the custom of the land that the verdict of the jury must be unanimous. Now we can purchase justice at a discount of 20 per cent, and my Lords of ACPO would have it at 33 per cent or 40 per cent.

I do not object to this innovation overmuch, although it was never based upon sound argument or research. We had managed, from the foundations of this state, without such watering, but then we had managed with hanging also. A miscarriage of justice, which might have been averted by one stubborn juror (and I have a note of such cases) might perhaps be corrected today without an exhumation order. I am willing to suppose that we may get justice from ten out of twelve of our fellow citizens. But I will not have the watering of the verdict at any higher rate.

For centuries the accused had a right to 'put himself upon his country'. This was a *right*, and it was claimed as the birthright of the 'freeborn'. The accused might not be a freeman of the city, nor an elector, nor even a male, but this right was jealously maintained. In 1977, without public discussion, in large categories of cases, this right was taken away.

This is by no means the end to the tinkering and watering. The custom of the land has been random jury selection, corrected by the right of challenge, to remove persons with evident bias against either party before the court. Lord Hailsham, as we have seen, by striking out occupations in 1973, removed the main ground upon which challenge (with or without cause) might be made. In the Criminal Law Act, 1977, section 43, the number of challenges without cause

THE MUGGERS

allowed to the defence was reduced to the unprecedentedly low figure of three. Challenge (or 'standby') on the part of the Crown remained uncontrolled.

Over some seven hundred years the right has been established of summoning a jury of inquest, and in particular in cases of murder or manslaughter — as, for example, when disturbance, or the use of troops or police against crowds, raised issues of public concern. Such a jury remained mandatory until the Criminal Law Act, 1977, section 56 (2), when the right was quietly mugged.* Puff! And seven centuries are blown away! This is the reason why the inquest upon Blair Peach has been repeatedly delayed, and why we have had this scandalous interval in which memories of identification fade and beards have been allowed to grow.

From 'the foundations of this state' practices were evolved to protect the integrity of the jury, and — at least in theory — to safeguard it from undue influence from the Crown. In 1974 an Attorney-General dropped his guidelines into the privy conduit which runs from his office to the Director, the chief constables and the prosecuting counsel.

And why, so suddenly, has all this discounting, vetting, and tampering been going on? Is it because of some unprecedented dangers to the state, which must make Mr Silkin and Sir Tony Hetherington and Lord Hailsham constitute themselves into a Committee of Public Safety? Is it because the public mind has been agitated, and the public will has demanded revolutionary change? Is it because authority is afraid of *us*?

Alas, I fear it is not even that. The learned editor of the standard edition of the Criminal Law Act 1977 tells us that there is one reason only for this wide-ranging measure: 'modernization'. Modernizing authority finds democratic practice to be inconvenient. It has no use for Lord Devlin's fusty old lamp. It can manage us better in the dark, when it has put out all our rights.

Antiquity, in a place of this sensitivity, does seem to me to be a serious matter. Take the jury away, and I would face a

---

*See 'Law Report', above pp. 187-8.

crisis of identity. I would no longer know who the British people are. I cannot find polite words for these who, in the space of a few years, have chucked one part of this away and are tampering with the rest. They are the muggers of the constitution and the vandals of the jury box. These are the miscreants who are seeking to undo the rule of law.

4 Anarchy and Culture

It is because I am sentimental about juries that I began to look into other things. Attorney-Generals and judges who can mug the jury system are capable of anything. I began to look about me. I began to subscribe to *State Research*. I studied at the feet of Chapman Pincher and Sir Robert Mark.

It is a time to watch out for footpads behind the hedge-rows of legislation, to peer anxiously into the dark courts, and to expect assassins of our liberties in the short cuts of administration. It may even be a time to watch out for provocations. It was to enlighten the public mind as to the threat to public order that the Nazis put the Reichstag in flames.

It is not necessary to suppose that high positions in our state have been infiltrated by persons of fascist persuasion. A few such 'sleepers' may have lodged themselves in the security services and the Special Patrol Group. But in general the ideologists of order today are authoritarians of an *ad hoc* kind; they suppose that they are not ideologists at all. They do not consult their consciences, they consult immediate convenience.

The thing about our rulers today is that every one wishes to be an 'executive'. They want to be managers and issue orders. They want to modernize things. That is why they wish to bring our constitution into contempt.

It is true that our constitution is of a peculiar and indefinite kind. Indeed, it is widely supposed that, because we have no written constitution, with subordinate clauses and amendments, we have none. That is an error which, two centuries ago, might have drawn down upon one an indictment for sedition.

Written constitutions are either for nations which are young (or reborn after imperial rule) or for regimes which are stiff-jointed and insecure and need a suit of armour to hold them up. Unwritten constitutions nourish ambiguities; they mark out the limits of the field, but the field remains in a state of play.

The law-and-order brigade, in 1979, is uncertain which way to jump. They oscillate between being Written Constitutionalists and no constitutionalists at all. If the trade unions look vigorous, or if Money is uneasy, then the cry goes up for a new suit of armour for property to put on. Not long ago, when Lord Hailsham was temporarily out of office, he volunteered to occupy his leisure hours in writing a new constitution for us. That was handsome in him, and unhandsome in us to pass the offer by.

But Lord Hailsham is back in office and has something else to occupy his time. Interest in the question has become slack, with the general turn of the conservative tide. If persons of sound and authorized view are dominant in almost every field of life, from the civil service to the judiciary, from ACPO to the BBC, a constitution of that kind could even be an impediment. If one is slaughtering the opposition, left and centre, why should one bring onto the field a strict referee?

It is simpler to act as if (some small pieces apart — the monarchy, the House of Lords) we have no constitution whatsoever. What then becomes legitimate is whatever authority can get away with. Since governments and ministers are in the public eye, execution can more easily be carried out by surreptitious means. It is all done today by senior civil servants and the like, and by a new set of instruments — discretionary powers, enabling acts, guidelines, circular instructions, injunctions, *in camera* decisions, Orders in the law vacation.

If a private citizen tries to peer into the state today, it seems like nothing so much as a huge aquarium, filled with

inky water and flourishing weeds. The weeds are the Official
Secrets Acts and the water is dark with 'confidential matter'.
The aquarium is populated only with shadows. Some little
fish flick past in schools, but they are anxious of the great
predators which lie upon the mud or which, like Permanent
Secretaries, dart from the shadows of a Ministry to the tangled
shelter of private industry.

Big fish eat little fish and the great fish eat the big. But all
fish have a common interest in the dirty water and the
weeds. The water is the sink of ideological legitimation in
which alone they can survive and maintain their predatory
style of life. The weeds protect them from public scrutiny
or account. Clean up the tank and put them in water of a
clear constitution and they would not live.

This is known to careful observers, and some part of the
public is getting a sense that this is so. But it is not easy to
follow a shadow through an inky maze. In a remarkable
paper in the current number (October/November 1979) of
State Research these skilled icthyographers follow one
shadow through its habitat of Emergency Powers and Army
Regulations in the matter of the use of troops and police
in strikes.

It is an important document, and it is a civic duty to study
it. The most lucid précis could not do justice to the tortuous
procedures by which our liberties today may, at the cough of
an 'emergency' (or even without), be put into the hands of
unknown and unaccountable bodies like the Civil
Contingencies Unit in the Cabinet Office. In short, troops
and police may now be employed for almost anything, and
especially as strike-breakers, and without any constitutional
controls.

I will comment on one matter only. The crucial points
where our constitutional rules and precedents have been
exchanged for arbitrary powers have been outside the debates
of Parliament and shielded from public knowledge. Thus it
has been a crux of our evolving constitution that the troops,
in civil disputes, should be subject to the civil power. That
the police must be subject to the civil power — and are,
indeed, one of its arms — has gone without question.

The standing army was brought within the control of Parliament in 1688, and this was one reason why our ancestors thought that settlement was 'glorious'. The police, from its origin, was held within the control of elected local authorities. Where force was used against a crowd, this force was supposed to be under the authority of civil magistrates or perhaps of the mayor, who was *ex officio* a JP. This has not been, in our history, a small matter at all, a mere procedural *caveat*. There are hundreds of precedents, some passionately contested, out of which this constitutional principle has evolved.

So matters drifted down to us, with arguments — modifications — accessions of civil power and reversals, until some time around 1973. Still, at that distant date, troops and police might be brought into a number of normally extra-legal functions, including strike-breaking, but only during a 'State of Emergency', which state must be proclaimed and renewed each month by Parliament. In 1977 the government (Labour), during the firemen's strike, by a brutal misconstruction of a different Act (passed in order to empower the use of troops during natural disasters such as floods), dispensed with parliamentary sanction for an 'Emergency'. Even so, the employment of troops was contrary to Queen's Regulations, so that the Defence Council quietly rewrote Regulation J 11.004b *some months later* (June 1978), without reference to Parliament.

Parallel to this another adjustment was made. The constitutional position in those ancient times (1973) was that troops and police might act in such extra-legal ways only in response to requests from the 'civil authority', which authority had become defined as a magistrate or mayor. But in the Administration of Justice Act (1973) the *ex officio* office of JP was removed from mayors. A hiatus was left, through which the most terrible disorder might flow.

Good citizen, relax. In 1976 it emerged that the 'civil authority' had been redefined *as the police*! It is unclear who redefined it so — perhaps some piranha fish lurking in inky obscurity. It was announced, in a letter to the Cobden Trust, from the Ministry of Defence, as a trivial matter of routine administrative tidying-up.

The police, in such cases, had therefore become their own authority, the authors of their own powers. But the troops might resent being placed under the orders of constables. So a further adjustment was made, in the deepest recesses of the inky tank. Roy Jenkins announced (*Hansard*, 8 April 1976) that the power to request the employment of troops now rested with him. We may hope that this was in his office as Home Secretary, since it would be inconvenient if he had carried off the powers with him to Brussels.*

So what we had supposed to be a critical constitutional principle of this country was spirited away, after three hundred years. As our icthyographers report, 'these changes were made without reference to Parliament and were in conflict with the common law'.

An illustration of how things are now may be taken from Great Yarmouth, on the weekend of 27 October 1979. The National Front held their annual conference here, with a maximum of 400 delegates. The local trades council and Anti-Nazi League organized a peaceful picket and protest demonstration of a few hundred people.

In response to this 3,000 police were alerted, of whom 1,500 were marched in battalions up and down the streets. Road-blocks were set up; cars were stopped; persons were searched. Patrol boats and police divers lurked in Yarmouth Bay, to ward off a sea-borne attack. The environs of the pier were cordoned off; fishing was banned; the seafront was a no-go area; local residents were admitted only on proof of identity; a wedding reception was forced to look for new quarters; the Saturday business of traders came to an end.

Floodlights surrounded the 'prohibited' area; visors and

---

*According to Peter Hennessy, in an important series of articles in *The Times*, the police *may* call directly on the military after all. This has been decided, not in Parliament, but privately in Whitehall', in a recess too muddy for the observation of even skilled icthyographers. A chief constable who 'sees his men becoming overwhelmed' may call in the military without asking a JP, mayor, the Home Secretary or Defence Secretary (*The Times*, 20 November 1979). It was because JPs thought that someone might be 'overwhelmed' that the Yeomanry were sent in at Peterloo. Major-General Kitson is now training staff officers at Camberley for such eventualities.

dog-handlers were in evidence. Special magistrates courts awaited eagerly for custom. 'The area resembled a scene from Belfast', wrote a reporter in the *Yarmouth Mercury* (2 November).

But nothing happened. Not an egg was thrown. Nor did anyone local *expect* anything to happen. The cost of the operation was variously reported as being one-quarter and one-half a million pounds. The national media, BBC TV excepted, did not report the story, and I fear that it may be an Official Secret — although if one brick had been thrown at a policeman we may be sure that this would have hit every front page.

Yet it is not quite true that *nothing* happened. For it was either a grotesque case of over-reaction, or else it was an exercise, almost a war exercise. As the *Yarmouth Mercury* noted, 'there is no harm in providing the police with a real, live situation to test them to the limits'. It was a rehearsal for the 'real, live situations' ahead, whether in strike-bound Norwich or in response to anti-nuclear demonstrations at Lakenheath.

It was also another little test of the constitutional questions which I have been noting. For this operation was very certainly not under the direction of the 'civil power', which power will, however, have to meet half of the bill. Before the event the Mayor and Chief Executive of Yarmouth met the police and were *told* something of their operational plans. But, as with county police committees these days (whose constituencies rarely correspond with those of the forces supposedly within their control), all 'operational' matters have passed beyond scrutiny or even inquiry by the civil power.

This is all in a state of normalcy. No 'State of Emergency', whether direct or devious, was here. The police were sole authors of it all. But the present point is to observe the *style* of things these days. Some peculations of our liberties obtain formal parliamentary sanction, but in such obscure ways that MPs may be forgiven for not knowing that they are doing them.

This sort of privy fiddling is going on *all the time*. The

mugging of the jury of inquest in 1977 is one example (above, p. 235). Or there is another of Sam Silkin's exploits, when Attorney-General in 1978. He then wrote out new 'regulations' which relinquished certain powers to bring the Director of Public Prosecutions to account. Then early in 1979 a bill was introduced, heaping new powers upon the Attorney-General to transfer, by Order, new powers upon the Director. It was intended that all this should pass 'on the nod', and would have done so, had not two back-benchers (Christopher Price and Jeff Rooker) as well as certain Lords (for we still have that constitutional defence) obstructed the way. We may expect the bill to return in this session (see John Griffith in the *New Statesman*, 19 October 1979).

Or turn to *The Scotsman* (17 and 18 October 1979). Here are details of Crown Office Circular No. 1643, headed 'Warnings to Accused Persons'. This document may not be especially heinous: I known nothing of Scottish law. What it does, in certain minor offences (which may include breach of the peace), is to authorize police to issue Warnings in lieu of prosecutions. No legal process will be involved, whether due or undue.

It is a gentle measure and no penalties are attached. What is new is that the Warnings will be recorded, and entered in a national register, and they may have a force not unlike that of a previous conviction. It is an elegant means of enforcement, since, with neither juries nor magistrates to contend with, the 'success rate' is likely to be high, and even higher than that of Mr Canham, a stipendiary taking cases arising from the Southall affair, whose success rate has been reported at only 93 per cent.

What is nice about Crown Office Circular No. 1643 is the date of its issue: 3 May 1979, the date of the general election. It was signed by a person called a Crown Agent. It came out of a hiatus between governments. While Scottish electors were zealously trooping to the polls to elect a government to rule the law, this little bit of law popped up, unheralded, and out of a hole.

But I have been carried away by the fun of the thing and am misleading readers. For this Circular did not pop up, on

3 May 1979, at all. It popped up, on 17 October, on the front page of *The Scotsman*, and, one presumes, it did so only because of a leak by some public-spirited official. The comment of the Scottish Solicitor-General, Nicholas Fairbairn, was severe, not in the matter of a national register of Warnings, but in the matter of anyone allowing the public to *know* that one was being prepared. 'I regard a breach of trust as a major offence,' he said. One could not have a fairer sort of bairn, to administer the law, than that.

Well, that is how it is done these days, by Orders and instruments, by something called Box 500 of which the immigration service stands in awe, by Regulation J 11.004b and Crown Circular No. 1643. Some are done 'on the nod' and others are done in secret, and *we do not know what other guidelines and circulars may be about*. It is an offence for any official to tell us, an offence to publish our knowledge, and, if the Official Information Bill had been passed, it would have become an offence to know.

If Englishmen were to be subjected to an opinion poll and asked if they were 'freeborn', the majority would reply: 'Don't know'. As for the freeborn Scot, he need not feel offended in his national pride that he was left out of the Criminal Law Act, 1977. A particular package is in preparation for him, in the Scottish Criminal Justice Bill, although what delicacies this package will contain (apart from new police powers of arrest and search without warrant) has not yet (at the time of writing) been disclosed.

The Scots, from well before the time of the great Braxfield, have been jealous of their own peculiar laws and process, and for all I know they may find the new package under preparation at Westminster to be wholesome. I only hope that they can keep it, like haggis, to themselves. We are already too much in their debt; they have sent us Sir David McNee.

In any case, in all these arguments, both Scots and English may be well behind the times. For our laws, our liberties, and our constitution may have been passed over, some time ago, to the care of the Commissioners in Brussels. Roy Jenkins may already have set up a committee to bring them under review, and the taxi-copters may be flitting now from one hotel-suite to the next. Questions were asked about that in the late referendum, but the answers were all left to lie.

The point I have been addressing concerns our constitution. I have said that we have, or used to have, a constitution, of an indefinite and ambiguous kind. Some parts of it are as plain as the letters of old Acts: as that the monarch may not be a papist nor marry one. If these no longer suit the times, our legislature has the power to make a new enactment.

Other parts are obscure and decided case by case, each case establishing a precedent: as that the monarch may not marry a divorcee. Precedents are heavy things, but they may be upset.

Other parts exist in a mixed medium of statute and common law, in practice and precedent, and in the memory and expectations of people: the jury system is such a part. If the legislature wishes to tamper with such parts, the responsibility is heavy. The people expect to be consulted in any change. Change without consultation is regarded as arbitrary rule.

Our constitution provides a few rules, like markers here and there, but not rules for every eventuality. It provides a set of limits and expectations as to how conflicts may be fought out without the use of force or repression, and a fund of safeguards and examples to prompt the present. It includes places of especial sensitivity: prod them, and we feel the pain today as yesterday. I am thinking of such places as the jury: as *habeas corpus* (which itself has been well watered in the last decade): and as all those freedoms the media are always on about but which they practice less and less.

I started out by speaking of a constitution and have ended by speaking of a political culture, with evidences that are both material and ideal. This is not just our history: it is history-as-now, when traditions still burn in our minds as norms and expectations.

A political culture is not the same as that rather large and important sociological entity, a 'consensus'. A consensus may be a very provisional affair, which the media reconstruct from time to time for our diversion. A political culture is grounded at an altogether deeper level, and it is within its limits and determinations that consensuses are manipulated —

and sometimes arise unbidden. You cannot change a nation's political culture without changing the character of the people.

Of course, I don't suppose that we all agree as to what is our constitution and which are its most sensitive parts. That is one reason why we fight about the meaning of our history — and few nations fight harder. The Prime Minister herself has recently complained about 'socialist academics and writers' — 'a whole generation has been brought up to mis-understand and denigrate our national history'. I am expect-ing every day an Act to be passed enabling the Regius Professor at Oxford to decide what our history has been and to order the suppression of the rest.

The law-and-order brigade would like us to think that the constitution is a generous provision, made at some time by Them to Us. But they know in their hearts that the opposite is true. They know that one way of reading our history is as an immensely protracted contest to subject the nation's rulers to the rule of law.

This contest has swayed backwards and forwards, through a thousand episodes, and with each generation it has been renewed. We have subjected feudal barons, overmighty subjects, corrupt Lord Chancellors, kings and their courtiers, overmighty generals, the vast apparatus of Old Corruption, inhumane employers, overmighty commissioners of police, imperial adventurers and successive nests of ruling-class conspirators to the rules of law. Every now we have notched up a victory, and every then the ratchet has slipped back.

Today our rulers find the rules and expectations grounded in that long struggle to be an impediment. That is why the word has gone round . . . we have no constitution, we can burn the lot up. But what is then left is anarchy: the anarchy in which the oldest rules of our society are changed in secret, constitutional safeguards disappear without public know-ledge, and circulars pop out of holes.

It is anarchy when Permanent Secretaries and Directors do whatever they can get away with, when inquests are uncon-scionably postponed, when the police and security organs of the state are beyond democratic scrutiny, when men are murdered in the streets without inquiry or redress, when truth is hidden from the people by Acts of State, and when there is no clear and rule-governed place of account.

The choice we are faced with is between anarchy and culture. By political culture I mean a constitution that is alive in the conjunction of memory and practice, and in the jar of argument over contrary precedents and interpretations of 'consensual' rules. And I mean more than this. I mean not this practice and that rule, but the structure of the whole: the political character of the people. It is this character which the anarchs who are our rulers now mean to destroy.

5 The End of an Episode?

That is the state of the nation today. We are approaching a state of anarchy, or arbitrary and unaccountable administrative rule, in which the constitution, or political culture, of the nation is being surreptitiously destroyed.

As to what the state of the nation will be tomorrow, I will sketch only the briefest scenario. We are well incorporated within the managed society already, and I need only offer one example of how it will be.

Early in October, 1979, when I commenced these articles, an 'expert' sort of young man came upon the BBC news, and informed us that we are to have 140 Cruise missiles with nuclear warheads stationed on our soil. These are to be called Tomahawks, a reassuring cowboys-and-Indians sort of name. They are to be our 'contribution' to NATO, in addition to whatever genocidal toys we are to keep for our own private national pride when Polaris becomes obsolete.

As is the manner with the 'news' these days, this young man offered us all this in a comforting, normative kind of way. That is, he told us with the same twist of the tongue both the 'facts' and what we were authorized to think about these facts. He was kind enough to rehearse us in approved responses. We were to accept these missiles as a gesture of solidarity with our West German allies.

But the Dutch, it seems, may neglect to take their proper quota of Tomahawks, since the Dutch have 'moral objections' to genocide. Nay, the loyalty of Belgium was also in the balance, since some Belgians (persons called Flemings) were Dutch-speaking, and through the medium of language a moral contamination might spread. In that event, the British and the Italians were in duty bound to come forward and to take even more than their proportionate share. Perhaps 240 missiles should be dotted around the East Anglian and Oxfordshire countryside.

With so many calls upon our duty, from NATO and from ACPO, from Brussels and from Bonn, it is difficult to know which way a loyal Englishman may turn. I have a half-acre coppice in Worcestershire, and — for each Cruise missile must be tidily hidden — perhaps I should let NATO know?

But, then, will 240 be truly enough? For whereas it is not to be supposed that Italians would have 'moral objections' I think it probable that Italians will have an almighty political bust-up, so protracted that it will lead to the fall of governments by dozens and will outlast the patience of NATO. Three hundred and forty for that. And, at the current rate of inflation in the mutual balance of terror, we would be wise to settle for a round 500 by 1983.

It would be laughable to suggest that the British, as an old imperial nation, should have 'moral objections' to anything. But there could be Flemings even in our own midst. There will be such. There was a Flemish immigration some centuries ago, and these intermarried with the natives. 'Moral objectors' have been known in our history. They may arise again.

Now these Tomahawks are not especially large. They can be dragged around our country lanes on giant transporters. They are like a species of very large beetle, which projects itself into the air and then unlocks its horny wings. They were not (our 'expert' thought) to be kept together like cockroaches in little nests, but be dotted individually around the place, near Bury St Edmunds and Burnham-on-Crouch, one in Three Mile Bottom and another in Hurdlemaker's Spinney.

The enemy may not be permitted to knock out forty or fifty of them with one lucky shot. That would be unsportsmanlike, like potting sitting pheasants, and we cannot take it upon trust that the enemy will be a sport. The enemy

must obliterate all East Anglia and South and Central England
to find them out. The place of each one must be kept as an
Awful Official Secret. The transport drivers and technicians
and plumbers and typists who service the military personnel,
and the farmers who happen to work the neighbouring land,
must be laid under the most terrible oaths.

But there is more to it than that, oh, very much more. A
Cruise missile is a death-intensive weapon. It is quite small. It
is not like a submarine or an aerodrome, which is likely to
stay put submissively in the hands of law and order. It could
be attacked by terrorists. It could even be carried off by
persons unknown. Direct actionists could sit down in front
of it or even make moral objections to its behind. I may be
insufferably weary by then and need to sit down myself.

Civil liberties and 250 Cruise missiles cannot coexist in
this island together. East Anglia is not Arizona nor the
Nevada desert. You cannot put ten million persons out of
their homes nor surround them with twelve-foot barbed
wire.

This will be a great argument for the security services and
the police. Truck drivers and motorists will be stopped at
road-blocks, canteen staff will be positively vetted, all of us
will carry identity cards. Not only pacifists, anarchists,
Marxists, Irish and Welsh persons (not to mention Flemings)
but all those thought susceptible to moral objections must be
vigilantly watched; their letters opened and their telephones
tapped; their moral temperature monitored, charted, com-
puted and filed.

Informers will be put in. To legitimate all this in the eyes
of the public a provocation or two will be worked up. Experts
will be put into the BBC and press, like constables into
schools. The most awful trials will become habitual.

It is then, as the toll of summary punishments for offences
against 'public order' mounts and the trials before vetted
juries unroll, that the British people will look back nostalgic-
ally and wonder where their constitution has gone. I am not
speaking of our children's children. I am speaking of the
immediate future: let us say 1984. And many of them will
turn upon their most immediate oppressors. They will call

it a police state, and they will put all the blame upon the Director and the cops.

But in this they will be unfair. For we will have done this to ourselves. The brokers of repression will have been the television controllers who rushed forward to offer Dimbleby lectures and chat-show places to the police; the MPs who could not, once, in the matter of the jury, divide the House; the editors who served up every official hand-out in return for paltry inside leaks; the judges who, when asked for justice, gave us back a hole; and all the law-and-order brigade, warming their hands before the burning constitution.

These offenders will never be called to account. If by some lucky stroke there should be an identity parade at the end of the next decade, they will all have had time to grow beards by then. And the beards, in that event, will be liberal. They will always be able to keep up with the mode.

But I do not know that the mode of libertarian Britain will ever return. It has had a long run, and we have been lucky for that. But that immensely-prestigious foreign personage, the Tomahawk, cannot be expected to pig it together with the jury system in Three Mile Bottom.

The more immediate scenario is obvious to everyone. The law-and-order brigade are about to lean hard on the trade unions and their pickets. They will revive old nineteenth-century laws and put them in modern visors. Very shortly, and perhaps before winter is out, trade unionists in hundreds will be learning in their own persons the meaning of summary jurisdiction under the Criminal Law Act, 1977, and the Repression of Picketing Act, 1980. Late in the day those powerful trade-union officials who have slept through each civil liberties issue which did not directly affect their own members will begin to cavil and complain.

That will do them no good. For under the leadership of Mrs Thatcher and her fellow militants, we are entering a classic period of class war. A few of my comrades on the left may take comfort in this. They will scent a 'revolution' ahead. But a revolution of that kind is not what they will get. It will not be permitted by ACPO or NATO. They are more likely to get the kind of justice that was administered to Mr

Jimmy Kelly and Mr Peach. What we will all get is a foul authoritarian state.

And why should we *not* get this? In the past half century great European nations, with vigorous democratic and working-class traditions, have succumbed to a repressive statism without precedent. If we have had libertarian traditions, we have had traditions that are brutal and imperialist also. There is no need for the British to invent authoritarian ideology and practice out of some state of original innocence. Our past contains sufficient precedent for sin.

Indeed, one might argue that we *must* be the next to go, our authoritarian traditions being drawn to a head like a boil in the foetid climate of post-imperial inferiority and economic decline. Time has swung round and turned its back on Germany, Italy and Spain: we are now being beckoned in our turn.

Maybe a counter-revolution is exactly what we *have* been undergoing in the past decade, which has subverted the constitution beyond the point of recall. The state of the nation is no longer in question. This has already been decided, although it may never be clear by whom or how. The nation is to be a property managed by the state. And the state is to be a station of NATO, a station with a blue light over the door and sirens moaning in every street.

Readers must forgive me if my scenario does not turn out to be, in every jot and item, accurate. I can do no more than peer at shadows in the inky recesses of the state. There has been, in recent months, an immense thrashing in the depths of the tank, as sharks and piranha joust at each other.

Not every shadow tells the same story as the 'expert' on the October news. Now we are told this and that. The missiles *will* be in cockroach nests (Upper Heyford and Lakenheath) and will run around the place in 'Emergencies'. And so on. We are sprayed with conflicting obscenities and awesome official secrets every day.* The service chiefs are fighting over budgets, NATO is deciding this or that, one day or other we will be told whatever we are permitted to know.

*See below, 'The Doomsday Consensus'.

What we are never given is honest information, in a form which we may debate in advance of its decision, on matters critical to our national identity or even survival. While people goggle at their Sunday supplements, and speculate upon who was the Seventeenth Man in 1933, the foulest sort of traitors lurk at the top of our state: the foulest, boldest and most hardened liars, preparing their genocidal treasons ... but 'authorized' treasons, each one of them 'in the public interest'. Which interest the public is not permitted to decide, nor even to know.

Well, that is where we are. The paradox is this. In times of disturbance in the past our ancestors were often seized with apocalyptic visions. We now inhabit daily a civilization which is, for the first time, technically equipped to enact the apocalypse: the opening of the heavens, the cremation of infants, the rivers of blood. And our vision is null. Apocalypse has become normal.

If there was to be another kind of future — but I scarcely think that there can — it could only be like this. There would have to be an ignition of our old political culture and an incandescence of all that is libertarian in our traditions. There would be a critical struggle to impose the rule of law upon our rulers.

This struggle would be enacted at every level of society. It would even divide the police and seep through into the odd judge's brain. Mayors would act as civic officers, and the 'civil power' would assert its ancient prerogatives and powers. Parliament would divide again and again, not on party-political stratagems, but across party lines as constituents served Warnings on their members. The press and the courts would be at issue. With extreme exertion the forces of 'law and order' would be put back into their proper place.

In a contest for a human order, laws must be changed and disputed of course. Particular laws may and will be broken, as a matter of conscience, as has been done in the past. There must be inflexible opposition to attempts to trench upon basic constitutional rights; and if they do trench, then we must disobey. And equally, if in such a contest the democracy were to be victorious, the victors would honour these rights and rules in their turn. Money might be disfranchised but persons and parties would not.

If one places these two scenarios beside each other one knows in one's heart that the Tomahawk has everything going on its side. It is already on the assembly-line, whereas there is not a tested prototype of a democratic *common*-wealth anywhere in the world. I suppose that we have come to the end of the road — at least to the end of that long episode of peculiar British history. We must make our terms with the future and adjust to it as best we can.

Indeed, that it what is now going on at every side. The managed society requires some kind of moral legitimation; some large part of its resources are spent on managing exactly that. For this it may be helpful, for a few more years, to allow universities to posture as independent, to let little journals make faces, to secure the jury for vestigial purposes, and to let Parliament meander impotently on.

But I cannot say that this adds up to 'the institutions of our country' when these are considered in a full perspective. I have, over the years, become attached to certain of these institutions, and even sentimental in my regard. I have been chided by my comrades for my insularity, liberal illusions, and the rest. It may be properly so. I have never been able to get my decimal table right. I was brought up at a time when twelve true units made a foot, a shilling, or the verdict of a jury.

In excuse, I have thought that most of these 'institutions', from the franchise to the free press, from rights of picketing to certain rights of women, were wrested in protracted contests from our rulers. And then, I have felt a benefit from what history has passed down. Things have always been rigged, money and power have always had thumbs on the scales, but something could be done. I have lived through times when something more than chauvinism made one glad that one was not a German, a Russian, an American or a Czech.

We are living now through a contemptible decade of British history. I do not know that public persons are more corrupt, time-serving and mendacious than at other bad

times, but their technological means for managing and
mendacity are immensely enlarged. They think they can tell
us any damn lie they like and throttle our liberties 'on the
nod'. I am not making a party-political statement. The injury
to liberty, the corruption, and the law-and-order cant has
come from an all-party 'consensus'.

I have said that you cannot change a political culture without changing the character of the people, and perhaps this is
what has at last been done. The freeborn Briton has been
bred out of the strain, and the stillborn Britperson has been
bred in. The people have been drugged into an awe of office,
and into that diminished reality-sense known as 'normality'.
They can look at a nicely-groomed expert on TV who is
telling them about weapons of genocide, and they can
suppose that this is 'authorized' by 'responsible persons' and
in the normal course of things. An operation has been done
on our culture and the guts have been taken out.

Maybe it was time. The freeborn Brit was full of self-
congratulation, and other nations found him a hypocrite
and bore. At home he used to strut about and rant of 'birthright' and of 'transmitting British liberties to posterity in
their pristine purity'. In the eighteenth century, if a gentleman had cause to take issue with the Crown, and had reason
to expect arrest, the style was to seat oneself in one's study
and be taken while reading Magna Carta to one's son. No
one has a son or daughter who would put up with that sort
of camp now.

Yet they did, those exhibitionists and hams, have a point
of sorts. They stood in a certain position. They had a certain
stance towards authority. The position was that the state was
for them, they were not for the state. The stance was that of
vigilance; they suspected authority's every move. They
thought that the best state was weak, and that it was under
weak central power that consensual order is best maintained.

'Pristine purity' makes one wrinkle one's nose. Yet it does
so happen that we *are* their posterity, and that they *did* hand
something down. And might we not also have some kind of a
duty — I am sorry to use such a heavy word — to pass on
down the line what we have inherited, in the way of rights

and rules upon power? If we, with our universal literacy and high technology and great institutes of learning and comfortable homes, should seem to respect ourselves less, as citizens in the face of authority, than seventeenth-century petty gentry and yeomen, than tradesmen and artisans in the 1790s, than Clerkenwell bakers or Chartist working women and men — might we not have to wrinkle the nose at ourselves?

As I left my typewriter and walked down the lane this evening, multitudes of starlings were settling in the autumn trees. The air was full of chittering and hissing, as if the whole sky was saying 'sus-sus-sus'. The scene was menacing, as if an energy was out of control. Myriads of black wings swirled around the television aerials, like images of violence flocking towards the screens.

I must say, in honesty, that I can see no reason why we should be able to bar that foul storm out. I doubt whether we can pass our liberties on and I am not even confident that there will be a posterity to enjoy them. I am full of doubt. All that I can say is that, since we have had the kind of history that we have had, it would be contemptible in us not to play out our old roles to the end.

ACTIVE NEUTRALITY

The Doomsday Consensus

I am concerned with the management of opinion. This has a
long history. But the history which concerns me now is that
which led up to Britain's zealous advocacy, at Brussels on 12
December 1979, of the deployment of Cruise missiles on our
own soil and on that of NATO allies.

We may commence in October 1979. On 6 October
Brezhnev attempted to pre-empt NATO plans by announcing
some limited and unilateral local withdrawal of his forces
from East Germany. This was like a nuclear 'red alert' to the
propaganda organs of NATO and the British state, whose
operators — television 'experts', defence correspondents,
editorialists — were 'scrambled' and instantly sent aloft upon
their long-prepared offensive against the public mind.

We were informed that NATO was just on the point of
deciding to deploy about 600 nuclear-tipped Cruise or
Pershing-2 missiles upon nominated hosts within NATO:
108 Pershings and 464 Cruises (or Tomahawks) to be exact:

> Britain would take the largest number of cruise missiles (160),
> followed by Italy (112), West Germany (96 plus the 108 Pershings),
> Holland (48), and Belgium (48). [*Guardian*, 14 November.]

These figures, 'released in the Hague', might not be wholly
acceptable to Holland, and even created a little concern in
Belgium (we were informed in mid October by a defence
'expert' on BBC news) but they were (it seems) wholly
acceptable to 'Britain'. The fact that these missiles, of the

---

First published in the *New Statesman*, 20 December 1979.

NATO 'alliance', would remain within the control of US forces, who would alone keep the ignition keys, aroused concern in Italy but not (it seems) in 'Britain'.

The processes by which 'Britain' made up its mind, and came to this remarkable consensus, remained obscure. Wherever one looked, the decision had already been taken, or was just about to be taken, by someone else. 'Britain May Take Cruise Missiles' was the headline for Clare Hollingworth's account in the *Telegraph*, but her account commenced: 'The Government *will agree to* . . .' (31 October). 'Britain *has already agreed* to accept Cruise missiles,' she announced two weeks later (12 November). Then Henry Stanhope of *The Times* announced that 'Britain *has been* one of the strongest supporters of the American package,' and had even volunteered to take *more* of the missiles than originally intended 'because West Germany found that it did not have room for its whole quota' (14 November). The question 'is largely decided', Gregory Teverton, Assistant Director of the International Institute for Strategic Studies, informed *The Observer* (18 November): 'Britain and Germany are committed . . .'

The 'mind of Britain' (and its 'quota') was, it seems, made up, not in this country but in the Hague, by a NATO committee known as the High Level Group, whose instructions were passed on in turn to a thing called NPG, or NATO's Nuclear Planning Group (*The Times*, 13 November). Three features of the strategy by which 'Britain' was instructed that its mind was already decided may be noted.

The first we will call subliminal indoctrination: that is, the decision was presented as if agreement was already *assumed*. Viewers and readers were informed that 'Britain' had decided, and it was a matter of consensus. The second was that of suppression. The facts were disguised (so far as possible) from public knowledge that Norway, Denmark, France and Turkey had refused to have these missiles on their soil, and that the decision of Holland and Belgium hung in the balance of an alert and disturbed public opinion. The third was that of devaluing the issue. The decision was presented, not as one of high and controversial political concern, but as a trivial question of *technology*. The key-word in this strategy has been 'modernization'. Only Luddites or seditionists could oppose *that*!

Within this obliterating barrage of opinion-management there was one discordant theme. This concerned the question of a successor to Britain's own independent nuclear weaponry (Polaris). The mind of 'Britain' on this matter did turn out to be divided — not as to whether we should burn money up on an 'independent' nuclear arsenal ('Britain' has, it seems, a seamless consensus in favour of doing that), but as between two options: should we replace Polaris with Trident missiles, at a cost of £5,000 millions, or take the cheaper option of buying a few Cruise missiles of our own, to which the Americans might even allow us to have our own ignition keys?

This question (it turned out) had also been 'decided'. 'A firm decision has been taken at the Ministry of Defence' in favour of buying Tridents, David Fairhall informed the *Guardian* (1 November). Even so, the mind of Britain remained divided, because the Chief of the Defence Staff is an admiral, who, for obvious reasons, is keen on the Trident submarine strategy, whereas army and air force chiefs would prefer Cruise missiles which would fall within their own constituencies, and which option would also leave hundreds of millions over for their other expensive toys.

This savage in-fighting over the war budget, as our service chiefs seek to mobilize miniscule sectors of elite 'public opinion' upon their side, builds up a terrific pressure in the bladder of Official Secrecy. Suddenly, on such occasions, ordinary viewers and readers find themselves sprayed from on high by conflicting official leaks. We are once again back in the universe made familiar to us by Chapman Pincher. Admirals and generals and senior officials of the MOD stand against the wall of Fleet Street and leak in the public interest.

A lot of 'Official Secrets', in the form of Official Information, have been sprayed around in the past two months. We have been told the exact range of Cruise missiles; what kind of warhead is going on the Tridents; where the Cruise missiles will be sited (Lakenheath, Upper Heyford and Sculthorpe). We are told that 'a US air force team has been touring the UK', examining possible firing-sites ('at least a dozen'). We are given a précis of highly secret reports from NATO secret committees. And on and on.

Since these breath-taking secrets usually appear simultaneously in rival establishment sheets, I think that we may take it that all this leaking is very much in the public interest. There is no imminent danger of Ms Clare Hollingworth, Mr David Fairhall or the secretariat of the International Institute for Strategic Studies being clapped into jail for betraying the secrets of our country.

Let us now consider this material. We may commence with some observations on Official Secrets.

First, an Official Secret is not defined by any objective criteria of secrecy, such as 'the national interest', but according to who tells it and how. If it is to *inform* public opinion it is an awesome secret, defended by state sanctions and threats of up to fourteen years' imprisonment. If it is to *manage* public opinion, by established persons, then it is not.

If Mr Duncan Campbell or I had come into possession of information as to decisions of the defence staff, the plans of NATO secret committees, or as to the warheads of missiles and their siting, and if the editor had been incautious enough to publish these, then we should all now be under arrest and awaiting trial before vetted juries.

Second — and following upon this — the foulest damage to our political life comes not from the 'secrets' which they hide from us, but from the little bits of half-truth and disinformation which they *do* tell us. These are already pre-digested, and then are sicked up as little gobbets of authorized spew. The columns of defence correspondents in the establishment sheets serve as the spittoons.

That is, the Official Information which we *do* get is only the other side to the medal of the Official Secrets Acts. A new breed of journalist has emerged in the last decades (and, very certainly, not only in 'defence'). These never have to get off their arses, poke around, move about the world, or investigate anything. They simply taxi to official briefings in Whitehall, Westminster, Brussels or the Hague. They serve as supine vectors to convey to their readers official pre-masticated pap. Their only skills are those of managing minds, or of chatting up public relations persons at this ministry or that, so as to express from their official bladders the last few drops of exclusive leak.*

Official Secrecy is not only a way of denying us honest information. It is a way of selling us pre-packaged decisions, accompanied by dishonest data and normative noise. Official Secrecy, in controlling *all* information in forbidden areas, controls even more what we *do* know than what we don't. In the moment of offering us any information whatsoever it attempts to control also what we are permitted to think.

Third, the function of Official Secrecy is not to deny knowledge to any 'enemy' but to delude and manage the opinion of the native population — that is, us.

A nice example of this primary function came some weeks ago when the *Omaha World-Herald* disclosed that we came within a hair's breadth of radioactive disaster in July 1956 when a B47 bomber crashed at Lakenheath. If the TNT component in three nuclear bombs had been ignited by fuel blazing all around their hideaway, then (a retired US Airforce general said) 'it is possible that a part of eastern England would have become a desert'. Plutonium would have been released into the air, 'spreading radiation over a very wide area, giving cancer to those in contact and making the locality uninhabitable'.

Now this is, exactly, what an Official Secret *is*. It has been a well-kept secret, even though (it seems) it was known to members of Eden's government, senior service staff, and officials at the MOD. The secret was kept, of course, from us, and not from any 'enemy', just as the Soviet nuclear disaster in the Urals (which Zhores Medvedev has disclosed) is still kept as a secret, not from us, but from the Russian people.

In those distant days, I and other readers were tramping the Aldermaston road in support of the Campaign for Nuclear

---

*I have been accused by an inattentive reader of mixing my metaphors. This is not so. Official Secrets leak from one end of the official anatomy and Official Information is expectorated or spewed from the other. The confusion arises only because both kinds of evacuation are received in the same journalistic chamber-pot or cuspidor.

Disarmament. We carried some part of public opinion. We carried churches and trade unions. We carried the Labour Party conference, until the entire media swung around behind Gaitskell to fight our resolutions off. If the near-disaster at Lakenheath had then been known to the public, I have little doubt that we would have carried the country. Neither Cruise missiles nor £5,000 millions for Tridents would be on the British agenda today.

It is enough to make one tired. It is even enough to make one angry. One does not have all that much life to spend on little meetings and tramping down roads. What other near-disasters are being kept under civil service hats until the *Nevada Cosmos-Tribune* sees fit to let us know?

There is also that other little bit in the *Omaha World-Herald*. Official Secrecy was essential in 1956, it seems, because 'the Eden government had concealed from the British people the fact that American atomic bombs were being stockpiled in the UK'. As the former US air chief said, 'Orders came down to keep "nukes" out of the records. Officially they did not exist.'*

One does not have to be a defence 'expert' to see that what is going on now is imbecile.

There is the matter of where these missiles are going to be sited. At first we were told, on telly, that they were going to be scattered around in woods across East Anglia and the South Midlands. Then (David Fairhall) that the missiles will be kept together in a few sacred US sanctuaries:

*When, by the way, *did* they come, officially, to 'exist'? I disremember. In a letter to *The Times* (11 December 1979), Air Vice-Marshal Stewart Menaul of the Institute for the Study of Conflict notes that 'it is remarkable how many politicians in Europe appear to be unaware that from 1957 to 1962, the United States deployed medium-range ballistic missiles in Europe, targeted on the Soviet Union. Thor missiles were deployed in Britain on bases in Yorkshire, Lincolnshire and Norfolk and operated by RAF Bomber Command.' These were withdrawn after the Cuban missile crisis. Air Vice-Marshal Menaul's information appears to be greatly superior to that of the British public, as well as 'politicians in Europe'. For the extreme right-wing activities of the Institute for the Study of Conflict, and its putative connections with CIA-funded bodies, see *Review of Security and the State 1978* (State Research, Friedmann Books, 1978), pp. 13-17.

> The individual missile launchers are mobile and if war threatened they would be scattered round the countryside. But to minimise costs, and perhaps more importantly the political and environmental impact of this unfamiliar weapons system, the peacetime deployment plans now being prepared in the Ministry of Defence envisage concentrating them in two, or possibly three locations. [*Guardian*, 31 October].

And, reassuringly, the Cruise 'makes no noise and the only inconvenience the local population will experience is the occasional sight of the missile launchers on the roads' (*Telegraph*, 31 October). That is likely to be no small 'inconvenience' to the nerves of 'the local population', since we are also told that 'the missiles would begin to move around the countryside only in times of extreme tension' (*The Observer*, 18 November).

And what is a time of 'extreme tension'? Is it a time, perhaps, when there are sudden oil embargoes, or when truculent students occupy US embassies in Asian cities? If Cruise missiles were already here, the local population might have noticed much movement around the countryside in recent weeks.

If nuclear war breaks out it is not going to be after a formal ultimatum and a gentlemanly count-down to zero, so that missile launchers can be sent down minor roads and across hayfields and into prepared emplacements in the woods — and only then can we all start fair together. The only possibility of genocidal 'victory' lies in the pre-emptive strike. The warning-time, which was once placed at forty-eight hours, is now calculated by 'experts' at thirty minutes, or even at fifteen (*Telegraph*, 12 November; *Now!* , 16-22 November).

Whether war starts by accident or intent, it will start without more than a few day's warning, and (from the standpoint of the civilian population) it will finish in a day. (The high politicians and the service chiefs, in their deep strategic caves, submarine or stratospheric command posts, may slog it out for a few more weeks.) While NATO might be willing to write off the 'local population' (that is, us), it would not put its Tomahawks to an 'inconvenience' of that kind.

If the missiles come, they will be stationed to strike, or the whole operation is fantasy. I write this as a very knowledgeable military expert who, regrettably, has not yet found employment with *The Observer* or the BBC. In the last war I once arrived at a battle half an hour late, owing to the distance to be travelled and the difficult nature of Italian country tracks; fortunately the infantry whom my tanks were supposed to be supporting had not yet been overrun.

NATO knows better, and it is not going to have its expensive hardware bogged down to the axle in East Anglian byways. More happens in thirty minutes now than used to happen then. Nor is NATO going to start dispersing its missiles around the place only when 'extreme tension' has already arisen, since any such dispersal would be monitored by satellite observation and would be the instant signal to an enemy to press a pre-emptive ballistic button.

But, look where you will, there is no end to the insanity of the whole operation. One might suppose that 'modernizing' NATO's nuclear armament might, at the least, allow us to spend less on conventional weapons and armies. Not at all. Mr Francis Pym, the Defence Secretary, in an exclusive interview given (as it happens) not to the House of Commons but to Sir James Goldsmith's *Now!* (9-15 November), has explained patiently that the more nuclear 'deterrence' there is, the more dangerous the situation becomes, and hence the greater the need to raise the level of conventional armaments as an alternative option to nuclear war. It is 'very important not to let our conventional forces run down, because if you do the result is to lower the nuclear threshold and weaken deterrence'.

This is not just a closed circle of 'deterrence', like a horse-gin, in which we must plod round and round for ever grinding out terror until something snaps or the horse falls dead on its side. It is a manic spiral of proliferating terror and proliferating expense, with misjudgement, hysteria, or accident becoming statistically more inevitable every day.

And *why*, since there is already terror enough, ten times over, ballistically poised at both ends of Power's great divide, do we need this intermediate additive of terror at all? Ah, it is a safeguard to *prevent* the ultimate horror of a Soviet/US total nuclear war! It is to 'localize' nuclear war: that is, to keep nuclear war local to us, and to West and East Europe, and away from America.

Britain's 'primary role is to survive as a forward NATO base' (*Now!* , 9-15 November). Or not to survive, as the case may be. Mr Gregory Teverton (who, we should recall, is an *international* expert) tells us that the threat of a Soviet nuclear attack on Western Europe might 'put American cities at risk'. 'Missiles in Western Europe would give the American President an intermediate option' (*The Observer*, 18 November). No wonder the US service chiefs are determined to keep control of the ignition keys to 'our contribution' to NATO, since if such an option had to be taken, the 'local population' might not be so opt.

Three further comments. The first is self-evident. The whole operation of Official-Secrecy-cum-Prepackaged-Official-Information carries with it another kind of threat — that of internal terror. For if all the organs of the state and the media combine to impose a 'consensus' upon us, then it follows that the other side of the consensus (or those who fall outside it) must be 'treason'.

There is a lot of this kind of talk around, as you may have noticed. 'Britain needs to re-create its immunity from treason and disaffection,' the *Telegraph* editorialized (19 November): this has 'been thwarted by widespread beliefs here that any such concern is "McCarthyite" '. *Now!* is very explicit as to the motives of anyone opposed to the consensus: 'Severe disruption of national life by Soviet special forces, operating together with undercover KGB "teams" and fifth columnists would take place days or hours before the first air strikes on Britain' (9-15 November).

Good heavens, if such traitors and fifth columnists are lying in wait, then they must already be here! 'Speak for Britain, Mrs Thatcher!' squeals Peregrine Worsthorne (who has always had difficulty in distinguishing his own liver condition from the National Interest). 'Barbarians' are not only 'at the gate', they are 'within our own borders'. They burst forth, in their 'alien style', in the industrial troubles of last winter:

NUCLEAR DESTINATION

Those brutal, angry faces seemed scarcely human, let alone British, arousing reactions of dismay among all classes rather as would the emergence of strange creatures from the nether regions ... There seemed to be a stench of evil in the land. [*Sunday Telegraph*, 2 December.]

Much the same thought, in more elegant terms, has occurred to the Regius Professor of Modern History at Oxford, Hugh Trevor-Roper: 'It is the function of MI5 to keep an eye on suspect contacts, and who can say exactly where, in the amorphous Labour Party, the eastern frontiers are now drawn?' (*Spectator*, 24 November.) It is a chilling image, and chilling when it comes from that high table of cultivation. Against the geographic eastern frontier we must mount the Pershing-2 and the Tomahawk; against the 'eastern frontier' of the human mind and moral sensibility, what modernized weapons will Trevor-Roper now grant to MI5?

The second comment is that all this has gone on, and for months, not through any open democratic process but behind democracy's back. There has not even been, prior to the decision of 'Britain' at Brussels, any debate in Parliament. I don't know that this greatly matters, seeing how rabbity Parliaments are these days and how servile the opposition front bench. But there *are* some honest MPs, who would have asked awkward questions, to which answers must have been given. And for form's sake there could have been gestures — a White Paper, a debate.

Why does the Defence Secretary make his most luminous statements to *Now*! or to Brian Walden on ITV's *Weekend World*? And why can we be told, by the *Times* defence correspondent, (15 November), that, in relation to the siting of Cruise missiles —

Mr Pym is understood to be considering ways in which this should be presented to the British public — particularly in East Anglia and Oxfordshire ...

— when one might suppose that he would also be considering how to solicit the assent of Parliament?

But that is the giveaway phrase: 'ways in which this should be presented to the British public'. Politics has nothing left to it now but this: lies, disinformation, the management of opinion, the theatrical show of legitimation. Decisions are taken elsewhere: by NATO's High Level Group, by defence and service chiefs. Politicians are the servile and oily-tongued liars, the shady brokers who put these decisions across.

Which leads one to ask — *what* has the Parliamentary Labour Party been up to? Labour's official policy, as founded on conference decisions, and as declared in its 1974 manifesto, was unambiguous: 'We have renounced any intention of moving to a new generation of strategic nuclear weapons.' 'Renounce' is a word without ambiguity: my dictionary gives, *inter alia*, 'revoke', 'disown', 'reject', 'give up', 'consent formally to abandon', 'repudiate', 'refuse to recognize longer', 'withdraw from', and (please note) 'not to follow suit at cards'. That would seem to be clear. It does not say 'go along with in privy and devious ways, following every suit that NATO leads'.

My dictionary, like the Authorized Version, no doubt needs modernizing. And Mr Callaghan can show us how this should be done. For he modernized Labour's clearly stated policy in the election manifesto of this year (without consulting either the Parliamentary Party or his own National Executive) by inserting some slippery provisos:

> We reiterate our belief that this [i.e. renunciation] is the best course for Britain. But many great issues affecting our allies and the world are involved, and a new round of strategic arms limitation [*sic*!] negotiations will soon begin. We think it essential that there must be full and informed debate about these issues in the country before any decision is taken.

Yes. And how much has Mr Callaghan done to drive forward this 'full and informed debate'? Inside the House? No. Inside the Party? No. Outside the House? No. If we can trust some further Official Secrets leaked in *The Times* (4 December), his mind has been on other things. For it seems that, during the last eighteen months of his administration, a 'small ad hoc committee' of the Cabinet was being convened by Mr Callaghan so immeasurably secret that the Cabinet was not informed of its existence. This committee, or gang of four, was so very privy that it did not even have a name or number: it was an unconstitutional and secret faction of the Prime Minister, Mr David Owen, Mr Healey and Mr Mulley.

In Mr Callaghan's judgement the matter was too delicate to put before the Cabinet's Defence and Overseas Policy Committee, upon which sat one or two sticklers who might have reminded him of the party's manifesto commitment.

It was not, however, too secret to have a slate of senior civil servants in attendance on it, headed by Sir Antony Duff of the Foreign Office, nor too privy to be leaked, in due course, to *The Times*. The function of this committee, or gang, was precisely to prepare for the next generation of nuclear weapons.

With this, Official Secrecy advances its frontiers to the very verge of the authoritarian state. The 'eastern frontiers' are now drawn through the elected government itself. One 'stickler' who was denied knowledge of the Cabinet's own operations was perhaps the Deputy Prime Minister, Mr Michael Foot, and, if so, his exclusion from this gang is to his credit. What is now officially secret is what leading Cabinet members, and the Deputy Prime Minister, may not know.

For the 'all-party consensus', and *especially* the submission of the PLP to the 'consensus', is the lynch-pin of the whole operation. It is this fiction which legitimates all that is done to us — the suppression of information, the manipulation of the media, the exclusion of critical questions from the arena of national political life. And what an ineffably craven and captive set those PLP 'leaders' — those cringing uncles and tailor's models and thugs of the rostrum and inept conference wheeler-dealers — are!

The final comment is that, in the past three months, the British people have been publicly shamed, not only in their own self-esteem but also in the esteem of Europe generally. If we had had a debate, some kind of a row about it all, then — even if sanity had lost the day — people would at least have known that there was still a little breath in the lungs of British democracy. But there has not even been a little moan. There has been *worse* than a moan, for 'British public opinion', like one of those animated corpses in a Hammer horror film, has been sent around Europe to cajole *other* nations to act against their consciences.

Mr Francis Pym has proudly proclaimed that 'we' want to 'keep our allies up to the mark' (*Now!*, 9-15 November). At the West German SPD conference this month, Chancellor Schmidt has been able to use our name to confuse his own critics. And our press has seen fit to deliver editorial homilies to the reluctant Dutch:

> The Alliance does not usually ask much of the Dutch, who lead a comfortable and prosperous life at the heart of Western Europe.

Thus the *Financial Times* (whose readers are not noted for their austerity and self-sacrifice) which goes on to chide the Dutch for being 'smug and hypocritical' (19 November). I do not know what concerned Norwegians or Danes or Dutch think of 'Britain' today; but if they think of us with contempt I could not argue that this is unjust.

There are manifest and sufficient reasons for accepting the official Labour policy of *renouncing* a new generation of nuclear weapons (whether NATO or our own): reasons rational, ethical, and even tactical, which I cannot — and need not — now rehearse. But I must, at least, refuse the false choice which we are so often offered, between NATO and the unending inflation of mutual nuclear terror on one hand, and a moralistic 'gesture' of national self-exemption on the other.

I am not critical of moralistic gestures. They are often the signs of a deeper realism, and those Christians in Holland who advocate this have my respect. What I am opposing is the notion that renunciation of the means of nuclear terror entails *any* kind of opting-out from the discourse of the world.

The alternative which some of us have advocated on the Left for more than twenty years is the policy of 'active neutrality'. We argued this policy within the counsels of CND. We argued it again in the *May Day Manifesto* in 1967-8. And we argue it still. It has never been a position of sufficient propriety to permit its discussion (as a 'viable option') in the media, although I have noticed plenty of editorials and telly programmes aimed *against* its unexpressed and misreported theorems. For a good many years (I am sad to report) it was not possible to state the position even in this journal.

I will restate it now, as concisely as I can, as theorems.

1. The present nuclear status quo is inexpressibly dangerous and increasingly unstable. It is exceedingly probable that it will at some point detonate in global nuclear war, whether through accident, miscalculation or hysteria.

2. The status quo is not a stationary state. It is (from the standpoint of democratic practices) a degenerative state: that is, it generates authoritarian tendencies, and is supportive of secretive and authoritarian bureaucracies within both halves of the divided world. As I wrote in 1958:

> With each month that the Cold War continues, a terrible distorting force is exercised upon every field of life. As it drags on the half-frozen antagonists become more sluggish in their reactions. Political and economic life is constricted, militarism and reaction are infused with new blood, reaction and the subordination of the individual to the state are intensified, and the crooked ceremonies of destructive power permeate our cultural and intellectual life. [*Universities and Left Review*, Number 4.]

3. The bureaucratic elites engendered by this condition develop, in turn, a distinct *interest* in maintaining this condition. Moreover, in a curious manner, the two opposed elites (Soviet and US) develop a *common* interest in repressing any unseemly development or popular initiative within the system which might create instability within their delicate strategic equilibrium. Thus, the US held back from 'taking advantage' of the Czech unrest in 1968, and the Soviet Union did not 'take advantage' of this year's revolutionary situation in Iran. Both powers loathe democratic initiatives — and their possible contagion.

4. Hence to wait for ultimate détente from initiatives at the top — to wait for some Salt Treaty 17 in 2079 — is futile. For the state of permanent terror affords to these elites their purchase upon internal and external power.

5. Hence the system must be made to crumble at the bottom before it will give way at the top.

Twenty years ago we argued that Britain should not only renounce nuclear weapons, but should also renounce NATO and initiate new policies of active neutrality. We should resume initiatives towards a Europe which included Stockholm, Belgrade and Warsaw, as well as towards India and the non-aligned powers.

We were told, in those days, that this would leave Britain 'naked in the conference chamber' and without allies. That was rubbish then, but in the last twenty years developments in Europe and in the Third World have converged to enforce the realism of our policy. Greece and France have detached themselves from NATO, and the skies have not fallen. Yugoslavia has maintained its stubborn national integrity. Romania has edged into a curious position of truculent dependence. Within NATO itself, second and third tiers are discernable — Norway, Denmark, Holland; and Iceland, Portugal and (shortly) Spain — which are refusing nuclear hardware and keeping open other initiatives.

What a British Labour government might have done — might even still do — with a policy of democratic socialism at home and of active neutrality abroad would be to re-enter into an international discourse which would invigorate democratic practices both East and West. As a new neutralist heartland re-emerged in Europe, a hundred forms of political and cultural bonding would go on, not only between socialist and radical movements in West and South Europe, but also with the huge reserves of 'dissidence' in East Europe — and within the Soviet Union itself.

That such a policy would be complex, delicate and entail great risks, as the US and Soviet elites felt the ground begin to crumble beneath them, is evident. If we were to leave NATO, in fact as well as form, we could expect revenges from Washington and Bonn, just as the Soviet Union would exact revenges upon any Eastern European nation which responded in the same neutralist kind. There would be 'red alerts', and missile launchers would scurry down West and East German lanes.

But that will happen anyway. It will very certainly happen if Mr Pym and Mr Callaghan get their way. We are already at risk — Britain, Europe, civilization, the human project — whatever big name we wish to put upon it.

The difference is this. In the 'new generation' of nuclear weapons we might subdue for a while immediate and manifest risks while centralized authoritarian power (and its concomitant management of the mind) encroached further year by year, and we drifted towards some unpredictable and unplanned contingency, an ultimate detonation. In the policy of active neutrality we would take an immediate and conscious risk, which, if we survived, would engender a new generation of human possibilities.

Envoi

'The Ariane telecommunications satellite booster rocket, due for launch from the Kourou space centre in French Guiana yesterday, failed to get off the ground. Built by Britain, France, West Germany and other West European nations, the rocket remained static on its launch pad.

'Yesterday's failure followed the dramatic explosion in mid-air of Europe's first attempt to launch the Europa rocket from the same site in November, 1975.

'The $18 million, 200-tonne rocket was shipped across the Atlantic in sections and put together this autumn at the Kourou space centre opposite the once infamous Devil's Island penal colony.'

The Observer, 16 December 1979

European Nuclear Disarmament

Were it not for the fact that I have other pressing engage-
ments, I would volunteer for the International Brigade in the
Afghan mountains, where a horde of turbaned US senators
and Fleet Street athletes are already serving alongside Pathan
tribesmen. I am very much against sin, and especially against
Russian sin. When the Russian state does not give me a pain
in the head, it strikes my lower anatomy.

Now that my moral credentials are plain to the whole
world, let us discuss serious matters.

These concern Cold War chain-reactions, the nuclear
fission of diplomacy. The sequence has been this. From last
October there was a long run-up to NATO's decision to
'modernize' its nuclear armoury. Mrs Thatcher and Mr Pym
were the self-appointed cheerleaders of this operation,
although they disdained to consult the British Parliament at
any point. A 'new generation' of nuclear missiles, under US
ownership and control, was to be planted all over West
Europe, many on our own soil.

Soviet spokesmen repeatedly warned of the consequences
of this decision; proposed discussions; and even made small
gestures of concession. NATO spokesmen refused every
advance and argued that discussion could only take place
'from strength': that is, from a posture of menace, *after the
decision*.

This essay first appeard in the *Guardian*, 28 January 1980.

277

The decision made nonsense of the trivial provisions of Salt 2. But it became clear, meanwhile, that the US Senate was not going to ratify even these trivial provisions, thereby indicating that top level nuclear détente would prove futile in the face of the American military and arms lobby. As this became clear, a trickle of Soviet dissidents went off to gaol.

On 12 December, at Brussels, NATO ratified its menacing plans in full. On 19 December, *exactly one week later*, the Soviet decision to enter Afghanistan was taken. The hawkism of the West directly generated the hawkism of the East — according to one account, Brezhnev was actually overruled by his own hawks. On the Cold War billiard-table, NATO played the Cruise missile ball, which struck the Afghan black, which rolled nicely into a Russian pocket. It was as if Mrs Thatcher, Mr Pym and Mr Bill Rodgers were there, perched on the leading Soviet tanks, waving to the astonished people of Kabul.

There followed the heroics of the Cold War Olympics, with President Carter carrying a torch through Iowa and that remarkable athlete, Bernard Levin — the gold medallist of every moral pentathlon — hop-skip-and-jumping in *The Times*. The white Olympic ball has been squarely struck, and is still rolling round the table; but it is Academician Sakharov who has rolled into a Soviet pouch. Not the KGB but President Carter and Mr Levin took him, one at each arm, and directed him to internal exile at Gorkiy.

It is, to change the metaphor, like a motorway pile-up in a fog. Soon some Western genius is going to come careering down in a ten-wheeler loaded with threats and sanctions against the Warsaw powers, and will crash into the back of Yugoslavia, which will be sent spinning into the opposite lane. And if the athletes of Westminster and Fleet Street try hard enough, perhaps they can get Roy Medvedev and the remnants of Charter 77 sent to gaol as well.

Bravo for all this! We have seen it before. This logic of the Cold War has been manifest for decades — from at least 1956, when the Suez invasion immediately preceded, and licensed, the re-entry of Soviet tanks into Budapest.

Hawks breed hawks. Now one party and now the other

appears as the most guilty — on 12 December the West, on 19 December, the East. But all the time the warriors of both sides are feeding provocations and adventures to each other.

The logic has a deep structure. A general hawkism grows all the time. In each crisis the military, security and interventionist interests enlarge their powers, acquire new economic and political resources, and a greater ideological resonance. In this mirror-war authoritarian bureaucracies engage in shadow-battle with each other, but the effective gains which they make are largely within their own societies. When Mrs Thatcher eventually comes back from Kabul she will, no doubt, bring back with her a new Official Information Bill.

I have had, over the years, exchanges with dissidents in the East, and I think I understand something of their predicament. I can feel only humility before the towering courage of Sakharov, even when I have felt, on occasion, that his sense of political tactics has been unwise. But if we are to express solidarity with Sakharov (as we must), then we owe him the courtesy of attending to his writings.

What Sakharov has written about most of all has been 'peaceful coexistence'. And he has described the alternative:

> A complete destruction of cities, industry, transport, and systems of education, a poisoning of fields, water, and air by radioactivity, a physical destruction of the larger part of mankind, poverty, barbarism, a return to savagery, and a genetic degeneracy of the survivors under the impact of radiation, a destruction of the material and information basis of civilization — this is the measure of the peril that threatens the world as a result of the estrangement of the world's two superpowers.

Over the years we have had, from East and West, a series of similar warnings, in the most solemn terms. There is no way in which this list (which includes Bertrand Russell, Lord Louis Mountbatten and the Pope) can be fitted into any stereotype. Last month the scientists of successive international 'Pugwash' conferences moved the minute-hand of their warning-clock ominously close to the midnight of detonation.

Every warning has been disregarded. It might not have been made. We have seen a flippant example of this last week in Westminster. On 21 January *The Times* carried a full-page address, of the very first importance, by Lord Zuckerman, the government's Chief Scientific Adviser from 1964 to 1971. In tone this was extraordinarily reminiscent of the warnings of Sakharov. But what it also did, in close and deeply informed argument, was to tear into shreds every justification that has been offered for a 'new generation' of nuclear missiles. Lord Zuckerman showed that the process of the nuclear arms race 'clearly has no logic' and that Western policy was in defiance of the best scientific advice. Last Thursday a debate took place at last in the House of Commons in which the 'defence' spokesmen of Conservative, Labour and Liberal parties rehearsed the arguments which had been shredded in *The Times* three days before. Perhaps they did not know? Important politicians have little time to read, and no time at all to think.

The point is not that distinguished voices, East and West — Sakharov and Zhores Medvedev, Lord Zuckerman and the Pugwash scientists — are saying the same heart-stopping things about our common dangers and our common interest in survival. They are also saying that *they can no longer get through to political power*. All lines are blocked by hawkish interest-groups and ideological jamming. The world of politicians, East or West, has become impervious to rationality. The strategy of great-power détente, commencing at the top, has been tried, half-heartedly, and it has failed. For it is exactly at the top that rationality is weakest, and vested interests at their fullest strength. So . . . we must start at the bottom once again.

The strategy which I advise is this. We must campaign to detach more and more European nations from great-power nuclear strategy. Our aim must be to create in Europe an expanding zone free from nuclear weapons. The campaign will at first be most evident in the West (it exists already in Holland, Belgium and West Germany), but as it grows it will very quickly meet with a response in the East (from Yugoslavia to Romania, Poland, Hungary). The campaign must be conducted at every level — churches, sportsmen, trade unions, intellectuals — and it must certainly include the mobilization of popular movements, as well as international exchanges in which a common solidarity between 'dissidents' of East and West Europe will be expressed.

This 'neutralist' pressure in Europe will give a positive political space in which democratizing pressures in the Soviet bloc can renew their work. It will at length compel the United States and the Soviet Union to resume top-level détente, for fear of losing the allegiance of client states.

This strategy does not entail the immediate disintegration of NATO and the Warsaw Pact. Nations may maintain a loose allegiance to one alliance or the other, while refusing the stationing of nuclear missiles on their own soil.

But this refusal must certainly be made. And within each nation the expulsion of nuclear-missile bases from its own soil must be a prime objective of the popular movement. Since NATO's Cruise missiles are to be 'owned and operated' by US personnel, these are in any case a direct infringement of national sovereignty.

In the case of Britain we must turn our thoughts to Upper Heyford and Lakenheath. These are places which must be closed down. I do not argue this in any spirit of 'anti-Americanism'. We will be working, in the end, for American as well as British survival, and large sections of American opinion will support what we are doing. Some American visitors may join in the work themselves.

Since Britain is now the most abject client state in NATO, and the proud possessor of the most reactionary government in Western Europe (which grows more bellicose in direct ratio to its decline in real influence), we can expect the conflict here to be especially sharp.

We should be ready to meet this. It is time that we repaid a debt of honour to Academician Sakharov, to Charter 77, and to our colleagues in exposed positions in the East. These men and women have been acting, not — as *Izvestia* wishes its readers to believe — in support of 'the West' but in support of common survival. To issue a protest, in the heart of Moscow, against the intervention in Afghanistan is an act of the highest principle. To issue the same protest in Westminster or Iowa may be only an act of vote-catching and self-congratulation. NATO's decision at Brussels on 12 December was an act as menacing and as disastrous in its consequences as the Soviet actions which ensued. And what Western Sakharovs rose up in protest, in Iowa or Westminster, then?

Perhaps the time is coming when the only effective way of expressing solidarity with Academician Sakharov, Roy Medvedev and their friends, in common opposition to the most menacing and reciprocal great power strategies, will be in whatever form of internal exile Mrs Thatcher and her security services can devise for dissidents at home.

Notes on the Text

The Segregation of Dissent. When the New Left was first formed it was ignored by the BBC, as was to be expected. What (in our innocence) was less expected was that the BBC Third Programme then found time in 1960 for *three* broadcast talks by the Catholic philosopher, J. M. Cameron, which offered a general critique of the theories and positions of the New Left — which positions had never been given any presentation in the media. We did not object to Professor Cameron's criticisms (which were reasoned and open), but we did object to the BBC's procedures. With the agreement of the New Left Board, *The Segregation of Dissent* was submitted in reply. It was refused, and (after argument) again refused, although a specific reply to certain of Cameron's points was at length allowed. The rejected address eventually found a place in *New University*.

The Business University and *A Report on Lord Radcliffe*. A full account of the crisis at Warwick University in 1970 and the affair of the 'files' was hastily prepared by a team of students and academic staff and was published, under my editorship, as *Warwick University Ltd* (Penguin Books, 1970). This carries extracts from the offensive files and also fuller extracts from the Tyzack Report.

Going into Europe. In 1975, during the run-up to the referendum, the *Sunday Times* offered hospitality in its columns to an open debate on the question. The word limit was 1,000 words, which accounts for the staccato style of this piece.

An Elizabethan Diary, *The State versus its 'Enemies'* and *A State of Blackmail*. The occasion for all three pieces was the mounting of the Official Secrets trial against Crispin Aubrey, John Berry and Duncan Campbell. I had come to know, and respect, the defendants and their vigorous (and irreverent) defence committee in the previous months. (Accounts of this important case, by Aubrey and by Campbell, will shortly be published.) When the trial finally commenced, in September 1978, the practice of jury vetting came to light for the first time. In justification of this practice, the Attorney-General, Sam Silkin, revealed his 'guidelines' which had been secretly issued in 1975 or 1976. The judge presiding at the trial (Mr Justice Mars-Jones) made it clear (even to Mr Silkin) that he viewed the public discussion of jury vetting, while the trial was proceeding, to be a matter of contempt of court. It was evident that the mainline media, including BBC and ITV, had been warned off discussion of matters of acute public concern (including the integrity of the jury, 'Official Secrecy' and the activity of the security services — telephone-tapping, mail-opening — which had led up to the case) during the months that the case was *sub judice*. I therefore looked for ways of opening up the issues of the case, and penetrating the official silence, from an oblique angle. My first attempt, *An Elizabethan Diary*, met with rejection in several places (which perhaps it merited), and eventually was published last of these three, in the hospitable pages of *Vole*. *The State versus its 'Enemies'* went directly into the pages of *New Society* (with helpful advice from its editor): the discussion of jury vetting there could not be held in contempt unless Mr Justice Mars-Jones was willing to make public his *in camera* censure of the Attorney-General also — and perhaps *act* against Mr Silkin as well! *A State of Blackmail*, which signalled the double standards of the state towards 'Official Secrecy', went directly into the pages of the *New Statesman*, with equal help from its editor; a few passages of the original text, cut for reasons of space, have been restored.

The Great Fear of Marxism. On 28 January 1979, *The Observer* carried a philippic against Marxism, and against Marxists in the Labour Party, by its editor-in-chief, Conor Cruise O'Brien, under the title: 'No to a Nauseous Marxist-Methodist Cocktail'. I am grateful to Dr O'Brien and to *The Observer* for allowing me to reply.

A *Law Report.* The coroner presiding over the inquest on Mr Clement Blair Peach decided not to summon a jury in this case. On Appeal by the relatives of Mr Peach, the matter was reviewed before Lord Widgery (Lord Chief Justice) and Mr Justice Griffiths at Hammersmith on 15 November 1979 (*The Times*, Law Report, 16 November). The Court upheld the coroner's decision. Lord Widgery argued that the death of Mr Peach as a consequence of a severe blow on the head from a weapon wielded by a police officer did not amount to 'circumstances' the continuation or possible recurrence of which was prejudicial to the safety of the public. Such 'circumstances' (in his view) might be defined as 'meaning the circumstances surrounding a death involving effluvia from a nuclear power station, or by an outbreak of food poisoning'. Mr Justice Griffiths agreed, and added the example of a death resulting from inadequate flood precautions. 'The facts of the present case went no farther than revealing a possibility that a police officer might, in the course of the demonstration, have used a weapon other than a truncheon. There was no suggestion that it was police policy to issue such weapons, or, still less, to employ them so as to endanger the public . . . It was an isolated occasion of a police officer possibly using a weapon he should not have used and hitting too hard, and that being so it was not a case which fell within section 13 (2) (e).' My own *Law Report* appeared in the *Guardian* on the following Monday. But, in the event, it turned out to be less than accurate. For the case went to the Court of Appeal on 14 December 1979 (*The Times*, Law Report, 15 December) before Lord Denning, Lord Justice Bridge and Sir David Cairns. Here Lord Widgery's decision was reversed. A critical consideration, in Lord Denning's review of the evidence, was the fact that offensive weapons, including a metal truncheon encased in eight inches of leather, a pickaxe handle and a crowbar, had been found in police lockers after the demonstration. But the decisive influence upon the mind of the Master of the Rolls (Lord Denning) appeared to be, not the facts of the case, but the general public concern surrounding it: 'His Lordship said nothing about the merits. Everyone knew how well the police carried out their duties. But when allegations of the present kind were made against the police and fatalities occurred in circumstances in which a possible recurrence might be prevented, section 13 (2) (e) required that there must be a jury.' Mr Justice Bridge and Sir David Cairns concurred. I concur also, and judge that — since both the law and the facts of the case were the same before both courts — the decisive factor is the expression, in loud and measured ways, of public concern.

The State of the Nation. This is a single essay, first written in October 1979, and published as six articles in *New Society* in November and December 1979. A few passages, cut for reasons of space, have now been restored.